Antiquarian Bookselling in the United States

A History from the Origins to the 1940s

MADELEINE B. STERN

Greenwood Press
Westport, Connecticut • London, England

Library of Congress Cataloging in Publication Data

Stern, Madeleine Bettina (date)
  Antiquarian bookselling in the United States.

  Bibliography: p.
  Includes index.
  1. Antiquarian booksellers—United States—History.
  2. Booksellers and bookselling—United States—History.
  3. Book collecting—United States—History. I. Title.
  Z479.S79   1985   070.5′0973   84-19273
  ISBN 0-313-24729-3 (lib. bdg.)

Library of Congress Catalog Card Number: 84-19273
ISBN: 0-313-24729-3

First published in 1985

Greenwood Press
A division of Congressional Information Service, Inc.
88 Post Road West
Westport, Connecticut 06881

Printed in the United States of America

10 9 8 7 6 5 4 3 2 1

Copyright Acknowledgment

Acknowledgment is due to Jacob L. Chernofsky, publisher and editor of *AB Bookman's Weekly*, for permission to reprint in revised form, the following chapters which appeared in that periodical between 1980 and 1982: "New York City" (September 29, 1980); "Boston" (November 3, 1980); "San Francisco" (June 26, 1981); "Chicago" (September 7, 1981); "Los Angeles" (February 15, 1982); and "Philadelphia (July 5, 1982).

Contents

Introduction

That this book represents the first formal attempt to record the history of antiquarian bookselling in the United States should cause no undue surprise.[1] Unlike the publisher, whose name is immortalized in his imprints, the bookseller has almost always been a ghost, whose transactions as intermediary between source and market are seldom preserved. Booksellers pass a book from one to another, but the act of passing is a transitory gesture. Through their hands flow the written and printed testimony of our literature and our history, but nothing arrests a flow in its course. Many of these intermediary ghosts have helped to advance our civilization, but they are recalled only by a trade card or a directory listing, an auction record, a newspaper advertisement, a sales catalogue—by memorabilia as ephemeral as they themselves. Sometimes a traveler paints the portrait of a bookseller in his memoirs; sometimes an enthusiast embalms one in an article published in a learned periodical; the fate and fortunes of another may enter a scholarly work on some aspect of the trade; occasionally an individual bookseller is sufficiently significant to form the subject of an entire monograph or tome. Rarely, however, have business records been treasured and preserved by the institutions the bookseller helped to build.[2]

It is to reanimate those ghosts and trace the history of their fascinating trade that this book has been written. From scattered, often meagre sources, the attempt has been made to restore their tastes and their temperaments, their trials, their struggles, and their achievements, to clothe once again in flesh and blood the purveyors of antiquarian books.

If their biographies lend color to the fabric, the thread from which it is woven is history—the history of a business that served both muse and marketplace, that made of tradition a civilizing force. The history, which begins at the beginning, ends with the mid-1940s, although the trade assuredly did not. At that time a new wave of European émigrés enriched its ranks; the increasing democratization of culture extended its markets; conscious of its responsibilities, it established itself into professional associations.[3] Indeed, with the mid-1940s, antiquarian bookselling took on a new if somewhat altered life, and its annals from that time to the present deserve another history. That history must be written—but not by the present writer who herself took on the ghostly functions of an antiquarian bookseller at that period.

Indeed, the chronology covered by this first volume of antiquarian bookselling history is extensive enough. It begins in the seventeenth century when the eccentric John Dunton brought a "venture" of books to Boston, the city where the earliest catalogue of books in British America was printed in 1693.[4] It continues through the eighteenth century when delegates with a literary turn made speeches at the first Continental Congress and made purchases at Philadelphia's bookstores. It traces the exuberant development of the trade in that exhilarating nineteenth century when keelboat, steamboat and railroad interacted with the business of books.

Geographically, this history spans a continent. Its curtain rises in the East, in colonial Boston which, "founded in piety . . . flourished by Yankee shrewdness,"[5] and from Boston it passes to Philadelphia, and thence to New York. It follows the westward march of the pioneer booksellers, first to the midwest frontier of Cincinnati which, thanks in part to their efforts, was transformed from "Porkopolis" to the "Literary Emporium of the West." When the growth of railroad lines resulted in a shift northward to the lake plains, Cincinnati yielded to Chicago as a book center where the culture of the Middle Border was asserted. In a frontier town where books were less important than guns and saddles, books nevertheless were in demand, and so, freighted from Baltimore or Pittsburgh, New York or Philadelphia, shipped by river or sent via New Orleans, they too made the long journey westward to St. Louis. Indeed, in that "Memphis of the American Nile," books were sold even before there were bookstores! When the railroad entered Kansas City on the bend of the Missouri, the merchant entered too, with a frontier inventory that included books new and secondhand. In the wake of the Gold Rush, San Francisco became a city with bookstalls on every corner, and gold dust was exchanged for books that had come from the East in the cargoes of steamers and clipper ships. Pioneer booksellers joined the inevitable migration to the far reaches of the West, to the City of the Golden Gate, to the Hub of the Ranchos. Against the background of an expanding continent, over a period of 250 years, in the dynamic westward adventure that rounded out a nation, the antiquarian bookseller played a vital role.[6]

What was the nature of these antiquarian booksellers? What were their motivations, their methods, their achievements? From the troupe of individualists and eccentrics who people these pages, it is possible to attempt a composite portrait. One who flourished in the eastern United States may have hailed from Britain, as did that "stout, chunky" Scot,[7] Robert Bell, or from Central Europe, as did Charles Sessler of Philadelphia. One who flourished in the West may have migrated from upstate New York, navigating the Allegheny and Ohio rivers in a flatboat to Cincinnati, or pushing on to a farther frontier. Whether large and dynamic, or small and pensive, or dapper and rotund, booksellers seldom remained in the place of their birth.

Education often consisted of brief schooling followed by much independent reading. A few, like Dr. Rosenbach, attained advanced scholastic degrees, but many antiquarian booksellers were self-educated. Given $2 to buy a pair of shoes, they might well spend the money on books instead. Especially during the apprenticeship period the antiquarian booksellers educated themselves. For $3 a week they were engaged to sweep the floor of a local bookshop, wash the windows, run errands, and in the course of carrying out those duties managed—if indeed they were to become antiquarian booksellers—to read and study the riches that surrounded them.

When they struck out for themselves, they might begin as cartman, peddler, or scout. They might peddle books out of a basket or open a stall, as William Leary did in Philadelphia. Their place of business might be a dark and tiny hole in the wall, or it might be an elegant literary emporium with frescoed ceilings and multiple floors.

Wherever they set up a shingle, they required, for success in their trade, certain indispensable characteristics. Perry Burnham of Boston seemed to have been invested with them all: "He was quick, keen, shrewd, and had a remarkable intuitive knowledge of books. His judgment of the value of rare or old volumes was singularly true. The rapid way in which he would run through a pile of books offered for purchase—turning over a few of them, glancing at their contents, testing their condition—and estimate their worth was often surprising. He knew his . . . stock . . . intimately."

He also *remembered* his stock—past and present. Antiquarian dealers might be short in stature; they had to be long in memory. Indeed, the memory of the antiquarian bookseller has become legendary. As William Brotherhead summed up, "The old bookseller should be a cyclopaedia, able to answer questions about the general nature of books, and their authors. The whole field of history he should know, from Homer to Macaulay. The new discoveries in history, either biblical or general, he should know." George Littlefield of Boston used no "twentieth century methods of card filing, to aid him to supply [such] information. . . . He didn't have to; he had it all in his head." George D. Smith, czar of the American rare book trade during the early twentieth century, "could remember every title in a book catalogue, with its price, tell what it had fetched at auction, who the buyer was, and often the names of the underbidders." Elijah L. Shettles of Austin, far from a czar, could nonetheless supply the date of a rare pamphlet, tell where it was printed, recall how, when and where he had acquired it, at what price, to whom he had sold it, and note "casually certain printed items that had preceded it, and . . . a still rarer pamphlet published in reply to it."

To this prodigious memory antiquarian booksellers added a passionate belief in collecting that amounted often to monomania. Their shelves and cabinets eventually overflowed with their treasures. If the dealer's name was Samuel G. Drake, they would consist of works on the Indian and early colonial history; if Robert Clarke, archeology and Scottish books would compete with Americana in the library that was "the joy of his life"; if he was called Hubert Howe Bancroft, he revelled in books on the Pacific states. But whether from Boston or Chicago or San Francisco, the antiquarian bookseller was a collector of the "odds and ends of time."

To the tendency to collect was added the tendency to survive. The antiquarian bookseller arose to rebuild from many fires—the fire of 1711 that consumed every bookshop in Boston with one exception; the Boston fire of 1872 that turned the city into a smoking Sahara; the Chicago fire of 1871 that stimulated the sense of the past and the desire to preserve it. Many an antiquarian bookseller has survived not only his major nemesis, fire, but siege, revolution and war, the succession of panics that punctuated the economic history of the United States, the San Francisco fire and earthquake, the Montrose flood.

Perhaps antiquarian dealers have triumphed over such catastrophes because they love the work upon which they are engaged. They forage in the garrets of mansions and the basements of junkshops, in barn and storage house, in attic and trunk, in ghost town and literary emporium, and the adventure of their find becomes a "small miracle." Great books, great manuscripts, great libraries have passed through their hands, and they glitter through the pages of this history: Thoreau's own annotated copy of *Walden* in original binding; Poe's *Tamerlane*; the *Bay Psalm Book*; Shakespeare folios and quartos; a Caxton on vellum; the manuscript of *Alice in Wonderland*; a Chaucer manuscript; Lincoln's copy of Shakespeare; the Franklin papers; Washington's library.

Although lesser works lack the lustre of such monuments, they excite antiquarian booksellers' powers of detection and enthusiasm for research. From the nature of such occupation, as well as from the catalogues in which they describe their wares, the image of the antiquarian dealer as arbiter of learning emerged. Dealers in dusty tomes came to be regarded as dispensers of knowledge. Many scholar-booksellers parade through this volume: Samuel G. Drake, George Littlefield, Patrick Foley of Boston; Joseph Sabin and George Philip Philes of New York; Robert Clarke of Cincinnati; Robert Ernest Cowan, and that "frontier bookseller who turned historian," Hubert Howe Bancroft of San Francisco; Charles Heartman; that philosopher of bibliography, Henry Stevens of Vermont.

Such, at its most gratifying, was the *image* of the antiquarian booksellers. What were their actual achievements? They played a major role in the building of the nation's libraries, public and private. To their intercession the existence of such collections as the Hoe and Church, such libraries as the Morgan, Huntington and Clements is largely due. It was a firm of booksellers who helped amass for Thomas Jefferson the library of the University of Virginia. The antiquarian bookseller has built many such monuments.

Antiquarian booksellers are also responsible in great measure for the growth of interest in regionalism and the collecting of regional material in its multiple subdivisions from the literature of the Middle Border to the languages of the American Indian. They must be credited, too, with educating the public to the permanent value of the ephemeral.

It was Samuel G. Drake who collected all the pamphlets he could find relating to the history of Boston; it was William Gowans whose stock included "pamphlets innumerable." Elijah Shettles of Austin "had a strong leaning toward pamphlets, and . . . bought many." Out of the bookseller's knowledge and intuition came the realization that, though there was lustre in the monuments of learning, there was also *multum in parvo.*

Through the work of antiquarian booksellers, as the years passed, bibliomania (to which they were often subject themselves) was modified into bibliophilia. As Walter Hill of Chicago put it, bibliomania was succeeded by "the more rational and sympathetic spirit of *bibliophilia.* . . . The bibliophile nowadays insists that his collection indicate in a measure his efforts in life, his work, or his calling." Booksellers themselves effected this transition.

"By means of the printed word," it has been said, "the propaganda of enlightenment reached all citizens." Antiquarian booksellers who dealt in the printed word did much to achieve that end. As a nineteenth-century member of the trade wrote: "To be an educated bookseller in these latter days is something to be proud of. We are the almoners to the hungry souls who yearn for literary food." The fact shines through the ornate prose. Buying and selling the documents of our history, the printed records of our thought, booksellers spread the "propaganda of enlightenment."

That they thoroughly enjoy this calling is evidenced by the antiquarian booksellers' reluctance to retire from it. In a few instances their business is a family dynasty, but for the most part it is perpetuated by themselves, either alone or with a succession of partners. As a result, its ending coincides with their own. This terminal point dealers postpone as long as possible. If they retire—as Bill Smith of Cincinnati did in his eighties—the retirement is purely nominal, for they continue to purchase, sell, or appraise choice items. Moreover, they live as long as possible, and when they finally succumb to death, they die in harness and in style. Like Robert Bell of Philadelphia, they die en route to a book auction; like G. D. Smith of New York, they die "while in conversation"; like Robert Clarke of Cincinnati, they die in their library; like Julius Doerner of Chicago, they die in their Morris chairs, a book on their knees; like Charles T. Powner, they die in bed with a volume of Mark Twain propped up before them. And, having died, they go where all good antiquarian booksellers should go, to "where all first editions have proper points and . . . pristine dust wrappers."

All booksellers, to paraphrase the Illuminist Louis Claude de Saint-Martin, "speak the same language because they come from the same country."[8] It is a country they have created themselves, shaping its landscape, defining its borders. In a sense, it is from the nature of antiquarian booksellers that their trade has evolved.

Biography portrays the bookseller, but history traces the development of the trade. Its roots are buried in colonial times, when general booksellers combined the sale of books with printing and publishing, binding and engraving, often adding a circulating library to the attractions of their shops. Their shelves featured not only books but stationery and a variety of general merchandise that included patent medicines and spectacles, paper hangings and linens, beer, whale-bones and beaver hats. Books were often both new and secondhand. Antiquarian bookselling was an outgrowth of this trade in miscellaneous secondhand books. "Before there were rare booksellers, there had to be secondhand booksellers." Not until 1830 did Samuel G. Drake open his "Antiquarian Book-store" in Boston, the first store where trade was limited exclusively to the antiquarian.

Two operational methods imbedded in the general book business were largely responsible for the development of a separate, independent antiquarian trade: importing and specialization. Books imported from England found their way to colonial bookshelves, and books imported from New York or Philadelphia found their way to the West. With the importation of books came the importation of foreign thought and philosophy expressed not only in new publications but in used, secondhand, rare and valuable items. As the trade in rare books was shaped, dealers went abroad habitually for grand-scale buying. Henry Stevens took his climactic 1845 journey with forty gold sovereigns in his pocket. In a later day, Charles Sessler traveled abroad, often three times a year. As A. Edward Newton remarked, "Sessler . . . goes abroad every year with his pocket full of money, and comes back with a lot of things that quickly empty ours." Without imports, from Europe to America, from the eastern seaboard to the West, there could not have been a rare book trade.

Early on, dealers began to specialize. There were few special interests that could not be satisfied, either in the form of new or secondhand books: Spanish books and German books, law books, Presbyterian and Catholic books, scientific and medical books, maritime books, French books. Indeed, as early as 1794, Moreau de Saint-Méry opened his Philadelphia shop with the "beautiful signboard" where French émigrés could pick up French books. Importers who also specialized were well on their way to antiquarian bookselling, and by the nineteenth century George Littlefield, for example, connoted Americana and genealogy while Lauriat's connoted "leather."

Moreau de Saint-Méry's shop was not only a bookstore but a meeting place where French émigrés gathered "to chat . . . discuss the fate of the world and drink madeira." Almost from the beginning, the antiquarian bookstore was also a "lounging place of the literati." As William Loring Andrews wrote, it was at the old bookshops that "loungers with literary tastes congregated the livelong day, sipping knowledge as the bee sips honey." Audubon might patronize William Gowans; Mark Twain might drop in at Brown & Gross in Hartford; a group of bibliophiles inevitably metamorphosed their favorite bookstore into a literary rendezvous. In Boston or Cincinnati, in New York or Los Angeles, gathered those "fond of research in the pigeon holes of antiquity." They turned a "musty corner" of Brentano's Literary Emporium into just such a rendezvous; they created the famous "Saints and Sinners Corner" at McClurg's in Chicago. Such meeting places were affected, in turn, by the tendency of the bookseller to specialize, with the result that one bookstore—Colesworthy's in Boston—attracted Methodist ministers, while another—Elizabeth Peabody's "atom of a bookshop"—was a magnet for the Transcendentalists; John Campbell's Philadelphia establishment became a "center for hot-headed Democrats." Ralph G. Newman's Chicago premises was the mecca for a "club of customers" who sought refuge from the twentieth century.

Despite the nomadic nature of booksellers, who customarily moved from one location to another with the same frequency with which they changed partners and firm style, their bookshops, with their cluster of faithful habitués, tended to operate along Booksellers' Rows. Boston's Cornhill, New York's Nassau Street, Chicago's State Street, West Sixth Street in Los Angeles were all at one time flourishing centers of the antiquarian trade.

There they gathered their customers and their wares. The latter they obtained by importing from abroad, by foraging in likely and unlikely spots, by ordering through agents, by buying from colleagues, and by bidding at auction. Whether they bought under a pseudonym—as William Gowans did, under the name of "Mr. Chase"—whether they bid by means of "a peculiar muscular contraction in and around the left eye, vulgarly termed a wink"—as George Littlefield did—antiquarian booksellers have been both book auctioneers' most knowledgeable customers and most faithful patrons. Their histories are studded with triumphs and disasters in the auction rooms. Indeed, some booksellers have been so carried away by the possibilities of the public vendue that they have become auctioneers themselves. Robert Bell, who developed the book auction to "its colonial apogee," also attracted a delighted audience who found his sales "as good as a play." During a later century, Charles Heartman took on the role of auctioneer of rare Americana, holding several memorable sales crowned by his wife's dinners. On the other hand, some antiquarian booksellers mistrusted the competition of the auction from early days, Stephen Meech of St. Louis informing the public in 1841 that he would "sell as low, on the average, as the same editions sold under the hammer . . . and some editions even lower. Call . . . and be convinced that auction prices are not always the lowest."

Booksellers' attitudes toward auctions naturally differed, setting them apart from one another in this respect. In other respects there was much to unify the trade. Intramural buying and selling have always been customary among antiquarian booksellers. Sometimes those transactions, when on the grand scale, link one firm to another, as when Charles T. Powner of Chicago acquired the bulk of the stock of the Morris Book Shop, or when David B. Cooke bought out A. H. Burley & Co., successors to the pioneer Stephen F. Gale. Other connecting threads, woven through the trade, give to its fabric a fascinating pattern, and at the same time hold it together. Those threads are the threads of apprenticeship and employment, connecting house to house and past to future. Such connections are almost omnipresent in the small world of antiquarian bookselling. Robert H. Dodd, who managed the Dodd and Mead rare book department, numbered among his assistants several future New York booksellers including George H. Richmond, William Evarts Benjamin, James F. Drake, and the czar-to-be, George D. Smith. In the Far West, Paul Elder, who was trained by William Doxey, trained in his turn John Howell, under whom David Magee served an apprenticeship. Such relationships produce a nexus in the trade of antiquarian bookselling. They link not only people, but trade practises as well, and so they create a tradition that abides.

As individuals, the booksellers—great, near-great, and minor—who figure in these pages achieved much in the way of building libraries, stimulating an interest in ephemera and regionalism, metamorphosing bibliomania into bibliophilia, and spreading the "propaganda of enlightenment." What have been the achievements of the trade in general? Basically, it has accomplished on the grand scale what the individual dealer has attempted in a lesser way. It has brought books into wilderness areas. It has created a demand, and then supplied that demand. It has helped to shape taste, and so has been an educative force. It has taught cities to collect the records of their history even while that history was in the making, and thus it has been a force for preservation. As the editor of the first antiquarian booksellers' directory wrote in 1885: "The Antiquarian Book-shop . . . is the true preserver . . . of the books embodying the knowledge and wisdom, the errors and follies of past generations."[9] As a more recent commentator observed of antiquarian bookstores, they "index a city's personality."[10] At their best—when they make obeisance not only to the marketplace but to the muse—they are benefactors to humanity.[11]

In 1895, William Loring Andrews was asked: "What is the use of writing about these men [booksellers]? They were simply dealers, and bought and sold books as so much merchandise for profit, and that was all there was to it." He answered: "Not quite all. . . . I am loath to believe that one can pass his entire life among books, even in the way of sordid trade, without imbibing . . . a modicum of the wit, wisdom and philosophy they contain, and thereby becoming a less commonplace fraction of the mass of humanity." A few years earlier, when William Brotherhead's *Forty Years among the Old Booksellers of Philadelphia* was published, *Publishers Weekly* remarked: "he sketches a few of his contemporaries in the old-book business, thus partially filling up gaps in the history of the trade that some future historian may find useful."

That future historian has now ventured to fill up some of those gaps, and adumbrate "a less commonplace fraction of the mass of humanity." Others have hoped to do this before. William Clark Breckenridge of Missouri gathered material for a book on "Old Time Book Dealers and Old Time Book Stores . . . of St. Louis, From the First Book Store Down to the Present Day," and it was Aaron Mendoza's ambition to write a history of New York City bookselling, to which end he filled his roll-top desk with notes and sources.

Now the attempt to record the history of antiquarian bookselling in this country has at long last been made. Such sins of commission as it may contain are entirely involuntary. Such sins of omission as it does contain are purposeful. Admittedly, there are, and must be, omissions in a work of these dimensions. Antiquarian bookselling in Detroit and Milwaukee, Indianapolis and Des Moines, Minneapolis and Seattle might well have been included, but such chapters would have extended the volume without changing its thrust. Many dealers whose careers peaked during the late 1930s and early 1940s are missing from these pages and should be portrayed in a sequel devoted to a later golden age of antiquarian bookselling. Finally, there is another omission in this volume, for no simple and precise definition of antiquarian book or antiquarian bookseller has been attempted. Quoting a Chicago dealer, Paul Angle defined rare books as "those which are 'important, desirable, and hard to get,' "[12] and that definition—while it too omits much that might be added—has the merit of being succinct and comprehensible. To define antiquarian booksellers is more difficult. It is hoped that in the pages that follow the flavor of their personalities and the facts of their lives will emerge, the nature of their calling be recorded, and that those who have preserved the learning of the ages will themselves here be preserved.

NOTES

1. Henry Walcott Boynton's *Annals of American Bookselling 1638–1850* (New York: Wiley, 1932) is, as the author himself admits, p. v, "an informal chronicle." Its focus is the eastern seaboard. Some chapters of the present book have appeared in modified form as articles in *AB Bookman's Weekly*.

2. There are, of course, notable exceptions. At the New-York Historical Society, for example, are 535 items relating to Thomas H. Morrell, New York City bookseller who specialized in the history of New York and the Revolution. The Adolf Growoll Collection of *American Book Trade History*, preserved at the Melcher Library of R. R. Bowker Company, and made available to the author through the courtesy of Jean Peters and Margaret Spier, former librarians, was an invaluable source for the present work. The writer wishes to thank both Jean Peters and Peggy Spier for their generous and unending cooperation.

3. See, for example, "National Association Proposed by Antiquarian Booksellers At Meeting," *AB* (5 March 1949), pp. 677 f.

4. The catalogue of Samuel Lee's library.

5. Dorothea Lawrance Mann, "Our Ancestors and Their Book Business," *The Bookman* (1930–1931), Vol. 72, p. 372.

6. To take into account the exceptions, the mavericks who operated from locations remote from antiquarian book centers or were associated with such locations, the chapter "Lone Stars" was included in this volume.

7. All quotations in this chapter are, unless otherwise indicated, from the text that follows.

8. Louis Claude de Saint-Martin said: "All mystics speak the same language because they come from the same country." See Morris West, *The Clowns of God* (New York: Bantam, 1981), p. 205.

9. C. N. Caspar, *Directory of the Antiquarian Booksellers and Dealers in Second-Hand Books of the United States* (Milwaukee: Caspar, 1885), p. [5].

10. Brian Burnes, "Leafing through the city's used-book stores," [Kansas City] *Star* (15 March 1980), p. 9 (courtesy Philip Tompkins, Associate Director of Libraries, University of Missouri-Kansas City).

11. See R. M. Williamson, *Bits from an Old Book Shop* (London: Simpkin, Marshall, et al., 1904), p. 16.

12. *American Book-Prices Current*, ed. Colton Storm (New York: Bowker, 1944), p. xx.

1

Boston

In 1686 when that amiable and eccentric bibliophile-bibliopole John Dunton left London to bring a "venture" of books to Boston, his father-in-law gave him the following advice: "I think it will be less trouble to you to wish there that you had brought more, than to fret at the want of a market for too many."[1] The advice proved gratuitous, for by 1686 Boston had already developed an avid taste for books and provided a substantial market for the antiquarian as well as the new. It boasted, for example, the Mather library, and when Dunton visited Increase and his son Cotton, he commented: "As the Famous Bodleian Library at Oxford, is the Glory of that University . . . so I may say, That Mr. Mather's Library is the glory of New-England, if not of all America. I am sure it was the best sight that I had in Boston."[2]

Books were available in Boston, and they were made available through the instrumentality of the bookseller-publisher who imported sheets from abroad, along with books, stitched and bound them in his shop, and offered to a town of some seven thousand, sermons for its clergymen, textbooks for its scholars, works on navigation for its sea captains, pharmacopoeias for its physicians as well as a place of resort and a background for bookish conversation. Besides selling many books to Harvard College through its librarian John Cotton, John Dunton provided a vignette of the Boston literary scene in his letters home where he selected a handful of Boston booksellers to immortalize: John Usher, who "makes the best figure in Boston. He is very rich; adventures much to sea; but has got his estate by *Bookselling*"; Joseph Bruning, "a Dutch bookseller from Holland, scrupulously just, plain in his cloaths . . . versed in the knowledge of all sorts of Books, and may well be styled a complete Bookseller. He never decries a Book because it is not of his own printing"; Duncan Campbell, "the Scotch Bookseller . . . very industrious, dresses *à-la-mode*, and I am told a young Lady of a great fortune is fallen in love with him."[3]

Dunton's bibliopolic acquaintances had many predecessors who had helped make Boston receptive to learning and cultivation. The very first announcement to the world that a bookseller's shop had been opened in Boston was made in 1647 with publication of Samuel Danforth's *Almanack* which, printed by Matthew Daye at Cambridge, was "to be sold by Hez. Usher at Boston."[4] And even before Hezekiah set up shop, John Harvard had in 1638 made the bequest that would lay the foundations of the library that bore his name—a library that included Erasmus' *Colloquia*, Isocrates' *Orationes*, as well as North's *Plutarch* and Bacon's *Essays*. At his death in 1643, William Brewster left a library of nearly four hundred books, and the old soldier Miles Standish left about fifty, among them Caesar's *Commentaries*, Homer's *Iliad* and Calvin's *Institutes*. At the busy and prosperous port of Boston, throughout the seventeenth century, many cargoes of books were unloaded to supply the demands of a reading public for Greek and Roman classics, theology and history, philosophy and non-frivolous literature. Only a decade after John Usher's father Hezekiah opened the first bookshop in colonial America, a Town House including a library was built in Boston around which booksellers tended to cluster.

They accelerated the flow of books to the colonies, those thirty or so booksellers who cried their wares from shop or warehouse as the century rolled on. That there were antiquarian books among those wares appears highly likely. In February 1676/77, for example, Richard Chiswell wrote to Increase Mather regarding books shipped to John Usher: "You may see them at his shop, and I hope may help some of them off his hands, by recommending them to your publick library, especially the new ones, which cannot be there already."[5] With such emphasis upon "the new ones," it may be deduced that old ones were also present. Combining bookselling with printing, importing, confronting fire and—in the case of Benjamin Harris—censorship, they carried on: John Usher and Samuel Phillips, Samuel Sewall and Richard Wilkins, Joseph Bruning from Amsterdam, Duncan Campbell from Glasgow, Andrew Thorncomb from London, creating a kind of booksellers' row in Boston and, what is more important, helping to set the stage for a town that would become known as the "Athens of America."

In 1693 the earliest printed catalogue of books in British America—that of Samuel Lee's library—was printed in Boston.[6] Seven years later, the inventory of bookseller Michael Perry's estate disclosed that he had assembled a mélange of volumes to please every taste, from European imports to his own issues, from primers and catechisms to sermons and chapbooks, and among the titles included were some that might have been considered rare even in 1700: a Godfrey of Boulogne, an Ovid *De Tristibus*, an Aesop.[7]

The flow of books to New England increased during the early part of the eighteenth century. Cotton Mather's "mighty Thirst after the Sight of Books" could be quenched.[8] Then, in 1711, fire consumed the Town House, and every bookshop in Boston with one exception was destroyed. That rara avis, the bibliopole, however, has much of the phoenix in his nature, and before long an eighteenth-century dramatis personae of the booktrade emerged. The picturesque Daniel Henchman, who was characterized by Isaiah Thomas as "the most eminent and enterprising bookseller in Boston before 1775,"[9] plied his trade on "Cornhill, Corner of King-Street, opposite to the Old Brick-Meeting-House," handled both new and secondhand books, and supplied customers who ranged from the governor of the province to "small artisans."[10] By 1713 collections of books were auctioned in Boston at the Crown Coffee-House, the Royal Exchange, the Sign of the Magpy.[11]

Historian Thomas Goddard Wright gives a roseate picture of literary culture in Boston: "New bookshops were opened in addition to all those established before 1700, and these were supplemented by auction sales of imported consignments of books, generally at some coffee-house. Catalogues of these collections were printed for free distribution, and the sales were well advertised in the Boston papers."[12] A catalogue of books on the arts and sciences issued in 1734 for T. Cox, bookseller "at the Lamb on the South Side of the Town House" included some eight hundred titles.[13] Jeremy Condy, who operated "Near Concert-Hall," kept a supply of what Isaiah Thomas described as "valuable books, chiefly English editions," while William Lang, "at the Gilt Bible, Marlboro'-Street," specialized in Scottish editions.[14] James Rivington employed a Boston agent to sell his "valuable collection of books printed in England . . . At the London Book-Store."[15] Hawkers of almanacs, dealers who offered "small books from a stall in the market place," all joined the eighteenth-century parade of Boston booksellers who dealt not only in new but occasionally in antiquarian.

In 1764 the Harvard College Library burned, and five thousand volumes were consumed by fire. The next day, a broadside listed some of the losses which included Bibles, Orientalia, classics and theological treatises, the *Transactions of the Royal Society*, the works of Boyle and Newton, and a few ancient and valuable manuscripts.[16] Surely some of those antiquarian items had passed through the hands of Boston bibliopoles.

Perhaps the most distinguished bookshop of the 1760s was that opened by the Scotsman John Mein at the London Book-Store on the north side of King Street. Mein's "large and valuable collection of European books" vied with his "handsome assortment of stationery," his Irish linens, and his bottled "Bristol beer near two years old," and at his premises was also available the earliest circulating library in Boston.[17] In 1771 the obese, full-blooded, florid Henry Knox opened his "London Book-Store" in Cornhill, which became the resort of British officers who could find there a "large and very elegant Assortment of the most Modern Books in all Branches of Literature, Arts and Sciences" just imported by the "last ships" from London.[18]

Before the Revolution there were some ninety-two booksellers in Boston, importing and distributing, publishing and acting as selling agents, taking orders for binding, selling on long credit to country booksellers, offering patent medicines and paper hangings along with many modern books in all branches and a few antiquarian tomes. Having withstood fire, they now confronted, after Bunker Hill, a Boston in a state of siege. Yet neither fire nor siege nor revolution itself, despite their devastating consequences, ended the Boston booktrade. At length it emerged again, clustering by the end of the century about the Old State House of Old Cornhill.

One of the many booksellers who served the needs of the late eighteenth-century collector was the Franco-American Joseph Nancrede who, at his French and English Book-Store, introduced to his customers the work of French writers and philosophers along with "old Books" and "scarce Tracts." Indeed, Nancrede's catalogues mark the beginning of an attempt at bibliographical description, for they included notations regarding imprint, format and binding.[19]

The nineteenth century was to mark several antiquarian beginnings. In 1801 fourteen Boston firms established the Association of the Boston Booksellers. In 1804 the Boston bibliopoles published the first book trade catalogue, entitled *Catalogue of all the Books printed in the United*

States. Later in the century the first specialist antiquarian dealer in the United States would set out his shingle in Boston, and the first overseas hunters for old and rare would embark from the port of Boston. Meanwhile, as the century advanced, the milieu of the trade shifted to "a new street laid out from Court Street to Cornhill . . . named Cheapside,"[20] renamed Market, and finally renamed Cornhill or New Cornhill.

At No. 1 Cornhill in 1812, the firm of Cummings and Hilliard took over a well-known stand, inheriting a business originally founded by Ebenezer Battelle. Cummings and Hilliard sold, along with blankbooks and penknives, quills and paint boxes, books for "cultivated folk purchasing for private libraries." Among those books were some ferreted out by Hilliard from ancient monastic libraries in Germany. The firm's stock included not only the *Letters of Junius* and the *Works* of Bacon, but a 1491 Anselm "lately received from Germany" priced at $3.75. Obviously an interest in old and rare existed on Cornhill.

One of the most interesting episodes in Boston's bibliopolic history was played out by William Hilliard and Thomas Jefferson. In 1824, Joseph Coolidge, a Harvard graduate (class of 1817) soon to become Jefferson's grandson-in-law, recognized the enterprising qualities of William Hilliard and his firm. In that year, Jefferson's great achievement, the University of Virginia, was well on its way to completion but needed a library and a bookstore. Coolidge suggested to Jefferson the name of William Hilliard, and upon that "recommendation . . . and explanation of the means he had established of procuring books from the several book-marts of Europe," Jefferson accepted the proposition that Hilliard supply the books for the University of Virginia. Apprised of this honor, Hilliard wrote to Jefferson on 14 July 1824:

I rejoice for the republic of letters, that an Institution of this description is to be established in the ancient dominion, independent of all personal advantages, I may receive. I have for many years supplied Harvard College with their Classical Books. . . . In a recent tour through Europe, I have purchased a large stock of English, French, & German Literature, ancient & modern; & have established such a correspondence, as will enable me to procure a regular supply of the best works. . . . The advance, which I have received in importations of this description has been 10 pr ct upon the cost & charges. . . . [21]

On 8 April 1825 an agreement was drawn up between Jefferson and Hilliard arranging for the purchase, for about $15,000, of books for the

University of Virginia library. Jefferson preferred "newer and better" editions, wished unbound books to be bound "with back & corners in calf," and promised Hilliard a catalogue of desiderata—along with a 5 percent commission plus charges and expenses. Jefferson's catalogue, covering an enormous variety of books in many languages and a wide range of authors from Grotius to Pascal, from Mather to Rousseau, was sent in June, and at Hilliard's entreaty another $3,000 was allocated for the purpose. However, as his commission was reduced from the anticipated 10 percent to 5 percent, Hilliard refrained from going abroad in person. Nonetheless, many of the books were obtained from abroad, some supplied from stock, some from auction, but most imported. As the bookseller reported, "Our correspondents in France & Germany have advised us, that the auctions, during the winter season, of several private Libraries, will give them the opportunity of purchasing many valuable Books, not otherwise to be had." Moreover, some works "could not be procured, except as opportunities occurred of purchases from private libraries; & perhaps some of this description may embrace some of the most valuable & expensive works." And so, from purchases at auction, orders from the principal marts of England, France and Germany, and from his own stock, the collection of the University of Virginia was assembled by a Boston bookseller. Despite Jefferson's predilection for new editions, the collection included several scarce antiquarian items, among them the *Lexicon Heptaglotton* of Edmund Castell (London 1669), the *Biblia Sacra Polyglotta* of Bryan Walton (London 1657), an *Anthologia Graeca*, an Albertus Magnus, and a 1689 *Heptateuch*. All the books arrived in the Old Dominion in good order, except for "one which being tumbled carelessly by a waggoner at Richm^d. burst, without falling asunder."

Though they were not privileged to serve quite so eminent a collector, other bookshops of more or less antiquarian nature cropped up in Boston during the first part of the nineteenth century. W. G. Colesworthy was to inherit a business dating back to 1825, founded by his father, and his shop would become the favored resort of Methodist ministers. It was also favored by the Transcendentalist Bronson Alcott, father of Louisa May, who in 1875 wrote to Samuel Longfellow:

I was yesterday in Boston, and left your umbrella at Colesworth's [*sic*] book store.
Here I found an antique Volume of Dr. Donne's Sermons. . . . I fancied the

worn calf-skin . . . covered a dollars' worth of wit at least, and brought the book away.

This Colesworthy it seems deals in rhymes of his own as in other men's literary loves and, in doing up my parcel, added his Poem—Donne and Colesworthy in one envelope. . . . I think I shall call at his shop again.[22]

The Old Corner Book Store was first used as a bookshop in 1828 by Carter & Hendee who offered English, French, Spanish and Italian books along with globes and stationery. At the age of fourteen, James T. Fields was taken into the shop which was to undergo a series of metamorphoses under various publishing firms, including that of Ticknor and Fields, and to become a distinguished literary rendezvous.

One of the most influential bookshops of Boston before the midcentury was that established by the Massachusetts bluestocking Elizabeth Palmer Peabody at 13 West Street. Her combination library and bookstore became the scene of Margaret Fuller's Conversations, the meetingplace of New England's reformers, and, between 1842 and 1843, the place of publication of *The Dial*, the organ of Transcendentalism. It was also the principal disseminator of foreign literature, "the only [shop] in Boston carrying a [comparable] stock of foreign books." As Peabody put it: "About 1840 I came to Boston and opened the business of importing and publishing foreign books, a thing not then attempted by any one. I had also a foreign library of new French and German books."[23] The Peabody Foreign Circulating Library in the front parlor of 13 West Street in Boston's South End became a "centre of intellectual and reformatory interest," its patrons including Emerson and Alcott, Holmes and Lowell, Hawthorne and Horace Mann. At this "atom of a bookshop" collectors and readers could find the works of Dante and Petrarch, Herder, Schiller and Goethe, Molière, Mirabeau and Voltaire—the seeds of foreign thought that came to flower in Transcendental New England.

And so, Boston was indeed becoming the "Athens of America." It needed a bookseller who limited his trade exclusively to the antiquarian, and in Samuel G. Drake (1798–1875) that need was fulfilled. Drake was not only the first bookseller in the country to confine his stock to old and rare, but the scholar-bookseller *par excellence*. Indeed he is remembered rather as scholar than as bookseller. Toward the end of his life, the collector could seek him in his library, for he was collector as well as bookseller.

You first ascend a semi-vertical flight of forty stairs . . . and you find yourself in a large, six-windowed oblong—the hive of genealogy—crowded with shelves and cabinets—overflowing with antique books, pamphlets, periodicals, maps and MSS.—waiting, like learned ghosts for some patron of the arts to lead them to a more commodious and secure asylum—then turning away from the Round Table—you see a kind of sesame door . . . and then mounting up another steeper flight to another higher story—you reach the threshold of a long attic chamber lighted at either end and bearing a similitude to the cloister of some erudite monk.

For, there you will behold a solitary man—arrayed in black—small in stature—but well proportioned—of an elastic step—quick in motion—his hair touched by the cold finger of time—his face kindly, but featured by deep thought— . . . sitting by a desk near a window—pen in hand—in winter an open stove of live coals at his right—and before, behind and around him, lie books in piles, books on shelves—MSS.—ancient documents and pamphlets from floor to ceiling all arranged in rows or neatly labeled in cases;—and there he sits—in his cushioned arm chair—philosopher like—ready to lay down pen and receive the caller . . . answer his questions about the past—or sell him a long sought gem of antiquity.[24]

Born in 1798, Samuel Gardner Drake had tried teaching as well as the study of law and medicine before he decided to become a bookseller. In 1830, after a short period as book auctioneer, he opened at 63 in Boston's Cornhill the Antiquarian Book-store. As he wrote on the flyleaf of a duodecimo in his library: "In 1830 the first Antiquarian Book-store was established by me in Cornhill, and the letters on my sign were fashioned from those in this book."

The Antiquarian Book-store reflected the antiquarian passions of its founder. Samuel G. Drake early appreciated the interest of American schoolbooks as mirrors of American education, and amassed in time a collection of some four hundred volumes. "About 1843, an agent of the British Museum, seeing the value of the collection, bought up the whole of it to take to England. It had previously been offered at a much lower rate to a learned institution at home, but such matters not being appreciated then as they are now, it was refused." Fascinated by the history of Boston, Drake collected all the pamphlets and ephemera he could find relating to the city. During a hunter's journey abroad between 1858 and 1860, he searched for old and rare, American books, English history and antiquities, archeology. Writer and scholar, a founder of the New England Historic Genealogical Society, Drake collected an important library of some twelve thousand volumes and fifty thousand pamphlets principally concerned with the Indians and early colonial history. He wore many caps, not the least remarkable of which was his cap as antiquarian bookseller. Between 1864 and 1875 he issued *Catalogues of rare, useful and curious books, and tracts, . . . in American literature, chiefly historical and descriptive of the United States*. His Antiquarian Book-store became the rendezvous of Bancroft and Prescott, Sparks and Edward Everett, Orestes Brownson and Nathan Hall, of "people from remote places . . . fond of research in the pigeon holes of antiquity." Between 1830 when he began business and 1875 when he died, "he maintained a large family, but he laid up no wealth"—no wealth, that is, except the books which were his monument, "a monument to which all the world has contributed a stone."

In the same period that Samuel G. Drake set out his shingle on Cornhill, Thomas M. Burnham opened there a small shop called the "Antique Bookstore" dealing in secondhand books, curiosities, shells, coins, and Indian relics. This would become the nucleus for the large and important establishment of Thomas' son, T.O.H.P. Burnham (1813–1891). Born in Essex shortly after Perry's victory on Lake Erie, young Burnham was named Thomas Oliver Hazard Perry Burnham. Perry Burnham had every qualification for the antiquarian bookseller. "He was quick, keen, shrewd, and had a remarkable intuitive knowledge of books. His judgment of the value of rare or old volumes was singularly true. The rapid way in which he would run through a pile of books offered for purchase—turning over a few of them, glancing at their contents, testing their condition—and estimate their worth was often surprising. He knew his great stock, crowding shelves, corners, and nooks of his large shop, intimately."[25] Just how intimately becomes obvious from a Burnham anecdote. When Dr. Ezra Gannett inquired about "a certain book supposed to be out of print," the proprietor replied: "Gannett, you've got the wrong book. Go up to the third story, turn to your left, and on the third shelf near the end you'll find the book you want."

During his lengthy career Burnham moved his shop several times, from Washington Street to the corner of School and Tremont, adjoining the Parker House, and finally to the basement of the Old South Meetinghouse. There, in "rambling, dimly lighted vaults" could be found "his immense stock of old books and pamphlets, making . . . 'over fifty wagon-loads.' " (Usually his exceptionally rare books were guarded from the ordinary eye in "choice corners, not for sale.") And there could be met the ubiquitous proprietor, "a small, slightly built, wiry, nervous, high-strung man," outwardly "abrupt and brusque," generally dresssed "in a 'pepper-and-salt' suit," wearing "a tall silk hat, sometimes almost as antique as his shop, often in doors as well as out." Throughout his career he was an habitué of the auctionhouse, in his early days paying cash to the auctioneer for each volume he purchased and placed by the side of his chair. When he died—"a millionaire"—in 1891, his books were fittingly dispersed at auction by the terms of his will. The successful bidders, however, were three of his long-term employees. One of them, Richard Lichtenstein, had entered Burnham's in 1858, age eleven, receiving $2 a week for his labors. With another Burnham assistant, Henry F. Dodge, Lichtenstein was to take over the business and, after the dissolution of their partnership in 1908, he would continue on his own, becoming in his turn dean of the Boston book trade.

In the second half of the nineteenth century there were other shops in Boston to which collectors could turn for their specialties. N. J. Bartlett and Company on Cornhill drew the Episcopal clergy to its array of theological works. The grey-bearded proprietor sat silent near the door, merely nodding to customers, while his partner, William H. Chase, the "genius of the place," displayed the beauties of the Aldines and Elzevirs, the Baskervilles, Bodonis, Bulmers and Pickerings he had purchased in London for stock.[26]

At still another bookshop, that of William H. Piper and Company on Washington Street, the new as well as the "rare and curious" were sold. Inclined to flamboyant advertising, Piper's, one of the largest establishments in the 1860s, was a bustling emporium, and it was there that a significant Boston bookseller received his training.[27]

After six years' experience with William Veazie and eleven with W. H. Piper and Company, Charles E. Lauriat (1842–1920) in August 1872 formed a partnership with Dana Estes as Estes & Lauriat. At 143 Washington Street, opposite the Old South Church, the young men offered the "choicest selections of books from the English and American markets." Their timing was, in a way, unfortunate, for on 9 November 1872 fire swept through the business district of Boston, and flames devoured not only general merchandise but "Italian illuminated manuscripts," early printed and extra-illustrated books. Estes & Lauriat, it has been observed, started business "on the edge of the smoking Sahara of ashes, brick, stone and twisted iron." Nonetheless, the following year Charles Lauriat made his first book-buying trip abroad, and the retail division of Estes & Lauriat began to attract the habitués of the Saturday Club, the New England Transcendentalists and the Boston Renaissance gentlemen. It was difficult to resist Charles E. Lauriat or his books. Indeed it was said of him, "Whoever falls into his hands in searching for books may as well surrender at once, for with Mr. Lauriat 'success is a duty' and he never fails to sell." What he sold consisted to a large extent of leather-bound glories: "Tall green Dickens, Tall blue Thackeray, Tall gray Ruskin. Leather novels. Leather essays. Leather memoirs. Novels, essays and memoirs that once stood in the wainscotted library and filled the walls to the frosted ceiling. . . . Lauriat really means . . . Leather."[28]

In 1898 the partnership was dissolved, and Lauriat took over the retail department, offering the "choice and extensive stock of New and Old Books, which has for many years made their famous 'Old South' bookstore a favorite resort for book lovers." At Lauriat's on Washington Street, the collector would mount a flight of stairs in the rear to the "Balcony Book Room" where association copies vied with Pompadour bindings, sporting books with colorplate books, limited editions and sets in "new extra leather bindings" with presentation Dickenses, Rackhams and Dulacs. Other treasures were housed in a large room in the front of the basement known as "Lauriat's Old Book Room."

Frederic Melcher, later of the Bowker Company, was employed by the Lauriat firm between 1895 and 1913. He was fond of reminiscing about his days at Lauriat's, and he has left a vivid picture not only of "Mr. Lauriat . . . a fine-looking man with a full, white beard," but of the "Lauriat bookstore at which I arrived . . . every morning at eight."[29] He recalled its

two show windows, one devoted to the old and rare stock and the other to current books. Under one side was a sidewalk-level window which swung open to let in the wooden cases and bundles of arriving books or to let shipments out. Coal for the one central hot-air furnace was poured down through a manhole. . . . Dark oak bookcases ran the full length of the store. . . . The flat counters of heavy oak ran both sides of a main aisle and so near to the shelves that customers felt like intruders if they went back to browse. The counters had broad drawers that might house picture books, prayerbooks and hymnals, or perhaps were used for the cloth sheets that were thrown over every counter at night to catch the dust from Jim Dooley's sweeping of the hardwood floor. Dust was pursued and flicked off with flat feather dusters from morning to night. . . .

The dust settled upon a different kind of stock in the bookshop of George Emery Littlefield (1844–1915). Born in Boston in 1844, a graduate of the Latin School and of Harvard (1866), he began dealing in books as early as 1868, later setting up at 67 Cornhill. There he specialized in Americana in general and genealogy in particular, a dealer more akin in his predilections to Samuel G. Drake than to Charles E. Lauriat. Although the store was small, with a "dingy and un[pre]possessing front," in the city of Cabots and Lowells it became "the center of an entire generation of collectors. . . . Some twenty feet back from the front was a raised half decked floor. On the left hand corner of this, close up to the Brattle Street window, stood Mr. Littlefield's desk, and here he was wont to hold Communion with kindred spirits of the book hunting and book loving fraternity."[30]

While he was "not as diplomatic as he might have been," he conveyed in plain direct speech his "marvellous knowledge of books" and his "unfailing judgment as to prices and values." He suffered neither fools nor hagglers gladly. A customer looking for "an old novel for a quarter, or a last year's number of Harper's Bazaar" failed to arouse his enthusiasm. When one client demurred at the price of 75 cents for a book, remarking, "they sell that book for fifty cents on Bromfield Street, . . . But . . . they haven't got any now," Littlefield replied: "When I don't have any, I might sell them for ten cents." Persistent hagglers discovered that Littlefield's books persistently increased rather than decreased in price.

When a trustee representing a well-known library instructed Littlefield to purchase a list of books at auction, the bookseller refrained from acquiring certain items, thus arousing the ire of the trustee.

"I thought I told you to buy them all. Why didn't you do it?" At this Littlefield queried: "Don't you get my catalogs?" to which the reply was, "I suppose so."

"Well, don't you ever read them?"

"I suppose our people look them over more or less."

"Don't you know that one of the books you wanted me to pay six dollars for has been in my catalog the last two or three years at two dollars and fifty cents?"

Littlefield issued his first catalogue in February 1878: a *Catalogue of Historical Collections, Town Histories and Miscellaneous Books, relating to the Early History of Our Country, selected from the stock of Geo. E. Littlefield, 67 Cornhill St., Boston, Mass., Dealer in Old, Rare, and Curious Books . . . American History A Specialty*. All his descriptions were accurate and concise, and it was said that "quite a number of tight-fisted Yankees used his catalogs at Libbie's auctions, and made a rule of bidding from one half to two thirds of the price at which the books were therein valued." He himself was a familiar figure at Libbie's sales, where he "usually sat on the front row," presenting to the rooms his bald head fringed with grayish-black at the base, and bidding by means of "a peculiar muscular contraction in and around the left eye, vulgarly termed a wink."

One librarian said of George Littlefield that "he had forgotten more in his line of business than all the rest of us ever knew." His biographer amended this statement, remarking: "I never knew Mr. Littlefield to forget anything. Nor did I ever see him stumped for want of a book he knew he had and couldn't find. I really believe that on the darkest night of any Friday, the thirteenth of the month, he could go to the store at midnight, and without aid of any light, find the particular book he wanted."

Actually there never was electric light at Littlefield's, which also remained uninvaded by typewriter or telephone. Without the aid of such appurtenances he not only sold books but wrote them too—his *Early Boston Booksellers 1642–1711*, his *Early Schools and School-Books of New England*, his *Early Massachusetts Press, 1638–1711*—all of which were published by Boston's Club of Odd Volumes. As his eulogist remarked after his death in 1915: "neither did he employ any of the twentieth century methods of card filing, to aid him to supply information on topics about which he might be consulted. He didn't have to; he had it all in his head."

In 1894, just a few years after the Burnham auction, while Estes & Lauriat and Littlefield were flourishing, an Irish émigré entered into a bookselling partnership with headquarters in downtown Boston. The partnership between Andrew McCance (1863–1939) and Alfred Smith lasted only from 1894 to 1896, but it was under that style that McCance continued in business until his death. Born in Killyleagh, County Down, Ireland, in 1863, with little opportunity for formal education, he arrived in the United States at age twenty-two and worked as a machinist in a Boston pianoforte factory. Then, as his neighbor and colleague Charles Goodspeed would relate, "An impelling love for reading, unsatisfied by brief schooling and the few books accessible to him in his boyhood, may have prompted him to turn to the trade in secondhand books."[31]

Smith & McCance operated at successive locations in Bromfield Street, Park Street and Ashburton Place. Whatever the firm's address, it was McCance's wit and cordiality—as well as his stock—that attracted his clientele of clergymen and actors, jurists and teachers. The stock itself was of the general or miscellaneous kind, except for his speciality of works on Christian Science, housed in a special room on the third floor. Nonetheless, among the rarities that passed through his hands was the "*rara avis* of American first editions," Poe's *Tamerlane*.

The McCance bookshop, with "thousands of old books" that filled the shelves from basement to balcony and overflowed in spaces beneath the counters, became the meetingplace of bibliophiles and friends. In the evening, after McCance had dined at a nearby restaurant, it was his custom to return to the shop to chat with callers. Among the latter was his closest friend P. K. Foley who would sit in the rear smoking a cigar while McCance stood by his side, both greeting visitors in "the mellow roll of . . . two soft Irish voices . . . like a sample of the Abbey players."[32]

Patrick Kevin Foley (1856?-1937) was not only McCance's close friend but a distinguished bibliographer and bookseller as well. He is better known for that "pioneer and authoritative reference book,"[33] *American Authors, 1795–1895*, than for his Hamilton Place shop. Yet that shop takes a place in the bookselling annals of Boston. Surrounded by "the implements of his profession," the proprietor worked "in retired dignity," and though he certainly described and catalogued more books than he sold—for his stock was exclusively rare, small and selective—he played a role on the bibliopolic stage of the hub of the universe.[34]

That role, as well as the roles of Burnham, Bartlett, Littlefield, McCance, and of that "genial soul" W. G. Colesworthy, were all observed by yet another note-taking colleague Charles E. Goodspeed (1867–1950). Indeed, it was at the shop of Estes & Lauriat that the young bibliophile saw a copy of Ruskin's *Seven Lamps of Architecture* priced at $75, and thereafter became "a haunter of bookshops and auction rooms."[35]

Born in Cotuit, Massachusetts, Charles Goodspeed was graduated from Newton Centre grammar school and became an office boy in a stationery store, earning $100 a year. Subsequently, for fourteen years, he worked in an agricultural implements company. While his formal education had been meager, his informal education was rich, and he frequented all places where books were sold, including "junkshops and odd-corners." By 1898, the year of Manila Bay and the discovery of Klondike gold, he was unemployed. Encouraged by the New York antiquarian dealer Isaac Mendoza, young Goodspeed invested his savings at Bangs' Auction Rooms and, with a capital of $600 and some Mendoza remainders, made the bibliopolic plunge.

He opened a bookshop at 5A Park Steet, Boston, and proceeded to juggle his meager stock so that his displays would appear more varied than they were. The Goodspeed motto, "Anything that's a book," was adopted. In October 1899 the proprietor issued his first catalogue.

As the years passed and the catalogues multiplied, a procession of great books and engravings passed through Goodspeed's hands. In an establishment where "the kitchen-hearth of the Quincys" had been rededicated to "the *Lares* of the bookshop," could be found from time to time "landmarks of American historical engraving"; a *History of the British Dominions in North America* (London 1773) with Josiah Quincy's note: "Purchased in Philadelphia out of the library of Benj. Franklin"; Thoreau's *Week on the Concord and Merrimack Rivers* inscribed by the author to his sister; Thoreau's own annotated copy of *Walden* in original binding; Emerson's *Nature* with a presentation inscription from Thoreau to a classmate at the time of their graduation; the first catalogue of the Library of Congress; Stephen Daye's printing of John Winthrop's *Declaration of war against the Narragansets*; and not one but two *Tamerlanes*.

Goodspeed's visitors were almost as distinguished as his stock. That friend of the Transcendentalists, Franklin B. Sanborn, sold to the proprietor Thoreau's college themes and the galley proofs of *A Week on the Concord and Merrimack*; Fritz Kreisler chatted with him about his collection of incunables; Houdini, the magician-collector, the naturalist John Burroughs, the poet Amy Lowell, Franklin D. Roosevelt— all called in at Goodspeed's from time to time.

When Charles E. Goodspeed came to write his autobiography he described himself as a *Yankee Bookseller*. With his Yankee shrewdness were mingled a strong strain of Ruskin's "moral fervor," a devotion to tradition, and a disinclination to enter that "dusty field where bibliographical points are hotly contested by eager warriors of a younger generation." He was also an extremely modest man and, as a result, his autobiography reveals as much, if not more, about others than about himself.

Goodspeed's autobiography recalls his enchantment with a copy of Ruskin found at Estes & Lauriat. Lauriat worked once for Piper. The present leads us by a route sometimes circuitous, sometimes direct, to the past. During a journey to New England in the early 1940s, Leona Rostenberg and I first saw a copy of *The Month at Goodspeed's* and so were introduced to the fascinations of the art of cataloguing. The bookseller does what he is fated to do—"picking up the odds and ends of time." The Boston antiquarian bookseller may seem less spectacular in his collections, less flamboyant in his promotion, than his New York peers. If he lacked show, he never lacked substance. He provided the roots for the flowering of New England. Like his prototype, Samuel G. Drake, he was a Prospero who called up "the spirits of the Puritan Fathers from the regions of the past"[36] and made of his bookshop his kingdom.

NOTES

1. Worthington Chauncey Ford, *The Boston Book Market 1679–1700* (Boston: Club of Odd Volumes, 1917), p. 22.

2. Ibid., p. 23.

3. John Dunton, *The Life and Errors of John Dunton* (New York: Franklin, 1969), I, 95 f.

4. Evans 21; George Emery Littlefield, *Early Boston Booksellers 1642–1711* (Boston: Club of Odd Volumes, 1900), p. 25.

5. Ford, *The Boston Book Market*, p. 15.

6. Evans 645; Samuel A. Green, "An Early Book-catalogue printed in Boston, with other Bibliographical Matter," *Proceedings of the Massachusetts Historical Society*, Second Series, X (April 1896), pp. 540–547.

7. John Dunton, *Letters written from New-England A.D. 1686* (New York: Franklin, n.d.), pp. 315–316.

8. Thomas Goddard Wright, *Literary Culture in Early New England 1620–1730* (New York: Russell & Russell, 1966), p. 177.

9. Isaiah Thomas, *The History of Printing in America*, ed. Marcus A. McCorison (New York: Weathervane, 1970), pp. 195–196.

10. William T. Baxter, "Daniel Henchman, A Colonial Bookseller," *Essex Institute Historical Collections* LXX:1 (January 1934), pp. 1–30.

11. George L. McKay, *American Book Auction Catalogues 1713–1934 A Union List* (New York: New York Public Library, 1937), pp. 2, 39, 40.

12. Wright, *Literary Culture in Early New England*, pp. 176 f and passim. For further details of colonial bookselling and taste in Boston, see Henry Walcott Boynton, *Annals of American Bookselling 1638–1850* (New York: Wiley, 1932), passim; Jacob L. Chernofsky, "Books and Bookselling in Boston," *AB Bookman's Weekly* (6 November 1978), pp. 2771–2774; Dunton, *Letters written from New-England*, pp. 77–81; Hellmut Lehmann-Haupt, *The Book in America* (New York: Bowker, 1951), pp. 47–49; Thomas, *The History of Printing in America*, pp. 183–213; Justin Winsor, *The Memorial History of Boston* (Boston: Osgood, 1883), I, 455, 500–501; II, xix, 413 f.

13. Evans 3765; Winsor, *The Memorial History of Boston*, II, 414.

14. Thomas, *The History of Printing in America*, pp. 207–208.

15. Ibid., p. 209.

16. Winsor, *The Memorial History of Boston*, II, 432.

17. John E. Alden, "John Mein: Scourge of Patriots," *Publications of The Colonial Society of Massachusetts* XXXIV (February 1942), pp. 578–580; Charles K. Bolton, "Circulating Libraries in Boston, 1765–1865," *Publications of The Colonial Society of Massachusetts* XI (February 1907), p. 196; Thomas, *The History of Printing in America*, p. 210; Winsor, *The Memorial History of Boston*, II, xix.

18. Worthington Chauncey Ford, "Henry Knox and the London Book-Store in Boston 1771–1774," *Massachusetts Historical Society Proceedings* LXI (June 1928), pp. 225–304.

19. Madeleine B. Stern, *Books and Book People in 19th-Century America* (New York and London: Bowker, 1978), pp. 47–117. See also Lehmann-Haupt, *The Book in America*, p. 134.

20. George H. Sargent, *Lauriat's 1872–1922* (Boston: Privately printed, 1922), pp. 12–13.

21. Madeleine B. Stern, *Imprints on History: Book Publishers and American Frontiers* (Bloomington: Indiana University Press, 1956; reprinted, New York: AMS Press, 1975), pp. 24–35. See also Elizabeth Cometti, ed., *Jefferson's Ideas on a University Library* (Charlottesville: University of Virginia, 1950), passim.

22. Richard L. Herrnstadt, ed., *The Letters of A. Bronson Alcott* (Ames: State University of Iowa Press, 1969), pp. 650f.

23. Stern, *Books and Book People in 19th-Century America*, pp. 121–135. See also Leona Rostenberg, "Number Thirteen West Street," *Book Collector's Packet* IV:1 (September 1945), pp. 7–9.

24. John H. Sheppard, *A Memoir of Samuel G. Drake*, A.M. (Albany: Munsell, 1863), pp. 33–34, and passim. See also *Samuel G. Drake. His Life-*

Work and His Library (N.p., n.d.), pp. 1–6. Quotations about Drake are from these works.

25. Edwin M. Bacon, "Old Boston Booksellers," *The Bookman* IV:6 (February 1897), pp. 542–546; Adolf Growoll Collection, *American Book Trade History* VIII, 87.

26. Charles E. Goodspeed, *Yankee Bookseller* (Boston: Houghton Mifflin, 1937), p. 24.

27. Raymond L. Kilgour, *Estes and Lauriat: A History 1872–1898* (Ann Arbor: University of Michigan Press, 1957), p. 22.

28. Ibid., p. 183 and passim; George H. Sargent, *Lauriat's 1872–1922* (Boston: Privately printed, 1922), pp. 19, 42–43, and passim.

29. Frederic G. Melcher, "A Boston Bookstore at the Turn of the Century," *Proceedings of the American Antiquarian Society* 66:1 (18 April 1956), pp. 37–50.

30. For quotations regarding Littlefield, see Frank Jones Wilder, *An Old Boston Bookseller: George E. Littlefield As I Knew Him* (offprint from *Massachusetts Magazine* [N.p., n.d.]), pp. 177–184. See also Lehmann-Haupt, *The Book in America*, p. 394.

31. Charles Eliot Goodspeed, "Andrew McCance," *The New England Historical and Genealogical Register* XCIV (July 1940), pp. 211–214.

32. Ibid., p. 213 (quoted from *Publishers Weekly*).

33. Lehmann-Haupt, *The Book in America*, p. 394.

34. Goodspeed, *Yankee Bookseller*, p. 30.

35. Ibid., p. 14 and passim. See also Leona Rostenberg and Madeleine B. Stern, "Antiquarian Booksellers and Their Memoirs," *AB Bookman's Weekly* (22–29 December 1980), pp. 4196–4198. For the later development of Goodspeed's, and its departmentalization with the entry into the firm of Michael Walsh, Louis Holman, George T. Goodspeed, Norman Dodge, Gordon Banks, and others, see George T. Goodspeed, "The Bookseller's Apprentice," *The Professional Rare Bookseller* 5 (1983). *The Month at Goodspeed's* ran between 1929 and 1969 under the aegis of Norman Dodge.

36. Sheppard, *A Memoir of Samuel G. Drake*, p. 34.

2

Philadelphia

Boston was America's first important book center, a distinction which eventually passed to New York. But in between another city arose as the backdrop of enlightenment where books were imported and collected, circulated and read, bought and sold. In 1772 the Loyalist Jacob Duché wrote of Philadelphia: "the poorest labourer upon the shore of the *Delaware* thinks himself entitled to deliver his sentiments in matters of religion or politics with as much freedom as the gentleman or scholar. . . . Such is the prevailing taste for books of every kind, that almost every man is a reader."[1] As a more modern observer commented of the pre-Revolutionary city:

> An expanding market for reading matter . . . was assiduously cultivated by a group of enterprising printers and booksellers. . . . Books of domestic composition poured from native presses, and along with continuous importations lined the shelves of private libraries and bookstores. The range of private collections was geatly augmented by the services of subscription libraries, taverns and coffeehouses. By means of the printed word the propaganda of enlightenment reached all citizens.[2]

Philadelphia's geography exercised an influence upon this intellectual ferment. Its "proximity to the South and its situation at the head of the wagon road over the mountains to Pittsburgh and thence down the Ohio to the western country"[3] facilitated, and would continue for some years to facilitate, the distribution of books. The city's political position also played a part in its bookish supremacy. If the first Continental Congress assembled in Philadelphia in 1774, so too did delegates with a literary turn who took time off from the exigencies of statesmanship to pay a visit to bookstores.

In 1742 there were five "shops devoted exclusively to the sale of books" in the city; the number rose by the 1770s to "more than thirty." And as for "printers, publishers and booksellers, in various combinations of those functions, operating . . . for varying periods of time," 212 have been counted in Philadelphia between 1760 and 1820.[4] Indeed, as early as 1720, Andrew Bradford had sold imported books along with whale bones, Jesuit's bark and beaver hats. Six years later, Benjamin Franklin was working for the Quaker merchant Denham who had brought a stock of books from London. The following year, Franklin established the "Junto," and by 1730 founded his bookstore which the foremost historian of publishing has described as "one of the best in the colonies."[5] By 1748 David Hall was a partner in this flourishing establishment on Market Street which was "provisioned from British sources."[6] In the decades between the 1740s and the 1770s, the prevailing taste for books was satisfied. The city boasted James Logan's library—"the finest private library in the middle colonies,"[7] which in 1768 was opened once a week to the male public. The year before, Lewis Nicola opened a New Circulating Library on Philadelphia's Second Street. Philadelphia's "gentleman merchants" had long been inspired to invest in books— Isaac Norris, Sr., beginning his collection at Fair Hill in 1722, and William Peters constructing a library building to adjoin his Belmont mansion in 1745. And were not even the Hessians so impressed by Francis Hopkinson's "library of rare and fine books" that they struggled to save it during the burning of Bordentown in 1776?[8]

There is every evidence that, prior to the outbreak of the Revolution, there were rare books in Philadelphia: rare and ephemeral Americana in the library of the Swiss miniaturist Pierre Eugène du Simitière; scientific and medical works; Greek and Latin, French and Italian literature assembled by Philadelphians who had traveled abroad. And books were filched in pre-Revolutionary Philadelphia, too, for one citizen advertised in 1772 that "Altieri's Italian Grammar, of an old edition, bound in parchment, was a few years ago lent to some person of this city, by a Gentleman from Jamaica, who borrowed it of the owner. As it is a book very scarce, and was purchased . . . at a very high price, . . . the owner . . . will gratefully thank the person . . . for delivering it to the Printer."[9]

While there is no doubt that most of the rare books assembled in colonial Philadelphia had been imported from abroad or acquired by collectors in the course of European sojourns, there is also no doubt that some acquisitions of this nature were made at home. Certainly there were booksellers in the city whose shelves yielded not only patent medicines and paper hangings, penknives and sealing wax, but treasure in the way of broadsides, psalters, or "pretty Books" for children. Many are recalled only by a listing in a directory or a trade card, an auction record or a sales catalogue. Some few impressed their times more memorably with the flavor of their personalities, the vigor and productivity of their careers. Of these surely the chief was Robert Bell who has been described as "the first important buyer of private libraries and dealer on a large scale in secondhand books."[10] Bell, whose fame depended more perhaps upon his techniques as an auctioneer than upon his skills as a bookseller, has also been described as a "witty man of 'doubtful' religion," and, by Isaiah Thomas, as "a thorough bookseller, punctual and fair in his dealings; and, as a companion, . . . sensible, social and witty." Publisher of Paine's *Common Sense* (1776), he would be dubbed "Patriot Printer." He described himself as a "Provedore to the Sentimentalists" and his wares as "Jewels and Diamonds."

Born in Glasgow about 1732, the "stout, chunky" Scot Robert Bell had been a bookseller in Dublin before venturing overseas in 1767. Besides offering cheap reprints of English books at his High Street shop at the sign of the Sugar Loaf, he later opened a circulating library where he made available to subscribers literature tending "to dignify the human Mind" and "calculated to guide the Youth of both Sexes through the dangerous Whirlpool of agitated Passions."

Despite his credo, "the more books are sold the more will be sold," Bell found that "after waiting two or three years for the expected purchasers, the bookseller is convinced he was mistaken in the calculation of his customers, and then he determineth . . . to sell them by auction. . . . These sales by auction . . . realizeth dead stock into live cash." Robert Bell realized considerable dead stock into live cash as an auctioneer who not only developed the book auction "to its colonial apogee," but attracted a delighted audience to his lively vendues. One observer reported: "It was as good as a play to attend his sales." He was "full of drollery, and many . . . would buy a book from good humour. . . . There were few authors of whom he could not tell some anecdote, which would get the audience in a roar. He sometimes had a can of beer beside him, and would drink comical healths. His buffoonery was diversified and without limit." It was this "buffooning" bookseller who launched an attack upon the Act requiring auctioneers to be appointed and licensed. *Bell's Memorial on the Free Sale of Books: To which are added Sentiments on What Is Freedom, and what is Slavery* opposed monopoly in the booktrade and declared, en passant, that "Persons in Power, like female Beauties, seldom hear the Voice of Truth." It was somehow fitting that this flamboyant Scot should have died as he did, on 23 September 1784, en route to holding a book auction in Charleston, South Carolina. His mantle seems to have been assumed by William Prichard (or Pritchard), "Bookseller and Stationer at the American Circulating Library, opposite Letitiæ-Court, Market Street, Philadelphia, who gives a generous price for any Library or Parcels of Books."[11]

Another Scot followed close upon the heels of Robert Bell. By 1771, Robert Aitken of Dalkeith was ensconced on Front Street opposite the London Coffee House, where he offered for sale "imported books and those of his friendly local compatriots."[12] Moreover Aitken "sold to peddlers and storekeepers in western Pennsylvania and in villages from Maryland to South Carolina." His wares attracted delegates to the Congress, among them such illustrissimi as John Adams who obtained sealing wax from his shop, Benjamin Rush who ordered bindings from him, and Thomas Jefferson who in 1776 purchased from him a quire of paper. According to Isaiah Thomas, Aitken was "industrious and frugal." He was also productive, for the first English Bible printed in America (1782) came from the Aitken press. Printer and engraver, stationer, bookbinder and bookseller, Aitken may also have been— according to the speculations of a twentieth-century colleague—"the first antiquarian bookseller in Philadelphia."[13]

There were several other possible candidates for that role among the early booksellers who demonstrated a tendency toward specialization.[14] Quaker items, for example, were available from James Chattin, printer to the Society of Friends. Sparhawk & Anderton, purveyors of drugs, also offered at their London Bookstore on Market Street near the London Coffee House "a very large stock of books" including "a very great choice . . . adapted for the instruction and amusement of all the little masters and misstresses in America." Fine editions (if not yet antiquarian) could be had at high prices at the premises of Charles Startin: "Bibles, and the works of Milton, Terence, Catullus, . . . Horace and Virgil, 'printed by Baskerville . . . and bound in an elegant manner.' " According to his *Catalogue of new and old books for sale*

(1772), William Woodhouse offered "many uncommon books, seldom to be found." Searchers after German rarities might find a few among Henry Miller's numerous imports, for Miller, born on the upper Rhine, was not only a Whig but a Moravian, and his *Catalogus von mehr als 700 meist Deutschen Büchern* (1769?) might well have contained an early Teutonic sleeper. Among the children's books featured by Norman and Thomas Bedwell on Front Street, were to be enjoyed Lilliputian Auctions, Small Fables, Books of Birds. By the end of the Revolution, Thomas Dobson set up shop on Second Street, and there he, and his son Judah after him, offered many desirable items to Philadelphia bibliophiles. Indeed, it would be Thomas Dobson who in 1816 sold at the Stone-house on South Second Street "many very scarce and valuable books" from the library of the late Dr. Joseph Priestley, the English scientist and radical thinker.

Of all those who engaged in the sale of the printed word in post–Revolutionary Philadelphia, none was more famous than Mathew Carey, who built up a huge establishment from modest beginnings.[15] An Irish Catholic, he had fought English oppression of Irish Catholics. Sent to Paris, he had worked at Franklin's printing office in Passy. At twenty-four he had landed in Philadelphia with twelve guineas in his pocket. By 1792, without capital, he opened a "shop . . . of very moderate dimensions; but, small as it was, he had not full-bound books enough to fill the shelves—a considerable portion of them being filled with spelling books. He procured a credit at bank, which enabled him to extend his business; and by care, indefatigable industry, the most rigid punctuality and frugality, he gradually advanced in the world. For twenty-five years, winter and summer, he was always present at the opening of his store." As a result of his model proprietorship, by 1821, the year before his son continued the business, Mathew Carey's bookstore was a four-story brick building on Fourth and Chestnut streets. The founder had launched the *American Museum*, become first president of the American Company of Booksellers, and had not only printed books but sold them, too.

Many of his sales had been accomplished through the services of that incomparable agent Parson Weems, who for more than three decades carried his wares up and down the eastern seaboard. While Carey's stock can scarcely be described as antiquarian, the works he sold helped extend the taste for and love of books in general. Bibliophily sometimes begins in strange ways and strange places. Indeed, as Parson Weems wrote to Mathew Carey in 1809: "Remember that among the numbers running to your Bookstores for . . . Anti-bilious Pills or Vermifuges, some may pick up some of your good books that may purge their minds of the far worse worms of Error & Vice."[16]

To castigate his own notions of "Error & Vice," the vituperative English pamphleteer William Cobbett[17] set up shop on Second Street opposite Christ Church. Never one for self-deprecation, Cobbett boasted, "Few booksellers in the United States carry on that business with more life than I do." Certainly there was the hum not only of activity but of violent displeasure there when in 1796 the proprietor displayed portraits of George III and Lord Howe until a mob threatened him with tar and feathers. Cobbett's own political pamphlets had been printed by William Bradford's son Thomas, but when Bradford insisted upon anonymity and high payment, the writer became his own publisher. Besides printing and selling his effusions and his own newspaper at his Political Book-Store, Cobbett sold books—English books, pamphlets and periodicals imported through his London agent John Wright. One shipment, received early in 1799, was described as "the most extensive assortment of new, valuable, and elegant works ever imported into this country at one time." In spite of that, Cobbett shortly decamped to New York, and his shop was occupied after 1800 by Asbury Dickins.

Surely among all these imports from abroad there could be found some secondhand or antiquarian books. The "solid and continuous influence of England"[18] upon the American book market was matched if not superseded around the time of the French Revolution by the influence of France. Over a long period of time Philadelphia booksellers had offered their customers "an unexpectedly rich variety of titles by French authors of the sixteenth and seventeenth centuries." Molière and Fénelon, Voltaire and Rousseau, Raynal and Montesquieu were all available in Philadelphia, and with the outbreak of the French Revolution and in its aftermath, there was a heavy influx of French books into the city. As one scholar has put it, "The bookstores in Philadelphia were apparently more richly stocked with French books, especially in the last quarter of the eighteenth century, than was any-where else the case. . . . It would appear that this little city was very much in the current of the European world of interests."[19] Philadel-phians with a Gallic turn could find their desiderata at such a firm as Boinod and Gaillard which issued a *Catalogue des livres* in 1784.[20] A decade later a shop was opened on Philadelphia's First Street by another

French bookseller, Médéric Louis Elie Moreau de Saint-Méry. Born in Martinique, Moreau de Saint-Méry had gone to Paris to arrange for the publication of his books. At the time of the Fall of the Bastille he had received the keys of that prison and for the next three days had governed the city as king of Paris. Hounded by Robespierre, he escaped the guillotine by fleeing to America, and in 1794 he opened a shop with a "beautiful signboard" which became the meeting place of French émigrés who congregated there daily "to chat . . . discuss the fate of the world and drink madeira." And those exiles from the Revolution who had settled around Second, Third and Fourth Streets near the waterfront, making of Philadelphia a "French Noah's Ark," could also pick up French books from the bookseller-stationer-publisher Moreau de Saint-Méry.[21]

If no individual Philadelphia bookseller prior to 1800 can be singled out as primarily an antiquarian dealer, by the turn of the century a very likely candidate presented himself. Fortunately the Philadelphia collector William Mackenzie did not hold the dim view of booksellers harbored by James Logan. Booksellers, Logan believed, "were an unscrupulous lot who took advantage of his distance from them to send books in inferior condition and at inflated prices."[22] As a result, he gathered most of the books in his library from private owners or their heirs. Not so William Mackenzie. Mackenzie not only "reflected a revolutionary development in American book collecting" since he was "the first American to collect rare books as rare books"[23]—his library including incunables, chivalric romances, the first Caxton in America—but he also apparently trusted booksellers. At least he trusted Nicholas Gouin Dufief.

Born at the inception of the American Revolution, Dufief[24] had, by the time the French Revolution had ended, ensconced himself—via the West Indies and Princeton—in Philadelphia. Between 1798, when he appears at South Second Street, and 1828, when he is listed at Chestnut, he occupied some nine different Philadelphia locations, matching his geographical mobility with the protean nature of his occupations, for he is described as schoolmaster, translator, librarian, author-bookseller, stationer and bookseller. It was in this last capacity that he engaged the attention and the trust of collector Mackenzie.

Between 1801 and 1803 Dufief was involved in the dispersal of the William Byrd and the Benjamin Franklin collections. The Byrd library at Westover was, according to Edwin Wolf, 2nd, and Marie E. Korey,

"a shining outpost of European culture on the American frontier, representing the tastes and pursuits of a family of rich, intelligent and busy
Virginia gentlemen." Begun in the seventeenth century by the first
William Byrd and developed by the second of the name, it was eventually dispersed as the result of the prodigalities of the third William
Byrd. According to Wolf and Korey, "The books were bought *en bloc*
from his widow by the iron-master, Isaac Zane, who shipped them to
Philadelphia in 1781. They were first put up at auction under the
hammer of the exuberant Robert Bell, then placed in the hands of
various booksellers. By 1803 the library had been disposed of by frag-
mentation. In the final stage of the dispersal Nicholas Gouin Dufief,
professor of French literature and bookseller, handled what remained
of the library."[25] Among the items Mackenzie purchased from Dufief
was the manuscript catalogue of the Westover library, listing 2,345
titles in 3,513 volumes.

As for "The Franklin Library," "part of the select and valuable Library
of the celebrated Philosopher and Statesman" was offered for sale by
Dufief on 11 September 1801, the year he acquired it. He sold some
volumes to William Mackenzie as well as to the American Philosophical
Society. Another of Dufief's Franklin customers was Zachariah Poulson,
Jr., printer-publisher and librarian of the Library Company, who purchased from the bookseller "thirty-seven quarto and four octavo volumes, containing 'all the principal Pamphlets and Papers on Publick
Affairs down to 1715.' " One hundred fifty years later, those pamphlet
volumes, given by Poulson to the Library Company, were proved to
have come from Benjamin Franklin's library.[26]

More immediately, Dufief's efforts to sell the remainder of his Franklin collection to such potential purchasers as William Duane, Thomas
Jefferson, the Library of Congress, were largely unsuccessful. On 12
March 1803, therefore, the Franklin residue, including works in English, French, Italian, German, Greek and Latin, as well as several
manuscripts, was sold at auction by Shannon and Poalk of High Street,
Philadelphia, as "the property of N.G. Dufief, bookseller."[27]

In the decades that followed, while Dufief was still in business selling
books and seeing through the press one edition after another of his
Nature Displayed, in her mode of Teaching Language to Man, several
colleagues set up their stands in Philadelphia. Moses Thomas, who
would become the city's first major nineteenth-century auctioneer, began as publisher-bookseller in 1812. Fourteen years later, the Freeman

auction house began as Freeman, Son & Potter with the *Catalogue of a private library*, [that of Edward Penington] *comprising more than 6000 Volumes . . . in the different departments of Literature and the Sciences, many of which are . . . extremely Rare and Valuable*. A trade card, circa 1816, recalls the existence of E. Parker's Medical Bookstore. A year later, "America's First Catholic Bookseller," Bernard Dornin, set up a shop that included bookstore and lottery office on Walnut and Third Streets, two blocks from Mathew Carey.[28]

In 1816 John Grigg[29] arrived in Philadelphia; he would "effect rev-olutions in the book trade" by developing the "largest book distributing house in the world." Grigg was one of America's many Horatio Alger heroes. An English orphan farmer boy, he had run away to sea, and in 1816 had set out for Philadelphia. There he found work at Benjamin Warner's bookstore where he "soon learned the name of every book in the store, its price, and the place where to find it." Little wonder that Warner's Will singled out this able apprentice to carry on the business: "One or two young men," it stipulated, "in whom confidence can be reposed, might be found to take charge. . . . I consider John Grigg as possessing a peculiar talent for the bookselling business, very indus-trious, and . . . nothing in his conduct to raise a doubt . . . of his . . . correct principles." After the proprietor's death, Grigg settled Warner's business and then struck out for himself, applying his "industry" and "correct principles" to large-scale book jobbing. At his own retirement in 1850, his business would be transferred to Lippincott.

Long before then—in 1836—against the background of Jacksonian democracy, a bookstore was established in the City of Brotherly Love which would be dubbed, when it rounded out its century, "the very epitome of Philadelphia." Short and stout, persevering and industrious, William A. Leary[30] was described by an acute if vitriolic observer as one who "dealt in books as a grocer deals in sugar and candles, more by weight than from any intrinsic value." Nonetheless, William A. Leary survived. Arriving in Philadelphia from Maryland, he sold his first books out of a basket, but soon opened a stall on North Second Street next to the Camel Tavern. In time he would lease a whole building at the corner of New Street. To his bookselling activities he added publishing ventures, issuing a series of weighty tomes that have been characterized as "Leary's Bricks." Thanks no doubt to his sales of Bibles and dictionaries, he weathered the Civil War and, on his death in 1865, was succeeded by his son, William A. Leary, Jr. Junior's tenure, though brief, was not ineffective. Buying cheap and selling "at a good profit," he maintained his shop on the southeast corner of Fifth and Walnut Streets until, the victim of "stimulants," he died in 1876. At that time the business was purchased for $5,000 by Charles Mann, a Leary customer, and Edwin S. Stuart, a Leary employee. Leary & Co. was about to enter its heyday.

The character of E. S. Stuart made an indelible mark upon the character of Leary's bookstore. Here was another Alger hero who, through pluck and luck, ran the American gamut from rags to riches. In 1867 or 1868, young Stuart answered a Leary advertisement for "a boy to run errands and make himself generally useful." Hired for $3 a week, he swept and dusted the dingy looking store, and educated himself not only in books but in bookbuyers—among them Charles Sumner and Samuel Pennypacker, whose office was around the corner. At twenty-one, Edwin S. Stuart became manager of Leary's Old Book Store, and before long, with the financial help of Charles Mann, its owner. A poor boy was well on his way to his rise in the world. So, too, was Leary's Old Book Store.

Moved to South Ninth Street, Leary's boasted "one of the largest stocks of old and new books in the country" and the "largest collection of old books for sale in this city." A copy of the painting of The Old Bookworm standing atop a ladder, surrounded by books, had become the signpost of Leary's, a familiar trademark "inseparably identified" with the bookstore. At its outside stands, contemporary bookworms clustered. When they entered, they found "close to half a million volumes" filling store and ware-rooms: schoolbooks occupying the basement, the theological department on the second floor, along with medical and mechanical textbooks, law, art and music, while the ground floor was devoted to a general or miscellaneous stock. Several sections were given over to the old and rare, especially in the field of Americana. And there, through the years, could be glimpsed such collectors as Owen Wister and Howard Pyle, Houdini and Christopher Morley, Woodrow Wilson and A. Edward Newton.

The "Amenities of Book-Collecting" were available at Leary's. "Specially constructed electric light fixtures threw their beams on the open shelves or the glazed cases." No one was approached by a salesman; book lovers were encouraged to enter the domain as freely as if they were in their own libraries. Leary's bought as extensively as it sold, advertising "Books bought—Libraries purchased." Leary's "Pays cash and immediately removes the books purchased." At one time the private library of Justice Stephen J. Field of the United States Supreme Court was acquired and brought back from Washington in twenty-eight large packing cases; at another, the collection of Dr. J. G. Armstrong of Atlanta was purchased.

In 1891, Edwin S. Stuart, bookseller, became mayor-elect of the City of Brotherly Love, and it was commented that "Booksellers . . . will feel flattered that one of their fraternity has been raised to such high place." Stuart was raised to still higher place in 1906 when he succeeded the collector Samuel W. Pennypacker as governor of Pennsylvania. Meanwhile, Stuart's brother William continued the book business, purchasing abroad either personally or through agents, and introducing many new departments at Leary, Stuart & Co., including "the importation of standard editions . . . distinctive copies . . . and rare first editions from the book markets of London and Edinburgh." Often Leary's rarities were cased in bindings made by Riviere or Zaehnsdorf. And so, by 1936, the shop that had begun, so to speak, with a basket of books a century earlier, had become what John Winterich called "the very epitome of Philadelphia. To a good many thousand non-Philadelphians it *is* Philadelphia."

Leary's may have epitomized Philadelphia for many bibliophiles, but it was not alone in supplying the wants of collectors. By the mid-century some fifteen "old booksellers" with "well-appointed antiquarian bookshops" served a population of about 300,000. Philadelphia was a thriving city. From Vine to South Street the wharves lining the Delaware waterfront were "crowded with ships of every rig," some of them bound for the South. Conestoga wagons drawn by four or six horses rumbled along pike roads over the Alleghenies to Pittsburgh. The merchandise carried by those ships and wagons included books, and in the city itself, as the mid-century approached, a variety of antiquarian interests was stimulated by a variety of antiquarian booksellers. The Pine Street bookseller, William P. Caldwell, for example, could supply to the Library Company a set of first editions of McKenney and Hall's *History of the Indian Tribes.*[31] The firm of Davis & Porter had begun an operation that would become better known as Porter & Coates who, "as booksellers, specialized in art, trade, and rare books, many in fine bindings."[32] At the other end of the scale, Peter Thomson advertised himself as "The Cheap Bookseller," dealing in juveniles and floral keepsakes, and incidentally engaging as errand boy George W. Childs, future Philadelphia publishing magnate.[33] And it was in Philadelphia in 1847 that an unidentified bookseller sold to a visitor from Michigan a set of Calov's edition of the Luther Bible containing the ownership signature and "the most fascinating marginal annotations" of Johann Sebastian Bach—a unique item now known as "Bach's Bible."[34]

Thanks to the efforts of one bookseller who launched his business in 1849, a number of the antiquarians who plied their trade in Philadelphia between 1850 and 1890 have been caught in a net of words. William Brotherhead's little book, *Forty Years among the Old Booksellers of Philadelphia, with Bibliographical Remarks* is a catchall for those dealers who sat for sketches if not full-length portraits and whose idiosyncrasies are recorded by the keen observer who was their colleague. If he is short on facts, Brotherhead is long on racy, acerbic comments, and as *Publishers Weekly* remarked at the time of publication, "In his little book he sketches a few of his contemporaries in the old-book business, thus partially filling up gaps in the history of the trade that some future historian may find useful."[35] A "future historian" now takes the liberty of dubbing this collection of antiquarians "The Brotherhood of Brotherhead."

Brotherhead[36] himself, born in 1824 in Armsley near Leeds, England, came to America at about twenty. In 1849 he opened his stand at Sixth and Market Streets with a stock worth about $60. "As he had more shelf-room than books . . . he added cigars to his stock and filled the empty shelves with cigar-boxes." Soon, however, Brotherhead augmented his holdings at auction and was able to substitute for his cigar-boxes Catlin's portraits of Indians. Importing "English books . . . among them many curious books on America," he also expanded into the fields of autographs and engravings. In 1860 he started a circulating library and eventually, several removals behind him, he could boast not only his stock of books but "the largest and most valuable collection of autographs, engravings and prints in America."

Whether or not he lived up to his bibliopolic credo, it was indeed an ambitious one. "The old bookseller," he held, "should be a cyclopædia, able to answer questions about the general nature of books, and their authors. The whole field of history he should know, from Homer to Macaulay. The new discoveries in history, either biblical or general, he should know."

He should also know—as Brotherhead assuredly did—his colleagues and his customers. Among the latter he counted the witty and eccentric

E. D. Ingraham whose conversation "had the bouquet of Dibdin" and who had the peculiar idiosyncrasy of "borrowing" what he could not buy. As a result of his ardor, the Ingraham collection would do much to spur the Americana mania. Then, too, John McAllister, collector of local history, visited Brotherhead, coming "nearly every morning . . . with green bag" in which to deposit his purchases. Others were attracted to Brotherhead's stock, among them Judge Pennypacker seeking Pennsylvania imprints; Howard Edwards, old Bibles; Charles Mann, dramatic works; F. J. Dreer, autographs. Besides selling to such bibliophiles, Brotherhead doubtless imparted to them his pungent wisdom, including his memorable comment on the collecting of first editions: "Every cultivated reader knows too well that, in a literary sense, the *first editions* are the most imperfect of any author's work."

Brotherhead held in higher esteem than first editions Grangerized and facsimile volumes. He published a *Book of the Signers*, containing facsimile letters of each of the signers of the Declaration of Independence in 1860 and another in time for the Centennial of 1876. In the course of his long career he launched *American Notes and Queries* and sold many precious volumes, among them a presentation copy of Jefferson's *Notes on Virginia*, a Washington autograph love letter, numerous Franklin imprints, and a unique copy of the *Constitutions of the Thirteen States* containing an extra *Constitution*. This last, offered to the Librarian of the "National Library in Washington" for $50 was rejected and the work was later sold to James Lenox from whom it passed to the New York Public Library.

Brotherhead survived not only the business paralysis occasioned by the Civil War, but his own physical infirmity. In 1878 he fell on the ice, injuring his spine. Although he sold out his business at the time, he resumed it "quietly" the next year, and when he recorded his annals of *Forty Years* among books he expressed the hope of dying in harness. In 1893 he did so.

In his own more than forty years in the book business, Brotherhead had attained no small success. One of his more memorable achievements certainly was the book in which he sketched his recollections of his colleagues. They flit across his pages, this "Brotherhood of Brotherhead," some in shadow, some in bright, strong colors, and to the eye of the historian they summon up a picture of bookselling and of booksellers during the latter half of the nineteenth century in Philadelphia. The ghosts of booksellers past materialize in the present: the dark and sallow Apley, "a very dirty man, surrounded . . . by . . . old books," restored to his stand in the Arcade on Chestnut Street where he slept and lived among dirt and rubbish, smelling the smell of mustiness and of books; Duross, the "rough, gruff Irishman"; James Dalling the Scot whose "very select collection of old books . . . attracted the best class of book buyers"; the "courtly," "well educated" John Pennington, who featured French books, traded with the South, and attracted a literary coterie; John Campbell, "brusque and fearless," with "lion-like face," atheist, Copperhead, anti-black, author of the vituperative *Negromania*, whose bookstore on Chestnut Street became a "center for hot-headed Democrats" and who himself became the father of Franklin's bibliographer, William J. Campbell.

If Campbell attracted fiery Democrats, his antithesis Peter Doyle, soft-spoken, small and delicate, engaged the attention of "the black-letter scholars of his day" with his choice and rare editions. For a short time, between 1848 and 1850 and again between 1857 and 1861, the distinguished bibliographer Joseph Sabin, associated with New York City, carried on the business of books in Philadelphia, during the first period in the employ of George S. Appleton, during the latter on his own at South Sixth Street. No one ever questioned the ability of the expert Sabin, but Brotherhead, for one, did question his rectitude, remarking about some dubious financial dealings: "Had his rectitude been equal to his ability, none could have surpassed him in his business."

During the second half of the nineteenth century Philadelphia was the background for dealers who could offer a variety of specialties. For Spanish books there was Scanlan; for law books, Rees Welsh; for Presbyterian tomes, from Knox to the Old Covenanters, there was the "lean and lanky" W. S. Rentuol; for scientific and medical items there was the courtly, polished Walter B. Saunders whose windows displayed "the finest and most costly editions . . . illustrated most sumptuously"; for art books, C. J. Price; for German books, Schaefer & Koradi. Several, like John Hunt, who peddled his books through the country in a wagon when he was not attending his stand at the corner of Sixth and Arch Streets, came from Britain. One of his compatriots was Emanuel Price, who used the pseudonym of Peter Peppercorn for his poetic effusions and who, as late as the 1890s, was "still about the city, picking up old books and selling them where he can."

They rise again from the pages of Brotherhead's annals, these book scouts and book dealers, still clothed in their eccentricities. Some of them spanned the decades, surviving the Civil War when Southern trade was lost and the business of importing shifted to New York. Some of them passed on their expertise or their stock to assistants who followed them. Many were still on hand in 1882 when, having worked for Moses Thomas, Stan V. Henkels[37] opened his own auction house to serve a later generation of Philadelphians who would listen to his Southern drawl, smell his omnipresent cigar, and watch his goatee and drooping mustache. William Brotherhead arrested in their motion the fleeting images of his colleagues who traded in books. Under the circumstances it would be uncharitable to cavil that he did not do more. If the facts of many of these lives escape us, the flavor of their personalities survives. It is unforgettable.

Especially unforgettable was one member of this tribe of booksellers who came to the fore at the mid-century. Brotherhead remembered him, and so did others, for he left an unmistakable stamp not only upon his time but upon the future.

When, in the fullness of his eighty-six years, after a lifetime devoted to—inundated in—books, Moses Polock died in 1903, his nephew wrote the following letter to *Publishers Weekly*:

I regret to announce the death of Mr. Moses Polock, the oldest publisher in the country, and for many years a subscriber to the Publishers' Weekly. I think Mr. Growoll was acquainted with him. I enclose an obituary notice from one of the Philadelphia papers which you might use if you cared to. In addition to this it might prove of interest to note that the firm of which he was the last has continued through three centuries, a period almost unrivalled in the book-trade. Viz

(1) Jacob Johnson 1790-1808

(2) Johnson and Warner 1808-1815

(3) Benjamin Warner (1815-18)

(4) The executors of the above—to 1824

(5) McCarty and Davis 1824-1841 (about)

(6) Thomas Davis (1841-1850)

(7) Moses Polock (1850-1903)[38]

And so Polock's young successor carried his uncle's history back, not to his birth in 1817, but to 1790 when Jacob Johnson, Philadelphia printer and bookseller, stationer and inkmaker, entered upon his business. When in due course that business became a partnership, the Warner who shared the firm name with the founder was Benjamin Warner—the same Benjamin Warner who employed John Grigg and singled him out in his Will to continue his firm. It was after that firm had changed its style to M'Carty and Davis that it impinged upon the life of Moses Polock.[39]

According to William Brotherhead, Polock, born in Philadelphia in 1817, was "brought up" in the bookselling firm of M'Carty and Davis. He served that firm from 1831 when he was a boy of fourteen until the death of both partners, William M'Carty and Thomas Davis. Then, at the mid-century, Moses Polock bought in part of the firm's stock with capital left to him by partner Davis. A man in his early thirties, wearing "mutton-chop sideburns," Moses Polock was on his own. On Commerce Street below Fifth he began his business, publishing books, among them the collected edition of Charles Brockden Brown (1857), and gradually specializing in the antiquarian trade. "At any time after 10 o'clock in the morning," Brotherhead recorded, "you can ascend to his store; there you will find him bachelor-like all alone in his glory, breathing the atmosphere of his old books. He will meet you in the most genial manner, and will talk to you about his gems in the most intelligent spirit."

The gems he might have discussed over the years centered in the field of Americana, and included Franklin imprints, narratives of journeys across the Plains and Rockies, and William Bradford's 1694 printing of the *Laws & Acts . . . of New-York*. Despite what were called his "fanciful" prices, Polock sold this last for $16, and when the same copy was resold in the Brinley sale for $1,600, "the mention of this fact operated on Polock's mind as if he had taken bitter gall for his breakfast."

One of the traits developed by Polock over the years was a reluctance to sell, but despite, or perhaps because of that bibliopolic idiosyncrasy, his shop attracted such collectors as James Brinley, Samuel Pennypacker, and later Clarence S. Bement. As the years passed, Mo Polock became an "old, bearded man" and his shop "a mass of books and papers, piled on the floor, on tables, and crammed into all available space." Among his wares were "boxes of unsold books for children" which had come from the firm of Johnson and Warner, through M'Carty and Davis, and which would one day become the property of Mo Polock's young nephew.

By 1895, when Polock sold an American historical collection including Franklin imprints at a Henkels auction, he was assisted by that nephew. Eight years later Mo Polock died, and his nephew conscientiously informed *Publishers Weekly* of the passing of "the oldest publisher in the country," signing his letter A. S. W. Rosenbach.

Upon Abraham Simon Wolf Rosenbach the Polock mantle would fall, gilded by a splended alchemy. Unlike most of the Philadelphia booksellers who had preceded him, Moses Polock's nephew was fortunate in having his own special biographers who sorted from the legends that accrued about their subject the facts of his triumphant career.[40] In addition, since Rosenbach's triumphs were always newsworthy, they were emblazoned in the public prints, and so—despite the fact that one of his coworkers commented that "everyone who writes about him will have something new to tell,"[41] his story must remain a twice- or thrice-told tale.

To his intimates he was known as "Rosy," to his staff as "The Doctor," to the trade as "Dr. R." He combined in his nature a "genuine love and feeling for books" with an "equally . . . genuine love and feeling for the profits they brought him." In *Rosenbach A Biography*, Edwin Wolf, 2nd, with John Fleming has reanimated the character of Dr. R., restored to his shelf the great books that passed through his hands, and reminded investors of the profits they brought. In a sense his biography is the history of a succession of coups and the magnitude of his treasures—from a First Folio to a Gutenberg Bible, from a *Bay Psalm Book* to the original manuscript of *Alice in Wonderland*—is matched only by the magnitude of prices associated with them.

Rosenbach, we are told, always smoked a pipe and drank a bottle of whisky a day. In his heyday he was a "rotund little man with . . . pince-nez glasses, . . . stiff . . . collar, and . . . bowler hat." Earlier, in 1901, while his uncle was still alive, he made his first find—the Johnson-Garrick *Prologue and Epilogue spoken at the opening of the Theatre in Drury-Lane 1747*, previously known only from advertisements but discovered by the young doctor of philosophy as he leafed through a miscellaneous pamphlet volume in a Henkels auction. His first place of business consisted of a small back room in his brother Philip's establishment where lamps and inkwells, china figurines and bricabrac were sold. A month before his twenty-seventh birthday, in 1903, The Rosenbach Company, located at 1320 Walnut Street, was formed. The following year, Stan Henkels auctioned "A Collection of Valuable Americana gathered by the late Moses Polock, Esq., The Oldest Book-

seller in the United States." A goodly part of that collection became
Rosenbach's stock. Incidentally, the collection included seven volumes
from the library of George Washington, as well as a Washington letter
about Cornwallis. For those items the nephew of the late Mo Polock
solicited the bids of J. P. Morgan. Dr. R. was on his triumphant way.

Dr. R.'s 1906 catalogue featured an Aitken Bible. The next year he
made his first trip abroad, acquiring a Shakespeare First Folio. The
1906 catalogue was followed by landmark catalogues. The Shakespeare
First Folio was followed by ever greater acquisitions, from Harry B.
Smith's "Sentimental Library" of manuscripts and association copies of
Shelley and Keats, Lamb and Dickens, to the Marsden J. Perry Shake-
spearean Library. The Rosenbach treasures were matched by the collectors who sought to acquire them: young Harry Widener whom he
started on his collecting career, and, after his untimely death on the
Titanic, young Widener's mother; William M. Elkins; A. Edward Newton; John B. Gribbel; John B. Stetson, Jr.; Robert Hoe; Huntington
and Folger; Lessing Rosenwald.

By 1916, Dr. R. had provided for himself, his books and his transactions in books a fitting background. As Edwin Wolf reports: "During
the autumn of 1916 the final touches were being put to the book room
on Walnut Street to give it the appearance it retained thereafter. The
Tudor plaster ceiling was molded; the room was lined with floor-to-
cornice glass-fronted bookcases . . . the large window overlooking Walnut Street was hung with green velours; the little paneled room down
the hall was constructed to hide the several safes. . . . He looked as
though he belonged, sitting in an ornate needle-point-covered Chippendale chair at the big nondescript desk, his bald head reflected in
the glass of the cases behind him, his pipe belching smoke, while before
him lay a clutter of unanswered letters, book catalogues, a whisky bottle
. . . and a stack of Street and Smith detective weeklies."

At the beginning of the fabulous 1920s, the great New York bookseller George D. Smith died, and his throne was soon occupied by Dr.
Rosenbach of Philadelphia. As Wolf observes: "He wanted to sell only
great items," and since greatness—especially quantitative greatness—
has a strong national appeal, Dr. R. soon became "a national figure."
According to his biographer, "Gutenberg Bibles and Shakespeare Folios
became regular Rosenbach stock in trade." According to the collector
A. Edward Newton, "Rosenbach . . . has a stock of rare books unequaled
by any other dealer in this country." Newton added that Rosy was also

"the most scholarly bookseller in this country today. . . . Don't expect ever to 'discover' anything at Rosenbach's, except how ignorant you are."[42]

Rosenbach was scholarly indeed, and a lover of books. He was also a lover of publicity and of profits. During the 1930s his career has been described as a "Bookman's Progress" in the course of which he provided treasures for a new generation of collectors. In 1941 he attended the A. Edward Newton sales, and there the present historian—not yet a bookseller—saw him, the observed of all observers, the "rotund little man with . . . pince-nez" who had made such a great noise in the world of rare books. Until his death in 1952 he continued to electrify that world with his acquisitions, his prices, his style, his flair. For better or worse he helped transform the field of book collecting into an area for grandscale investment. His career wrote climax to the Philadelphia story.

Between 1850, when Moses Polock was about to enter business on his own, and 1890, when his fourteen-year-old nephew A. S. W. Rosenbach was already demonstrating his bookish inclinations, the population of their native city tripled. Not so the number of its antiquarian booksellers. For the fifteen who had served the needs of bibliophiles at the mid-century, only some twelve were on hand by the time the Mauve Decade had begun.[43] Among them were some of Brotherhead's colleagues, including Moses Polock. Among them, too, was a man in his mid-thirties, a "large man, with large features, and a deep vibrant voice" who would be dubbed "A Great Romantic."

Charles Sessler[44] came to America from his native Vienna in 1880 when he was twenty-six. He had nothing to declare but a college education and "a delighted first reading in English of 'Nicolas Nickleby.' " Employed by the George Kelley Publishing House of New York, he honed his skills of salesmanship on the firm's Catholic Bibles. The following year he moved to Philadelphia, striking out on his own as a bookseller in an upstairs office room at 1018 Chestnut Street. "His idea was 'sets' and his capital was exactly forty dollars."

Sessler's original "idea" expanded in time, along with his capital, his stock embracing prints of distinction and rare editions, art and illustrated books, Americana, incunables and illuminated manuscripts, paintings and autograph letters, and, of course, Charles Dickens. His background shifted from Chestnut Street to Walnut where the leading booksellers had begun to compete with a row of merchant tailors. When in 1906 he moved to 1314 Walnut Street, nigh to The Rosenbach Company, it was announced that "he has omitted no detail of arrangement that would serve to allow a plentiful addition to his stock . . . nor any item that would serve to make the shop inviting to old as well as prospective patrons." After three decades there, a leak on the premises drove Sessler to 1310, and there, seated in a huge Jacobean chair in a book-lined back office, he greeted his customers, some of whom—Harry Widener, A. Edward Newton and Henry E. Huntington—he shared with his neighbor Dr. R. As far as Huntington was concerned, it was Sessler who first suggested that the railway magnate collect not only art but books. The story of his conversion was printed at the time of Sessler's seventy-fifth birthday and still makes inspiring reading:

One snowy afternoon in the winter of 1907, Henry E. Huntington sat at a table in an upper Fifth Avenue club playing solitaire. It is said he looked up with little interest when Charles Sessler [on a visit to New York] spoke to him about the acquiring of certain rare books. Frankly, he was not interested. He had never been a rare book collector. However, it took just what Mr. Sessler has, a kind of passionate belief in collecting, to fire an imagination like Mr. Huntington's. That was twenty-two years ago. To-day $27,000,000 worth of books rests in a beautiful Greek Temple Library—The Huntington Library . . . is it any wonder that Mr. Sessler believes in Romance . . . ?

As for Huntington, he believed in value received, as a letter he wrote to Charles Sessler testifies:

I am glad to say that my dealings with you in books have been very satisfactory to me, and I imagine equally so to yourself. The books I purchased from you were what I wanted and while, of course, I paid you too much for some, I got a good many at figures quite acceptable to me. When I paid you the tall prices, I felt at the time I owed it to you as a tribute to your linguistic ability and your transcendent qualities as a salesman of literary commodities, both of which used to excite my sincere admiration. If I never run across a worse man than yourself to deal with, I certainly deserve congratulation, and if you always find as good a customer as myself, you will never want for the necessaries of life.

Almost as good a customer was Samuel H. Austin who started book collecting in 1915 with the purchase of a Dickens from Sessler, and in so doing became the subject of an anecdote worth repeating. At Sessler's shop, Austin noted a volume by Dickens priced at $150.

He looked askance. $150 for a book! That was ridiculous! . . . He left the office disdainful. A week later, highly triumphant, almost gloating, he returned, to lay on the table before Mr. Sessler what he thought to be a volume identically like the one he had seen the week before.

"And I got it from a second-hand dealer for $15," he almost shouted.

The hour had come for Mr. Sessler, . . . A quick glance at the Austin copy had assured Mr. Sessler that it was a "cripple." Slowly and prophetically, he rose and lifted down from the shelf his own perfect copy. . . . He opened the two books; . . . enumerated the points of the perfect copy; . . . cast these points into the very teeth of the owner of "the Cripple;" . . . made him see, sadly, that books . . . have their fine distinctions. . . . That hour a new collector was born.

In the two years that intervened between Samuel Austin's initiation into the niceties of book collecting and his death, he acquired a distinguished library.

It was in Charles Sessler's window that Lessing Rosenwald spotted an engraving that first stimulated him to collect fine prints. William Jennings Bryan, Sargent and Pennell, George Arliss and Leopold Stokowski were all numbered among Sessler customers.

To supply their wants, the proprietor traveled abroad, often three times a year, seeking fine bindings and choice literary editions. As A. Edward Newton commented, "Sessler . . . goes abroad every year with his pocket full of money, and comes back with a lot of things that quickly empty ours."[45] Especially Sessler sought editions and relics of Dickens, and his Dickens expertise and acquisitions gave rise to yet another anecdote. Upon one occasion, F. Hopkinson Smith read aloud at Sessler's his manuscript of *In Dickens' London*. "The reading concluded, Mr. Sessler said: 'Yes, good, very good, but for one thing. You speak about the *original* little birds' tombstone at Gadshill, Dickens' paternal home, and you have sketched a drawing of that tombstone. That is the only incorrect note in your book so far as I can see, for here is the original little tombstone.' " Dickens' daughter Mrs. Perugini had sent the memento as a compliment to Charles Sessler, her father's greatest collector.

As the legends accumulated, so did the fame. A letter from Australia addressed simply to Charles Sessler reached him. So did another, from South Africa, inscribed: "Mr. Charles Sessler, American Connoiseur of Arts, Associated with the late H. E. Huntington, American multi-millionaire, New York or London." There is no doubt that Charles

Sessler was an "American connoisseur" of English literary works, fine prints and engravings. Though his net was neither so deep nor so wide as Rosenbach's, it caught many bibliophilic fish. Under his own proprietorship and in later years under the direction of the amazing Mabel Zahn, Sessler's bookshop added, and still adds, stature and distinction to Walnut Street, Philadelphia.

The twentieth century brought other bookstores of distinction to Philadelphia. Just after the First World War, in 1918, William H. Allen[46] began a book business in Temple, Pennsylvania, issuing his first catalogue—consisting of his own library—in November. Allen, described as "one . . . who has smeared his hands, but not his wit, in the dust of many books," was conversant not only with French and German but with Latin and Greek. In 1920 he moved to Philadelphia, and his shop, near the University of Pennsylvania, became a "campus gathering place." Five years later his wife entered the business, and in 1935, after the founder's death, she continued it. She was joined in 1940 by her son George, not only a bookseller but a lover of bookselling history, whose "Talk for Bibliophiles" in the 1950s was entitled "Old Booksellers of Philadelphia." Specializing in literature and linguistics, history and philosophy, the firm issued a variety of catalogues on the Greek and Latin classics and the Middle Ages, English and American literature, Africa and the Orient. In 1941 it moved to 2031 Walnut Street where it continues today, still under the aegis of George Allen, still reflecting the scholarly interests of its founder, still one of Philadelphia's "well-known and loved" bookstores.

Shortly before the Second World War, in 1937, another bookshop destined for longevity opened on Philadelphia's Walnut Street. Having worked for Walter Hart Blumenthal, George MacManus[47] set up his stand at 2022, specializing in Americana. In 1940 the business was incorporated with Ben Wolf as partner, and, under the aegis of Ben Wolf's son Clarence, George S. MacManus Co. continues its illustrious course.

Still another twentieth-century addition to Philadelphia's bibliopolic scene was Jeremiah Cullen's shop.[48] Although it was shorter lived than Allen's or MacManus's and far less distinguished than the emporia of Sessler and Rosenbach, its history is of interest. The phases of Cullen's career were linked together by those intertwining threads that give a fascinating pattern to the fabric of bookselling. In 1877, at age thirteen, he was initiated into the trade when he was employed by the firm of

Rees Welsh. George Allen reports Cullen's reminiscences of those days: "In 1882, while he was tending the outside stand for Rees Welsh, . . . Walt Whitman came up and said, 'Sonny can you get me a copy of Ossian's *Poems*?' Cullen replied, 'Wait, Mister, I'll go in and see.' He had recognized Whitman and went in to tell Welsh and [David] McKay [then a Rees Welsh employee]. They invited Whitman in and soon made arrangements to publish a limited edition of *Leaves of Grass*."

Subsequently, when Rees Welsh went into the publishing of legal books, he sold his antiquarian section to David McKay who opened "McKay's Marvellous Book Store" and took on Rees Welsh's young assistant Jeremiah Cullen. "Cullen . . . used to recall how Whitman often came in to 'borrow' five or ten cents from McKay in order to take the ferry back to Camden after a visit in Philadelphia. Each time he signed an IOU, which was dutifully put into an old cigar box in McKay's desk. When Whitman died, they were thrown away as being of even less value than when he was alive."

In 1905, David McKay sold his antiquarian stock to Leary's, and Cullen went along with the stock. Five years later he opened, with his son John, his own firm of Cullen and Walsh at 15 South Ninth Street, moving in 1923 to North Ninth Street, and giving up the business in 1939.

According to George Allen, "Cullen's stock was not fine, but such men as Governor Pennypacker, Houdini, and A. Edward Newton . . . would drop in to buy books from time to time. While the more important men used to meet at Rosenbach's or Sessler's, Jerry Cullen's back room was the meeting place of the lesser breed." That back room, with its lesser breed, inspired the local historian Joseph F. A. Jackson to verse:

It is dusty and musty,
    Yet it breathes not of gloom—
In fact, it's inviting—
    Is Jerry's back room.

What a club can be found there,
    Each day around noon!
What talk about books
    Fills Jerry's back room! . . .

And, then, there's the books—
(I was closing too soon)—
First editions are kept
In Jerry's back room.

And the best of it all is
The Welcome's a boon
To all who've been guests
In Jerry's back room.

How many guests have found welcome in the back rooms as well as
the splendid fronts of Philadelphia's antiquarian bookstores. There was
room for both in the city that was once called the "Athens" of America.

NOTES

1. Quoted in Carl and Jessica Bridenbaugh, *Rebels and Gentlemen: Philadelphia in the Age of Franklin* (New York: Oxford University Press, 1962), p. 99.
The writer is grateful to Marie Elena Korey, Free Library of Philadelphia, for
her cooperation and aid in the preparation of this chapter.

2. The Bridenbaughs, ibid., p. 98.

3. Madeleine B. Stern, ed., *Publishers for Mass Entertainment in Nineteenth
Century America* (Boston: G. K. Hall, 1980), p. xi.

4. The Bridenbaughs, *Rebels and Gentlemen*, p. 83; John Tebbel, *A History
of Book Publishing in the United States* (New York and London: Bowker, 1972),
I, 100.

5. Tebbel, *A History of Book Publishing in the United States*, I, 104.

6. David Kaser, *Books in America's Past* (Charlottesville: University Press
of Virginia, 1966), p. 3.

7. The Bridenbaughs, *Rebels and Gentlemen*, p. 89.

8. Ibid., pp. 94 f.

9. Ibid., pp. 95 f.

10. Carl Bridenbaugh, "The Press and the Book in Eighteenth Century
Philadelphia," *The Pennsylvania Magazine of History and Biography* (January
1941), pp. 15 f. For Bell, see also *Bell's Memorial on the Free Sale of Books: To
which are added Sentiments on What Is Freedom, and what is Slavery. By A Farmer*
(Philadelphia: Bell, 1784); The Bridenbaughs, *Rebels and Gentlemen*, pp. 84–
86, 90 f; H. Glenn Brown and Maude O. Brown, *A Directory of the Book-Arts
and Book Trade in Philadelphia to 1820* (New York: New York Public Library,
1950), p. 17; Evans 15735 and 18352; Joseph Jackson, *Literary Landmarks of
Philadelphia* (Philadelphia: McKay, 1939), pp. 14 ff; "William McCulloch's
Additions to Thomas's History of Printing," *American Antiquarian Society Pro-*

ceedings (Worcester, Mass., 1921), pp. 97, 219; George L. McKay, *American Book Auction Catalogues 1713–1934* (New York: New York Public Library, 1937), pp. 2 f; Ellis Paxton Oberholtzer, *The Literary History of Philadelphia* (Philadelphia: Jacobs, 1906), p. 85; Isaiah Thomas, *The History of Printing in America*, ed. Marcus A. McCorison (New York: Weathervane, 1970), pp. 395 f.

11. Evans 18740; McKay, *American Book Auction Catalogues*, p. 3.

12. Edwin Wolf, 2nd, and Marie Elena Korey, *Quarter of a Millennium: The Library Company of Philadelphia 1731–1981* (Philadelphia: Library Company of Philadelphia, 1981), p. 179. For Aitken, see also Thomas, *The History of Printing in America*, p. 402.

13. George Allen, "Old Booksellers of Philadelphia," in *Four Talks for Bibliophiles* (Philadelphia: Free Library of Philadelphia, 1958), p. 18.

14. The Bridenbaughs, *Rebels and Gentlemen*, p. 83; Evans 11339; Jackson, *Literary Landmarks of Philadelphia*, pp. 85 f; J. Thomas Scharf and Thompson Westcott, *History of Philadelphia 1609–1884* (Philadelphia: Everts, 1884), II, 886; Shaw and Shoemaker 38706; Isaiah Thomas, *The History of Printing in America*, p. 388; Harry B. Weiss, "John Norman, Engraver, Publisher, Bookseller; John Walters, Miniaturist, Publisher, Bookseller; and The 'World Turned Upside-Down' Controversy," *Bulletin of The New York Public Library* (January 1934), p. 7.

According to "William McCulloch's Additions to Thomas's History of Printing," p. 105: "John Sparhawk . . . kept old and scarce books only, such as were not elsewhere in the market, and sold them at high prices. . . . He was rich and his collection of books very valuable."

15. For Carey, see Adolf Growoll Collection, *American Book Trade History* (Bowker Library, courtesy Jean Peters), II, 6; David Kaser, *Messrs. Carey & Lea of Philadelphia: A Study in the History of the Booktrade* (Philadelphia: University of Pennsylvania Press, 1957), p. 17; Emily E.F. Skeel, *Mason Locke Weems His Works and Ways* (New York 1929), passim; Tebbel, *A History of Book Publishing in the United States*, I, 110 ff.

It was with a loan from Lafayette and the press of Robert Bell, auctioned after the latter's death, that Carey began as printer-publisher in 1785. See James Gilreath, "Mason Weems, Mathew Carey and the Southern Booktrade, 1794–1810," *Publishing History* X (1981), p. 29.

16. Quoted in H. Glenn Brown, "Philadelphia Contributions to the Book Arts and Book Trade, 1796–1810," *Papers of the Bibliographical Society of America* 37 (1943), p. 291.

17. For Cobbett, see Mary Elizabeth Clark, *Peter Porcupine in America: The Career of William Cobbett, 1792–1800* (Philadelphia 1939), pp. 172 ff; Jackson, *Literary Landmarks of Philadelphia*, pp. 67 f, 78.

18. William Reitzel, "The Purchasing of English Books in Philadelphia, 1790–1800," *Modern Philology* 35 (1937), p. 159.

19. Howard Mumford Jones, "The Importation of French Books in Philadelphia, 1750–1800," *Modern Philology* 32 (1934), pp. 160, 177.

20. Evans 18371.

21. Madeleine B. Stern, *Books and Book People in 19th-Century America* (New York and London: Bowker, 1978), pp. 70 f, 93.

22. Marie Elena Korey, "Three Early Philadelphia Book Collectors," *American Book Collector* 2:6 (November/December 1981), p. 4.

23. Ibid., p. 8.

24. For Dufief, see Ibid., p. 10, as well as Brown, *A Directory of the Book-Arts . . . in Philadelphia to 1820*, pp. 43 f; N. G. Dufief, *Nature Displayed* (Philadelphia: Watts, 1806), I, iv; Madeleine B. Stern, "Nicholas Gouin Dufief, Franco-American Bookseller," *American Book Collector* (July/August 1985); Edwin Wolf, 2nd, "The Dispersal of the Library of William Byrd of Westover," *Proceedings of the American Antiquarian Society* 68:1 (1958), pp. 38 f; Edwin Wolf, 2nd, "The Reconstruction of Benjamin Franklin's Library: An Unorthodox Jigsaw Puzzle," *Papers of the Bibliographical Society of America* 56:1 (1962), pp. 4 ff; Edwin Wolf, 2nd, and Marie Elena Korey, *Quarter of a Millennium*, pp. 91, 131.

25. Wolf, "The Dispersal of the Library of William Byrd," *Proceedings of the American Antiquarian Society* (1958), pp. 19–45; Wolf and Korey, *Quarter of a Millennium*, p. 131, #105.

26. Wolf and Korey, *Quarter of a Millennium*, p. 91, #75.

27. McKay, *American Book Auction Catalogues*, p. 65, #148A; Wolf, "The Reconstruction of Benjamin Franklin's Library," *Papers of the Bibliographical Society of America* (1962), pp. 1–16.

28. *Early American Trade Cards from the Collection of Bella C. Landauer with critical notes by Adele Jenny* (New York: Rudge, 1927), pp. xiv and 22; Kaser, *Books in America's Past*, pp. 106–128; McKay, *American Book Auction Catalogues*, pp. 29, 31.

29. Growoll Collection, *American Book Trade History*, VI, 96; Oberholtzer, *The Literary History of Philadelphia*, p. 346.

30. For Leary's, see Allen, "Old Booksellers of Philadelphia," pp. 22 f; Jean H. Breig, "Philadelphia Book Stores," *Library Journal* (1 May 1955), p. 1051; W. Brotherhead, *Forty Years among the Old Booksellers of Philadelphia, with Bibliographical Remarks* (Philadelphia: A. P. Brotherhead, 1891), pp. 34 f, 59, 66 f; Growoll Collection, *American Book Trade History*, XI, 119; Joseph Jackson, *An Old Landmark A Famous Bookstore* (Philadelphia: Leary's Book Store, 1920), pp. 12–29; John T. Winterich, "Leary's Centenary 1836–1936," *Publishers Weekly* (6 June 1936), pp. 2264 f.

31. Wolf and Korey, *Quarter of a Millennium*, p. 163.

32. Stern, ed., *Publishers for Mass Entertainment*, pp. 245 ff.

33. Madeleine B. Stern, *Imprints on History: Book Publishers and American Frontiers* (Bloomington: Indiana University Press, 1956), p. 160.

34. Christoph Trautmann, "Bach's Bible," *American Choral Review* XIV:4 (October 1972), pp. 3–11.

35. *Publishers Weekly* (2 May 1891), p. 631.

36. Besides Brotherhead's *Forty Years*, see *Publishers Weekly* (2 May 1891), pp. 630 f, and (1 April 1893), p. 562.

37. Allen, "Old Booksellers of Philadelphia," pp. 32 f.

38. A.S.W. Rosenbach to The Publishers Weekly, 17 August 1903, in Growoll Collection, *American Book Trade History*, X, 70.

39. For Polock, see Allen, "Old Booksellers of Philadelphia," pp. 19, 24 f; Brotherhead, *Forty Years among the Old Booksellers of Philadelphia*, pp. 50 ff; Growoll Collection, *American Book Trade History*, X, 70; Tebbel, *A History of Book Publishing in the United States*, I, 385; Edwin Wolf, 2nd, with John Fleming, *Rosenbach A Biography* (Cleveland and New York: World Publishing Co., 1960), pp. 19 ff, 35, 48.

40. Wolf with Fleming, *Rosenbach A Biography*.

41. E. Millicent Sowerby, *Rare people and rare books* (London: Constable, 1967), pp. ix, 132 f.

42. A. Edward Newton, *The Amenities of Book-Collecting and Kindred Affections* (Boston: Little, Brown, 1937), pp. 41 f, 71.

43. Brotherhead, *Forty Years among the Old Booksellers of Philadelphia*, p. 13.

44. For Sessler, see Allen, "Old Booksellers of Philadelphia," pp. 33 f; Frederick R. Goff, "Rosenwald and the Gift to the Nation," *AB Bookman's Weekly* (28 September 1981), p. 2004; Growoll Collection, *American Book Trade History*, XI, 37; Ruth Brown Park, "A Great Romantic," *Publishers Weekly* (16 November 1929), pp. 2399–2403.

45. Newton, *The Amenities of Book-Collecting*, p. 46.

46. Information from George Allen; Breig, "Philadelphia Book Stores," *Library Journal* (1 May 1955), p. 1051; *The Marginalia of 1931* (Philadelphia: Chilton Press, [1931]), unpaged.

47. Information from Clarence Wolf.

48. Allen, "Old Booksellers of Philadelphia," pp. 28–30. The verses by Jackson are also quoted from that source.

3

New York City

The greatest booksellers are in New York, Philadelphia, and Baltimore. Northward of New York, there is none of any consequence; not any in Boston of note. . . . The booksellers throughout the Continent are generally supplied from one of the above three places, where there are many considerable stores of books daily imported from Europe; and there are few publications that cannot be purchased here except very heavy and expensive ones, of which they have none. . . .

The usual currency of sale is at the advance of 50 1. and in many instances 100 1. *per cent.*; and their sales are very great: for, it is scarcely possible to conceive the number of readers with which every little town abounds. The common people are on a footing, in point of literature, with the middle ranks in Europe; they all read and write, . . .

Prints are a good article to carry over, and so are engraved copperplates.[1]

These observations, putatively made by Henry Lemoine, "armchair" traveler from London, in 1789, suggest that there was even that early a taste for books in the young republic which was fed principally by the booksellers of New York. As yet there was no recognizable antiquarian book trade in the growing metropolis, but the roots of such a trade were there—buried in the general bookselling that had begun in colonial times and out of which antiquarian bookselling was to stem.

The New York colonial bookseller was usually also a publisher, a printer of newspapers and a bookbinder, and his stock was as varied as his many-faceted calling.[2] He dealt in "mariners' compasses and writing paper along with Virgil, Ovid and the Bible." The bookseller's shelf yielded not only sheepskin backs but "whalebone, geese feathers, pickled sturgeon, chocolate and Spanish snuff." "Near the Meal Market" where Robert Crommelin plied his trade, in Hanover Square where Hugh Gaine sold books, on Wall Street where James Rivington set up his shingle, spectacles and patent medicines vied with books to lure a public as yet unaccustomed to the device of specialization. By 1743 Catherine Zenger (wife of the champion of a free press, John Peter Zenger) opened the first bookshop not engaged in publishing, but hers was scarcely an antiquarian venture, since she dealt primarily in pamphlets and stationery.

To five New York booksellers in 1786, there were thirty by 1800 when a booksellers' row was identifiable near Hanover Square and bookselling was becoming competitive.[3] Indeed in 1802 the New York booksellers held their first Literary Fair in the Coffee House and sold half a million books in five days. Nonetheless, the books they sold could not be described as rare or antiquarian. Two years later, however, Samuel Wood opened a shop dealing in secondhand books, and so led the vanguard of secondhand booksellers who would cluster along Pearl and Nassau streets as the century advanced. John Doyle, who "began by peddling books in a market basket," was soon able to put up a sign lettered with the triumphant words: "The Moral Center of the Intellectual World" and "The Grand Center of Life and Knowledge." Out of such shops as they would eventually emerge the antiquarian dealer who, among the chaff of a multitude of secondhand books, searched for and valued the treasured grain of rarity. Before there were rare booksellers, there had to be secondhand booksellers.

Other aspects of the early bookshops too made a congenial background for the emergence of the New York antiquarian trade whose tenuous and shadowy beginnings are so difficult to trace. What other commercial enterprise provided a rendezvous where the like-minded could exchange thoughts and top tall tales of "finds"? As William Loring Andrews observed, "The old book shops . . . were commonly supplied with outside shelves and counters, which were laden with books and pamphlets. Here loungers with literary tastes congregated the livelong day, sipping knowledge as the bee sips honey, and forming a feature of New York City street life."[4] Once inside the shops, the "loungers" found greater attractions. Several of the early booksellers, for example, offered customers the facilities of a circulating library—James Eastburn, a gentleman of enthusiasm and bland manners, who founded the first reading room in the city; Garret Noel, who in 1763 started New York's first circulating library; Samuel Loudon, who "revived Noel's idea in

1773 at his shop at 'Hunter's Quarry' " and advertised that "ladies are my best customers." By the turn of the century, the Pearl Street establishment of Thomas and James Swords was a meeting place for "philosophers, artists and writers, as well as dignitaries of the Episcopal Church." As the century progressed, New York bookshops came to resemble more and more "lounging places of the literati." In the early 1820s in the back room of Wiley's shop known as the Den, the nucleus of the Bread and Cheese Club gathered—Cooper, Halleck and Paulding, later Bryant, Morse and Dana—for talk of publications new and old. By the 1840s the Astor House bookshop of Bartlett and Welford provided the backdrop for literary men and collectors. That firm, which would merge into Charles Scribner's Sons, carried a line of fine and rare books unlike the houses that confined their stock to bestsellers. Indeed, one collector complained that the "fashionable bookstores never have knowledge of books published some ten years before, but if you ask these fashionably-clad, empty headed ignoramuses the name and price of the latest sensational novel, they can tell it to you [in] an instant—almost as quick as your groceryman can tell you the name and price of a number 3 can of mackerel."

It was not mackerel but another kind of catch that the frequenters of such bookshops fished for. One such fisher was New York's mayor Philip Hone who under date of 3 June 1840 wrote in his diary:

Old Books. I purchased this morning at Bartlett & Welford's bookstore a fine old Oxford copy of Shakespeare in six volumes quarto, printed 1744; and the original subscription copy, in eleven volumes small folio, of Pope's translation of Homer's Iliad and Odyssey, printed by the celebrated Lintot in 1715 and 1726; a most rare and valuable old book, in fine preservation, beautifully printed, and containing many quaint but well-executed engravings.[5]

The combination of old books and literary rendezvous continued through the century until in the 1880s, at Brentano's Literary Emporium on Union Square, there was a "musty corner" where Henry Ward Beecher, Artemus Ward and Edwin Booth chatted, smoked and told anecdotes while General Grant dropped in to buy "a pack of cards and a box of chips."[6] It is to be hoped that some of the visiting potentates carried away an antiquarian book now and then.

Many of these bookstores served not only as rendezvous for habitués but as importers for knowledgeable collectors. Despite the 1802 resolution of a concerned Society of Booksellers "to discontinue the importation of all books, of which good and correct editions are printed in this country,"[7] importation continued and helped provide a fertile ground for the development of the New York trade in rare books. Schiller and Kotzebue were popularized by Charles Smith of Pearl Street, a pensive looking bookseller who resorted to tobacco to relieve his pulmonary suffering. Sometimes an importer—like James Rivington— overstocked his shop with foreign products and failed, but imported books continued to make up the largest part of the eighteenth-century book business.

In time, these importers began to specialize, and with specialization came the opportunity for the development of the dealer in antiquarian books. Hocquet Caritat who served for a short time as the New York agent of a Paris printer-publisher was followed by another specialist in French books, F. G. Berteau. For imports from Germany customers with a Teutonic taste visited Westermann's Broadway bookstore by the mid-nineteenth century. And other specialists had arisen: John Bradburn whose forte was maritime books and who did his best business along the waterfront or in the captains' cabins of incoming vessels. A searcher for rarities could sometimes find them in Bradburn's basket of books or on the shelves of his shop "tucked away among the volumes clad in prosaic legal calf." While Bradburn specialized in books of the sea, T. H. Morrell specialized in the history of New York and the Revolution. Timothy Reeve and Company not only specialized but imported, restricting their business to rare books which were sold both to the trade in general and to individual customers.

And so, out of the very nature of the bookshop, the New Yorker's dependence upon imports, the growing trend toward specialization, and the maturing taste of the time, the figure of the antiquarian bookseller began its slow emergence. So too did the image of the antiquarian bookseller as an arbiter of learning, a dispenser of knowledge, a man whose dicta embodied "the deepest researches of antiquarian disquisition." I. S. Lyon, the "Old Cartman" whose recollections reflect his dim view of the trade, nonetheless tempered his cynicism about booksellers in general with the remark: "I have rarely met with a bookseller who knew anything about the character of the books that passed through his hands, beyond the *price* fixed upon them by the publishers. The exceptions to this rule are generally to be found among the dealers in old second-hand books."[8]

Who were these antiquarian booksellers of Manhattan Island, that "confluence of the greatest number of the streams of knowledge,"[9] for which many of them played the role of fountainhead?

One of the earliest antiquarian booksellers of New York, William Gowans (1803–1870),[10] forms a prototype for the host of dealers who followed him. In many ways his career, his methods and his accomplishments prefigure those of his successors. Gowans was no native New Yorker but, at the age of twenty-five, came to the city from Indiana. He did not plunge immediately into the book trade but worked as gardener and stevedore, stone cutter and news vendor, and even as "super" in the Bowery Theatre before he set up a bookstall on Chatham Street. As William Loring Andrews commented, "Trade in second-hand books, doubtless, was coy and hard to win, and at the outset of his career he [Gowans] was obliged to seek a market for his merchandise by carrying it in a basket to the doors of his customers. . . . Initiated . . . into the secrets of the second-hand book trade" by "the father of Thomas Cole, the artist, who was a bookseller in a small way," Gowans prospered. His Chatham Street stand "was simply a row of shelves, protected at night and in the owner's absence during the day on his book-selling peregrinations with wooden shutters, an iron bar and a padlock." It gave way in time to other stores on Liberty, Fulton and Centre Streets, until the early 1860s when Gowans was established in a three-story brick building near St. Paul's Churchyard on the booksellers' row of Nassau Street.

He occupied the store floor, basement and sub-cellar, which in time became crowded with books and pamphlets from floor to ceiling. His stock grew and never diminished. Books lay everywhere in seemingly dire confusion, piled upon tables and on the floor . . . until they finally toppled over, and the few narrow alleys which had originally been left between the rows became well-nigh impassable. There was no artificial light in the cellar, and the book-hunter must fain grope his way—if permitted—through the bewildering maze by the light of a small tin sperm-oil lamp. The freedom of Mr. Gowans's bookstore was not presented to every passer-by.

Among the profusion of secondhand books there were treasures for the knowing collector which William Gowans garnered from a variety of familiar sources. As early as 1840–1841 he went abroad "with an eye to business," and in this country he was a constant purchaser at auction, especially at Cooley, Keese, where he frequently used the

pseudonym of "Mr. Chase." He was, like some of his latter-day coun-
terparts, also a constant interruptor. When the *History of the Taters*
came under the hammer, for example, Gowans queried the auctioneer:
"Is not that Tartars?", to which the reply was "No; their wives were
the tartars."

At all events, from Europe, from auction house, from trade purchases
and domestic foraging, Gowans assembled an enormous stock that included notable rarities. His "dusky depository" yielded a treasure described by Dr. William C. Prime[11] as "a small quarto volume, containing
two books bound in one, a work of Jerome Gebuiller [Gebweiler] on
the origin and ancestry of Ferdinand, Emperor of the Holy Roman
Empire, printed at Hagenau in 1530, and an account of the siege of
Vienna by the Turks, under Suleiman, in 1529, [by Helianus] printed
at Augsburg, 1530. The volume was bound in paper boards covered
with calfskin," and inside the covers were found several early printed
sheets pasted and pressed together to form the binder's board.

Gowans' visitors and customers made a distinguished roll call. Among
those who frequented his shop were Audubon, who confided to the
bookseller the financial failure of his *Birds of America*; the "mad poet"
MacDonald Clarke, who refused to read Shakespeare or Milton "lest I
should spoil my own originality"; Bryant, Bancroft, the Duyckincks,
Washington Irving, Longfellow, as well as the collectors John Carter
Brown, George Brinley and John Allan. Allan prided himself upon
such acquisitions as a folio containing three hundred portraits and views
relating to Mary of Scots; George Wither's book of emblems; the Eliot
Bible; the Kilmarnock Burns, and, "having secured a new accession,
. . . would come tripping into [Gowans'] store, with a foot as noiseless
as that of Grimalkin, and spirits as buoyant and joyful as a youth let
loose from school."

For customers such as these William Gowans issued his catalogues.
Between 1842 and 1870 he distributed twenty-eight catalogues, many
of them printed by Joel Munsell and most of them interspersed with
notes sometimes discursive and often repeated in subsequent catalogues.
His prices were marked in front of his books while the cost price in
cipher appeared at the foot of the twenty-fifth page. Once fixed, Gowans' prices were "as unalterable as the laws of the Medes and Persians."

At the time of his death, Gowans' stock was said to have included
300,000 bound volumes "besides pamphlets innumerable." Eight tons
of these were sold by his executors at four and one-quarter cents per

pound for paper stock. In 1871 the remainder of Gowans' books were auctioned. The catalogue consisted of sixteen parts and included nearly 2,500 pages. The sale netted the Gowans heirs about $33,000.

Although William Gowans certainly operated on a larger quantitative scale than most of his descendants in the rare book field, in many ways there is a sense of *déjà vu* about his career. In the manner in which he obtained his stock, in his relations with his customers, in his cataloguing, and in his bibliomania, he seems a familiar figure today and his progress something of a twice-told tale.

In one of his catalogue notes, William Gowans made reference to a neighboring bookseller whose knowledge of books evoked high praise. Gowans' opinion was firmly based in fact, for Joseph Sabin (1821–1881)[12] was modest and abstemious in everything but bibliophilic, bibliographic and bibliopolic work. He drank nothing stronger than water, never used tobacco, but was so addicted to bookish labor that when he died, his suggested epitaph was "Killed by a Dictionary." Publisher, cataloguer, book auctioneer, compiler of the great *Dictionary of Books relating to America* that is known by his name, Joseph Sabin was also an importer and seller of books.

Born in Braunston, England, he was apprenticed at age fourteen to an Oxford bookseller-stationer, Charles Richards. In 1848, with his wife, he emigrated to the United States, and by 1850 was settled in New York City where he became a cataloguer for the auctioneers Cooley and Keese. After a variety of bookish enterprises, Sabin in 1864 purchased for $9,000 the stock of the secondhand and new book dealer Michael Noonan, and set up his shingle on Nassau Street, the " 'Rialto' of the old book trade" that would yield to Fourth Avenue after the Civil War. Visitors who came on foot or by horsecar could watch in Sabin's bookstore as cases from London were unpacked; could join the browsing collectors—Almon W. Griswold and William Menzies of New York, Henry C. Murphy and T. W. Field of Brooklyn, occasionally James Lenox; could examine the treasures, for, as the "Old Cartman" commented: "There is always some satisfaction in *seeing* and *handling* a rare and valuable book, and hearing its secret history descanted upon, even if you are not able to become the owner of it."[13]

According to William Loring Andrews, Sabin's sales between 1864 and 1874 "aggregated over $1,000,000, and during this period he supplied with some of their choicest treasures many of the public and private libraries then in course of formation." Some of Sabin's "treasures" reflected the tastes and perhaps the follies of the time: the mania for elephant folios and for extra-illustrated books. Huge tomes described as "rivulets of text in a sea of margins"—the Musée Français, the Musée Royal, Boydell's Shakespeare—were staples, and when such folios were extra-illustrated, the cup of many a collector overflowed. Sabin's sale of an extra-illustrated Shakespeare for $3,000 was one of his coups, as was his purchase, for Robert L. Stuart, of the extra-illustrated nine-volume *Old New York* at $230 a volume. That work contained more than 2,500 prints, water colors and autographs, including letters or signatures of all of Gotham's mayors.

While such volumes were available at Sabin's, the bookseller concentrated upon English literature and rare Americana. Through his knowing hands passed "several copies of the first folio Shakespeare . . . including that of Sir William Tite" along with early Chaucers and Miltons, Ben Jonsons, Spensers and Drydens. As for Americana, "What book-hunter dreams nowadays," William Loring Andrews mused before the turn of the century, "of finding in a book-stall such nuggets as the first New York Directory, the first edition of Andre's 'Cow Chase,' Symmes's 'Late Fight at Piggwacket,' or a copy of Hariot's 'Virginia,' the rare English De Bry, which was sold to Mr. Kalbfleisch for $1,250, a long price in those days, but a short one in this year of grace 1895."

When Joseph Sabin was not buying and selling books, he was cataloguing collections (the catalogues of 150 or more libraries are credited to him) or presiding at auction sales. At his last sale, the Brinley, on 4 April 1881, Sabin offered the Mazarin Bible, at the time "the only copy . . . brought under the hammer on this side of the Atlantic." Sold to Hamilton Cole for $8,000, the work was resold at the Brayton Ives auction and "taken to Chicago at a ransom of $14,800."

Sabin's biographer describes him as "a better bibliophile than he was a merchant," a bookseller "more eager to discuss the bibliographical points of his literary wares than to effect a sale of them." Nor did Sabin suffer fools—or sceptics—gladly. "A youth once brought him for sale a volume of the Mexican Boundary Survey, published by the United States Government" and was informed by Sabin that the work was imperfect since it should be in two volumes. "The young man insisted that the book was perfect until Mr. Sabin closed the discussion by saying jocosely, 'Young man, if that work was contained in one volume it would make a book as thick as your head.' "

It was predictable that Joseph Sabin should die in harness. Two months after the sale of the Mazarin Bible, on 5 June 1881, he died, a bibliopolic scholar whose "love for rare books passed into knowledge . . . for the benefit of all who had the pleasure and profit of knowing him." He was followed on Nassau Street by his son Joseph F. Sabin, who, according to Charles F. Heartman writing in 1925, "sold more Americana than any dealer now living, will ever be able to sell" and who was the "first to recognize the importance of a letter as well as the name of the writer."

Another bookseller who helped elevate the practice of bookselling into a profession was George Philip Philes.[14] Born in Ithaca, New York, in 1828 and educated at both Ithaca Academy and the classical institute of Dr. August Maasberg of Göttingen, he was not only a bookseller but a fine linguist and bibliographer. His short-lived periodical, *Philobiblion*, presented a mass of bibliophilic information and anecdote between 1861 and 1863. Moreover, this New York City bookseller helped in the preparation of Henry Harrisse's *Bibliotheca Americana Vetustissima*, issued learned treatises on the Bhagvat-Geeta and the first English Bible printed in the United States, and compiled the catalogues of the Andrew J. Odell library.

New York's Booksellers' Row accommodated a variety of antiquarian dealers, from Joseph Sabin to Charles Lowell Woodward whose first catalogue, issued in February 1876, was entitled: *Inventory of a few old books and pamphlets mostly home-made and picked up in the neighborhood for sale at starvation figures quoted by Charles L. Woodward Book Peddler Up-stairs in a back room 78 Nassau Street New York.*[15] But it was on Astor Place that quite another type of antiquarian business centered its operations. From the firm of John Wiley,[16] through their London agent Henry Stevens, James Lenox acquired his copy of the Mazarin Bible. That company, importers of books from abroad, also helped launch James Lenox as "a new collector of Americana." Indeed Lenox confided that he "could at present find the five pound notes more easily than such books, but you must not tell anybody how much I have paid." The Wiley firm, which survived many metamorphoses since its founding in 1807, forsook rare books for publishing in 1884. Although throughout its history it ranked primarily as a publishing house, nonetheless its period in the rare book trade was highly productive and merits a place in the record of New York City's antiquarian bibliopoly.

Another house better known for publishing also played a vital role in the purchase and sale of antiquarian books imported from abroad by packet ship. Robert H. Dodd,[17] who managed the rare book department of Dodd and Mead, "possessed that occult sense which leads your genuine rare book man to the priceless treasure in the lonely farm attic and which whispers to him how high to bid in the auction room." In addition to such supernatural aids, Dodd was invested with certain natural endowments. "He knew his way about in the intricate price systems and he knew the needs and desires of the various collectors." As a result, Dodd was able to help build up the Hoe and Church collections, the Morgan and Huntington libraries. Indeed one collector of the day is said to have remarked to another, "Well, what's in the rest of your library, Dodd only knows."

Among Dodd's assistants were several future New York booksellers of note: George H. Richmond, William Evarts Benjamin, James F. Drake. Luther S. Livingston, who became Dodd's partner in the rare book firm of Dodd and Livingston, began *American Book Prices Current* in 1895. By 1914 he was librarian of the Widener Library at Harvard. Meanwhile he had worked on the Dodd, Mead catalogues, and "the extent to which his notes on rare volumes and peculiar editions have been copied by other book sellers is the convincing tribute to the thoroughness with which he exhausted each subject that he undertook to examine."

Of all Dodd's assistants perhaps none became more legendary in the trade than his errand or stock boy. Having worked briefly for Wiley until 1884 when that firm relinquished the sale of rare books, George D. Smith, a fourteen-year-old Brooklyn boy, spent a short time with Dodd and Mead. In 1885, when the impulsive and audacious William Evarts Benjamin set up business on his own at 744 Broadway, young Smith joined him. Such was the early apprenticeship of a bookseller who "could remember every title in a book catalogue, with its price, tell what it had fetched at auction, who the buyer was, and often the names of the underbidders."

George D. Smith (1870–1920)[18]—familiarly referred to as G.D.S.— was a large dynamic man with what has been called a "picturesque" figure and an irrepressible nature. He lived books eighteen hours a day every day for almost four decades. Like many monomaniacs, he was sometimes distrusted, often disliked, but never underestimated. Early in Smith's career, William E. Benjamin remarked to his colleague, one of the Leon brothers: "When you come back [from abroad] I shall be the American Quaritch," to which the reply was, "Not you, . . . that boy George will be the American Quaritch."

"That boy George" certainly became the czar of the American rare book trade. Between 1900, the time of the Augustin Daly sale, and Smith's death in 1920, over half the rare books auctioned in this country were knocked down to G.D.S., and to that staggering quantity must be added the private libraries he purchased as Henry E. Huntington's agent. At the Hoe sales of 1911 and 1912 he was the major buyer, acquiring—inter a great many alia—the Gutenberg Bible for Huntington at the price of $50,000. He obtained the Duke of Devonshire library en bloc and considered the purchase "one of the greatest bargains he ever secured." Since it contained the Chatsworth Shakespeare folios and quartos including the Hamlet quarto, he was doubtless right. In 1917 Smith bought the Earl of Bridgewater library which included a Chaucer manuscript. The selling price was $1 million, and Huntington gave Smith a profit of $500,000.

Having begun his bibliopolic career in an 8th Street basement store, George D. Smith followed the uptown march of the metropolitan trade until he arrived at 8 East 45th Street. There his clients clustered: the Pforzheimers, Beverly Chew, Theodore N. Vail, William Randolph Hearst, Edward E. Ayer, Brayton Ives, and of course Henry E. Huntington. There was nothing small about George D. Smith—his customers were munificent and the treasures that passed through his hands were grandiose.

Smith was as keen as he was majestic. He opposed the London clique who "rigged the auction market," and he is said to have spotted Thomas J. Wise's forgeries as forgeries before the Carter and Pollard exposé. Like his Monuments of Early Printing in Germany, the Low Countries, Italy, France and England 1460–1500, George D. Smith himself seemed monumental. His attitude toward his trade had a kind of majesty: "When the rulers of kingdoms today have crumbled into the dust," he said, "and their names forgotten of the people, the memory of a maker of a great collection will be a household word in the mouths of thousands." Unduly euphoric as this view may have been, G.D.S. unquestionably helped raise the stature of rare books in this country. Dynamic and impressive, he invested bibliopoly with style and grandeur. At the age of fifty he died, as most booksellers would wish to die, "while in conversation." A generation later—in 1945—Charles

F. Heartman distributed a privately printed Yuletide greeting entitled *G.D.S. 1870–1920 A Memorial Tribute to the Greatest Bookseller the World has Ever Known Written by a Very Small One.* The image of antiquarian bookselling in New York City had undergone some changes between 1920 when G.D.S. died and 1945 when Heartman wrote his tribute. Czars slowly gave way to lesser potentates as the process of democratization gradually made itself felt among buyers of old and rare. Yet some of those lesser potentates exerted a powerful influence upon the nature and technique of bookselling.

One of them surely was Isaac Mendoza whose Ann Street bookstore had opened in 1894.[19] Mendoza, son of émigrés from London, had been born on New York's Lower East Side in 1864. At age eighteen he began work in the book basement of Michael J. Hynes, and after twelve years apprenticeship in the book business launched his own shop in half a store at 17 Ann Street, moving shortly after to Number 15. That six-story red brick building whose gas-lit mantle lights illumined hundreds of thousands of books and whose treasures and semi-treasures attracted "bankers and brokers, railroad titans and robber barons, politicians and passers-by," was destined to long life. The firm was incorporated in 1908 as the Isaac Mendoza Book Company, and in it were trained Isaac's three sons Aaron, David and Mark. After the founder's death in 1937, the business was carried on by those sons. After Mark's death in 1956, Aaron and David carried on; after Aaron's death in 1960, David carried on. It had been Aaron's ambition to write a history of New York City bookselling, and to that end he had crammed his roll-top desk with notes and source materials. Although he did not live to write that history, he and the Isaac Mendoza Book Company assuredly helped, and still help, to make it.

Another bookshop was opened on Ann Street by quite a different personality in the trade. Charles Grenedier, born in Umen, Russia, in 1901, came to this country with his parents two years later, and there was metamorphosed into Charles Grand.[20] After studies at City College and Columbia, he followed the Mendozas to Ann Street, but moved uptown, first to 34th and Madison and then to 28th and Lexington. The lack of mobility enforced by a permanent location did not appeal to Charlie Grand, and he shortly changed his modus operandi to that of scout. Charles Grand, however, was a scout of stature, a scout on the grand scale. Through his hands passed such gems as Poe's *Murders in the Rue Morgue* and Poe's *X-ing a Paragrab*, manuscripts by the Maryland printer William Goddard on the freedom of the press, Gutenberg leaves. To him was entrusted the disposal of portions of the libraries of Herman LeRoy Edgar and I. N. Phelps Stokes. After his death in 1951, Grand's funeral was attended by many booksellers, among them Howard S. Mott, Walter Schatzki, Richard S. Wormser and Harry Newman, who, on the way to the services, concocted the plan of a Charlie Grand Memorial Fund, a project designed to help booksellers in need—an antiquarian booksellers' benevolent fund originated in memory of the book scout Charlie Grand.

Mott, Schatzki, Wormser, Newman—all had entered the bibliopolic lists, helping extend to a broadening world of collectors the joys of the book. Before and during the 1920s and 1930s the ranks of booksellers were enlarged by several major New York firms, among them those of Edward Eberstadt and Peter Decker, leading specialists in Western Americana, the antiquarian emporia of Dauber & Pine and Argosy as well as House of Books, Ltd., launched by Louis Henry Cohn and his wife Marguerite. Along Fourth Avenue, Jack Biblo opened a store in 1928 "with $300 he borrowed from his mother," and that store would become known as Biblo and Tannen. In 1932 Walter Goldwater started a black-studies bookstore "with $600 and the help of 'a Communist uncle by marriage.' "[21] Among the older booksellers, one or two kings still reigned, and a necrological list of the major New York dealers who died during the 1940s forms a stirring reminder of our predecessors great and not so great:[22] William Evarts Benjamin, died 1940; Max Harzof, died 1942; Walter R. Benjamin, died 1943. Brother of William E. Benjamin, Walter R. Benjamin began his pioneering autograph business in 1887 and launched *The Collector* in September of that year. His distinguished firm—and *The Collector*—continue under the aegis of his daughter Mary A. Benjamin; Ernest Dressel North, died 1945, the year the Philadelphia-based monarch of books Dr. Rosenbach bought Poe's *Tamerlane* at the Parke Bernet Galleries; Gabriel Wells, died 1947, the year Dr. Rosenbach purchased on a bid of $151,000 the *Bay Psalm Book* now at Yale. As for Gabriel Wells, it was he who presented to the New York Public Library three leaves missing from the Lenox copy of the Gutenberg Bible which he supplied from the Munich-Curzon copy; Lathrop C. Harper, died 1950.

Lathrop C. Harper is especially memorable. His biographer Charles F. Heartman reminds us that "his human qualities . . . so penetrated his bookselling activities as to be a part of them." For a sincere book collector Lathrop C. Harper would happily buy on commission at auction a dozen cheap items, but would never sell a book to a millionaire "whose millions . . . made him an international nuisance." Nor was he impressed by the "spread-eagle notes of the modern cataloguer." Born in New York in 1867, Harper at seventeen joined his brother in the book business on Barclay Street under the old Astor House, and four years later made his first book-buying trip abroad. From such beginnings he followed the pattern set by some who had preceded him and marked a pattern for many who would follow him. He helped assemble the libraries of Henry F. De Puy and Newbold Edgar and supplied the nucleus of the Clements Library.

Researching the New York careers of the Leon Brothers who issued the pioneer *Catalogue of First Editions of American Authors* in 1885, I had the privilege of interviewing Lathrop C. Harper a few years before his death. Harper of course remembered the Leon Brothers as I remember Harper. And so the thread of continuity is woven into the fabric of the New York antiquarian booktrade. The memorable becomes also the remembered. The ghostly bookseller, whose name appears on no colophon, who has left no visible imprint except for his ephemeral catalogues, can still be conjured up.[23] In 1895 William Loring Andrews was asked the question: "What is the use of writing about these men? They were simply dealers, and bought and sold books as so much merchandise for profit, and that was all there was to it." And Andrews answered: "Not quite all, my good friend. An old bookshop is a mental tonic to one who merely whiles away an idle hour therein. I am loath to believe that one can pass his entire life among books, even in the way of sordid trade, without imbibing . . . a modicum of the wit, wisdom and philosophy they contain, and thereby becoming a less commonplace fraction of the mass of humanity."[24]

That "less commonplace fraction" has added another dimension to Manhattan Island and increased the stature of a city.

NOTES

1. Henry Lemoine, *Present State of Printing and Bookselling in America [1796]* (Chicago 1929), pp. 7, 17 f. For a source for some of these remarks see [Arthur Homer], *Bibliotheca Americana* (London: Debrett, 1789), p. 16. See also Lawrence C. Wroth, *The Colonial Printer* (Portland, Maine: Southworth-Anthoensen Press, 1938), p. 312 n. 2.

2. Edwin D. Hoffman, "The Bookshops of New York City, 1743–1948," *New York History* XXX:1 (January 1949), pp. 53–65.

3. Sidney I. Pomerantz, *New York: An American City 1783–1803* (New York: Columbia University Press, 1938), p. 440.

4. William Loring Andrews, *The Old Booksellers of New York and Other Papers* (New York 1895). For the bookselling scene of the period, see also Henry W. Boynton, *Annals of American Bookselling 1638–1850* (New York: Wiley, 1932), pp. 158, 163; John W. Francis, "Reminiscences of Printers, Authors, and Booksellers in New-York," *The International Magazine of Literature, Art, and Science* V:2 (1 February 1852), pp. 253–266; Hoffman, "The Bookshops of New York City," pp. 54, 57; Thomas E.V. Smith, "The Book Trade of New York in 1789," *Publishers Weekly* XXXV:17 (27 April 1889), p. 595; John Tebbel, *A History of Book Publishing in the United States* (New York: Bowker, 1972), I, 262; Isaiah Thomas, *The History of Printing in America* (New York: Weathervane Books, 1970), pp. 484 f.

5. Allan Nevins, ed., *The Diary of Philip Hone 1828–1851* (New York: Dodd, Mead, 1936), p. 483.

6. Hoffman, "The Bookshops of New York City," p. 60.

7. Pomerantz, *New York: An American City*, p. 440.

8. I. S. Lyon, *Recollections of An Old Cartman* (Newark, N.J.: Daily Journal Office, 1872), p. 101.

9. *The First One Hundred and Fifty Years: A History of John Wiley and Sons, Incorporated 1807–1957* (New York: John Wiley & Sons, Inc., [1957]), p. 1.

10. Andrews, *The Old Booksellers of New York*, pp. 3–29.

11. In a letter of 15 January 1886 to the *Journal of Commerce*, quoted by Andrews, *The Old Booksellers of New York*, p. 15.

12. Andrews, *The Old Booksellers of New York*, pp. 29–39, 43; Hoffman, "The Bookshops of New York City," p. 61. See also the excellent article by William S. Reese, "Joseph Sabin," *American Book Collector* N.S. 5:1 (January/February 1984), pp. 3–23. For Joseph F. Sabin, see also "Famous American Booksellers Past and Present," *The Americana Collector*, ed. by Charles F. Heartman, I:1 (October 1925).

13. Lyon, *Recollections of An Old Cartman*, p. 101.

14. *Appletons' Cyclopædia of American Biography* (New York: D. Appleton, 1888), IV, 755; Harry Miller Lydenberg, "George Philes: Bookman," *Papers of the Bibliographical Society of America* 48:1 (1954), pp. 1–48.

15. Adolf Growoll Collection, *American Book Trade History*, XIII, 78.

16. Andrews, *The Old Booksellers of New York*, pp. 46 f; Hellmut Lehmann-Haupt, *The Book in America* (New York: Bowker, 1951), pp. 390 f; Henry Stevens, *Recollections of James Lenox and the formation of his library* (New York: New York Public Library, 1951), pp. 14 f, 23.

17. Edward H. Dodd, Jr., *The First Hundred Years: A History of the House*

of Dodd, Mead 1839–1939 (New York: Dodd, Mead & Co., 1939), pp. 32 f; Lehmann-Haupt, *The Book in America*, pp. 391 f; *Luther S. Livingston 1864–1914* (Cambridge, Mass., 1915), unpaged.

18. "Famous American Booksellers Past and Present," *The Americana Collector*, I:6 (March 1926), pp. 232–236; [Charles F. Heartman], *George D. Smith G.D.S. 1870–1920: A Memorial Tribute to the Greatest Bookseller the World has Ever Known Written by a Very Small One* (Beauvoir Community, Miss.: The Book Farm, privately printed, 1945).

19. "Aaron Mendoza 1888-1960," *AB* (25 April 1960) pp. 1607 f.

20. Howard S. Mott, "Charles Grand 1901–1951," *AB* (4 August 1951) p. 265; Information from Phyllis N. Mott.

21. "Old Bookstores: A Chapter Ends," *New York Times* (31 May 1981).

22. The list, patently incomplete, could be extended and modified by other dealers with long memories. See "Famous American Booksellers Past and Present," *The Americana Collector*, I:4 (January 1926), pp. 139–143; and II:1 (April 1926), pp. 268–270; Lehmann-Haupt, *The Book in America*, p. 392.

23. To record and preserve the work of a later generation of antiquarian booksellers, the Rare Book Tapes were conceived by James Lowe and are currently being distributed by the Antiquarian Booksellers Center, New York City.

24. Andrews, *The Old Booksellers of New York*, pp. 49 f.

4

Cincinnati

In 1793, when Cincinnati was a wilderness, it would have required considerable faith in things unseen to visualize it as the "Queen of the West." Yet already a regular line of armored packet boats plied between Pittsburgh and that place, and within three years it was recognizable as a village of log cabins and frame houses. Cincinnati's fate was implicit in its location "on the river highway between East and West." The keelboat ushered in its destined preeminence; the steamboat brought it to fruition; the railroad ended it. In its heyday Cincinnati served as commercial and cultural capital of the frontier, and for a few decades it was not only the "Queen City of the West" but "the great mart for the book trade west of the mountains."[1]

In Cincinnati's early days, even before there were bookstores, books were available. Peddlers tramping back country roads had books in their sacks, and boats plying the rivers carried books in their holds. As early as 1793 there were a Cincinnati post office and a Cincinnati newspaper—*The Centinel of the North Western Territory*, "the first newspaper print north of the Ohio river." Its printing office was located "in the garret of a small building on Front street," and a "wheelbarrow would have moved all the types, cases and stands." By 1802, citizens met to organize a subscription library. As the population increased from 500 in 1793 to 6,000 in 1815, so too did the market for books. A latter-day bookseller would write of the town named after the Society of the Cincinnati: "The place was fortunate from its beginning," attracting literate young men. They came from the East—from New England and the Middle Atlantic States—and from the British Isles, and finally they came from Germany, the "*achtafurtiger*" or "forty-eighters," enriching the town of Cincinnati with their interest in good eating and good drinking, good music and good literature.

Despite Mrs. Trollope's disparaging remarks, good literature had long been available in Cincinnati. The author of *Domestic Manners of the Americans*, who sailed for the States in 1827, declared she "never saw any people who appeared to live so much without amusement as the Cincinnatians. . . . They have no concerts. They have no dinner parties. . . . I should have liked Cincinnati much better if the people had not dealt so very largely in hogs." And she added: "there are many reasons which render a very general diffusion of literature impossible in America. . . . they are all too actively employed to read, except . . . for a peep at a newspaper."[2]

As it happened, the acerbic Mrs. Trollope was wrong. The pioneer Cincinnati household library provided not only the omnipresent Bible, Shakespeare and Aesop, but often Johnson's *Dictionary* and Watts' *Hymns*, Cook's *Voyages* and Ashe's *Travels*. Such books could be found, not at bookstores which as such did not yet exist, but through newspaper advertisements, at auctions, or in stores that sold books as a sideline to drugs or general merchandise. A *Western Spy* advertisement of 1799, inserted by a traveler ready to leave the Northwest Territory, offered, along with a Milton and a Euclid, a Wollstonecraft and a Young's *Night Thoughts*, a Foxe's *Book of Martyrs* and the *Works* of Paine.[3] By 1823, Cincinnatians could purchase at auction "a large and valuable collection of BOOKS, among which are some of the most valuable and scarce scientific works ever offered in the western country," many of which had "elegantly colored plates" and handsome bindings.[4]

By that time, of course, there were bookstores in Cincinnati. If it were possible to sketch a prototype portrait of the early frontier bookseller, he might be described as a young Easterner who came west to make his fortune, perhaps navigating the Allegheny and Ohio rivers in a flatboat. Once in Cincinnati, he might set up as druggist or printer or newspaper publisher who tempted his clientele with a small sideline of books, and whose store might well become the center of a literary coterie. At all events, "by the beginning of the 1820's, the book trade was becoming firmly established in Cincinnati."[5]

Who were the booksellers who established it? As usual, it is difficult, if not impossible, to determine priority. The first Cincinnati bookstore—a store devoted exclusively to the sale of books and stationery— was apparently in operation by 1812, when John Corson advertised his

"Books & Stationery Store Only." Even before then, J. W. Browne & Co., booksellers, were in business next door to their *Liberty Hall* printing office. But "probably the earliest successful bookseller" may be identified as John P. Foote who, between 1820 and 1828, sold books on Lower Market Street. According to the Cincinnati historians Henry and Kate Ford, Foote's "stock was well selected and suited to the market... chiefly classical and standard works." That the market was literary is testified by the existence of Cincinnati's Semi-colon Club of which not only John P. Foote but, later on, Calvin and Harriet Beecher Stowe and Catharine Beecher were members. Besides editing the Cincinnati *Literary Gazette*, John P. Foote offered to customers not only "the choice literature on his shelves" but the delights of his own "genial and entertaining disposition." His bookstore—the prototype in this respect of so many bookstores across the country—became "a favorite place of meeting for a coterie of literary men of the day."[6]

John Parsons Foote had both his competitors and his successors,[7] most of whom resembled the prototype frontier bookseller who supplied the literary needs of a community grown from wilderness. There was, for example, the Englishman Thomas Reddish who had trained in Philadelphia before trekking west and whose Swedenborgian affiliations were reflected in the stock he offered at his Sun Circulating Library. Another product of Philadelphia training was William Hill Woodward, son of a Philadelphia bookseller, whose Cincinnati shelves were stocked from his father's store and who offered for sale not only books but coffee. Woodward would in time start an auction business before becoming a steamboat captain.

In 1827, E. H. Flint opened a bookstore at the corner of Fifth and Walnut streets where apparently the needs not only of the reader of new books but of the antiquarian collector could be satisfied. Moreover, Flint early stimulated an interest in regional collecting. The proprietor offered the usual "general assortment of school-books, geographies, atlases, stationery, &c." But, he announced, although "his assortment at present is small," it "comprises many interesting and valuable works, particularly upon the history and geography of the Western country. He has many books that were selected, to form part of a private library. He intends soon to import from Boston and Philadelphia a complete assortment of books, stationery, engravings, &c.... Having recently commenced the business of sending books to all the chief towns and villages in the valley of the Mississippi, he will be able to make up packages with neatness, and transmit them with safety and dispatch to any town in the Western and Southwestern country."

Importing from their native East, selling to the West, the Cincinnati dealers plied their trade. Josiah Drake of Massachusetts was one; his partner William Conclin of New York was another. Indeed it was Conclin who emigrated with his family from the banks of the Hudson to Cincinnati, traveling via Olean and navigating the Allegheny and the Ohio by flatboat.

The bookstore established by John P. Foote was purchased in 1828 by Nathan Guilford who hailed from Spencer, Massachusetts, had been graduated from Yale, and practiced law in Cincinnati before joining the ranks of pioneer booksellers. Guilford has been described as a member of "*the disinterested class in society*" who "lived not for himself alone, but for the good of others." Certainly he coupled his philanthropies with the successful operation of a Cincinnati bookstore which, under the aegis of his brother George and himself, survived well into the 1830s.

One of Guilford's competitors was Ephraim Morgan who journeyed to Ohio from Massachusetts at age fourteen and in 1828 opened a book and job printing office with a partner, John Sanxay, "in an old two story brick building on the west side of Main street." A member of the Society of Friends, Morgan was called "the noble Quaker." His book stock was less noble, consisting primarily of schoolbooks with a small stock of stationery, although he became "a most active publisher." As a younger colleague would one day observe, "Ephraim Morgan, with his serene countenance" was "as ready to speak the truth and impart good counsel as the quarto Bibles he made."

Selling quarto Bibles, schoolbooks, eastern imports and works of regional interest, such pioneer booksellers as these were transforming the Cincinnati of the 1830s into the "Literary Emporium of the West." As the mid-century approached, a writer on "The Book Trade of Cincinnati" would claim: "It has been apparent to observing minds for ten or twelve years past, that the time was fast approaching when the population of all the northeastern part of the Mississippi Valley, and also many of the most thickly settled localities on the lower Mississippi river, would look exclusively to Cincinnati for their supply of books . . . and discontinue their annual and semi-annual visits to the eastern cities for the purpose of laying in stock."[8]

Despite the characteristic chauvinism of the statement, it was no idle boast. For a period of time Cincinnati did indeed become just such a major supplier of books, new and antiquarian, west of the Alleghenies. For that development, a handful of outstanding Cincinnati dealers was responsible.

In 1979, the James Book Store[9] would be hailed by the *Cincinnati Enquirer* as the "oldest bookstore west of the Alleghenies." At that time it was "limping" toward its sesquicentennial. Actually, the James Book Store traced its origin to 1831 when Uriah Pierson James and his brother Joseph Arthur James, both from Goshen, New York, began a printing and stereotyping shop which would soon encompass publishing and bookselling. Indeed, by the mid-century, as J. A. & U. P. James, it would publish, print, bind, stereotype, and sell books besides manufacturing ink; it would employ over 125 hands and would engage agents throughout the Mississippi Valley.

The two brothers had traveled west by stage and canal, arriving in Cincinnati in August 1831. Their printing office would undergo several transformations, as would their partnership. Their shop would move from Pearl to Walnut Street and thence to Race and West Seventh as Cincinnati grew. By 1854 the firm would be dissolved, Uriah continuing the business on his own. It was Uriah who set his individual mark upon the firm. A modest man, avoiding show, he had strong antiquarian interests which were reflected in the books he published and sold. "Being an intelligent gentleman, of studious habits and extensive observation," he pursued studies "not . . . limited to bibliography" but extending to the natural sciences, especially geology and paleontology. A member of the Western Academy of Sciences, U. P. James published a *Catalogue of the Fossils of the Cincinnati Group* collected in the vicinity of the city, and amassed a large cabinet of shells and fossils.

As a bookseller, U. P. James offered not only a miscellaneous stock of new books but rare Americana, especially Western Americana which he also published. In 1886 this highly esteemed bibliopole retired in favor of his son Davis L. James, who continued not only the business but his father's interests. A latter-day bookseller would recall that Davis James "specialized in Americana" and had a bookcase in back of the store known as the "holy of holies" where a Richard de Bury was available for $3.75. The austere, dignified Davis L. James was followed upon his death in 1933 by his son Davis L. James, Jr., and the latter's wife who continued the operation under the firm name of the James Book Store until 1939 when Mrs. James took over. At the time of the latter's death in 1947 another member of the family was on hand in the business—James Pierson James, grandson of the founder—although the shop was managed by Mary Stix Holzberg. As the business that had once been styled the "Harpers of the West" approached its sesquicentennial, the name persisted but not the substance. Carrying few old books, it offered "new and standard works of all publishers." And so, although the name of Uriah Pierson James was remembered, his antiquarian interests were neglected. Now, moving toward the sesquicentennial milestone, the James Book Store was described as "an old bookstore—not to be confused with a store that sells old books, although James does have a sampling of those." But the rare Americana and the early *Philobiblon* were gone. The bookstore had survived the ages of keelboat and steamboat, railroad and jet plane but, unlike the leopard, it had changed its spots.

The life of another major Cincinnati bookstore was far shorter, but it too observed the city as it "grew apace, and . . . trade increased. Customers were numbered by hundreds, from New-Orleans in the South to Chicago and Galena, Ill., in the North-west." If the James Book Store spanned the rise and fall of Cincinnati as a cultural and literary center, the firm of H. W. Derby[10] coincided with its apogee.

In his teens, Henry William Derby trekked from his native Herkimer County, New York, to Columbus, Ohio, where in 1838 he clerked for the pioneer bookseller-publisher Isaac Whiting. Three years later he bought out his employer and set up his own shingle, stocking miscellaneous books, Bibles, schoolbooks, publications from the East, along with stationery and sheet music, flutes and fiddles, penknives and wallpaper, Currier prints and Macassar hair oil. Supplying not only Cincinnati but the entire state with books and stationery, Columbus was then the center of trade. Wagons from neighboring mills picked up paper rags and left in payment writing and wrapping paper. As a Derby apprentice, David B. Cooke would recall: "When trade became dull at home . . . it was our custom to take a load of our surplus stock, and start out into the country to work it off. In this way my employer and myself travelled over nearly every portion of the State of Ohio, selling books at auction from the tail of a wagon."

Within three years it became obvious that a substantial portion of the Derby business was coming from Cincinnati. Disposing of his stock to Joseph H. Riley, Derby and his young assistant left Columbus in "one of Neil & Co.'s old-fashioned stages" and "after several days of

weary travel over the national turnpike road," they arrived in Cincinnati on 13 October 1844. With a partner, Charles F. Bradley, who
had been trained in the New York house of Appleton, Derby established
the new firm of Derby, Bradley & Co. Subsequently Bradley would sell
his interest to Derby, and the style would be changed to H. W. Derby
& Co.

Its comparatively short history in Cincinnati, spanning the years
1844 to 1858, was "marked by brilliant and uniform success." In 1848
John C. Barnes, later of A. S. Barnes & Co., New York, joined the
firm, followed in 1851 by Fletcher Harper, Jr. In 1849 the house rose,
phoenix-like, from a fire that "completely consumed" the establishment. According to Derby's observant clerk David B. Cooke: "Our
advent in Cincinnati proved a marked era in the book trade of that
city, already possessing several bookstores carrying limited stocks. Our
elegant assortment and well-appointed establishment at once attracted
the readers and lovers of choice books, and for years our store was the
literary resort of the city." When, as the mid-century approached, "The
Book Trade of Cincinnati" was surveyed for the press, Henry W. Derby
& Co. was described as "a miscellaneous establishment, wherein all
standard works can be obtained in the various branches of literature,
with the current issues of the American press, importations from England and the Continent. . . . This is the largest house west of the mountains, and one of the completest and best systematized in the United
States. It has an elegance in the look, and a taste in all its appointments,
which is equalled by nothing of the kind in this country. . . . It is really
an intellectual treat to walk through its elegant rooms and glance at
the rich contents of its well-arranged shelves, counters, cases, &c.,
without even opening a volume." Those who did venture to open
volumes found—as they found in most Cincinnati bookstores—not only
an array of the new, but a sampling of the old and the antiquarian.
The firm's senior partner, with his "energetic and elastic spirit," had
indeed given an "impulse to the Book Trade" of the Queen City.

H. W. Derby made no attempt to withstand the shifts in the cultural
tide that came with the growth of the railroad and that would shortly
diminish the importance of Cincinnati as a literary center and enhance
that of Chicago and St. Louis to the West. By 1860 the firm of H. W.
Derby & Co. was dissolved. One branch of the business—the company's
interest in law books—was sold to yet another Cincinnati house whose
history marked the high water mark in the city's antiquarian annals.

Robert Clarke[11] must have been the exception that proved the rule, for his house—the most distinguished antiquarian firm in Cincinnati—did not begin its flourishing history until after the mid-century when Chicago had already begun to take precedence as a book center over the Queen City of the West. He came, not from the American East but from Scotland, having been born in Annan, Dumfriesshire, in 1829. At age eleven he migrated with his parents to Cincinnati where he attended Woodward College and became a bookkeeper for William Hanna. According to his obituary, the former institution stimulated his "scientific and historical tastes" while the latter occupation helped shape "the neat, methodical habits of his business career."

Both tendencies were given opportunity to develop when, in 1854, Robert Clarke bought out Tobias Lyon's interest in the book business of Lyon & Patterson, operating as Patterson & Clarke in Bacon's Building on the corner of Sixth and Walnut streets. This, Clarke's first bookstore, dealt chiefly in secondhand and foreign books and became "the first house in Cincinnati to import books direct from London and Paris." There, too, Clarke began that education in Americana which was to enrich the antiquarian trade in Cincinnati. Like most popular bookstores, Clarke's became a "favorite resort for literary men," and, despite the fact that in the 1850s "books were of less importance . . . than . . . lumber, flatboats and pork" to this western community, it prospered. In 1857 Clarke bought out Patterson, and the next year he acquired H. W. Derby's law book business. His partners in this enterprise were John W. Dale, and Roderick D. Barney who had clerked for H. W. Derby & Co. The new firm of Robert Clarke & Co. would endure until 1894 when it would undergo another transformation. It was already on its way to becoming "a power in the West."

Located at first in the former Derby headquarters on West Fourth Street, Robert Clarke & Co. were both law book publishers and wholesale and retail booksellers. Sustaining the usual removals and changes in partnership, the firm flourished in its multiple role and, in time, the entire third floor of the establishment was devoted to Robert Clarke's major interest—Americana. As for the rest of the "large, attractive retail department," that was described as "a literary center, where do chiefly congregate the Cincinnati bookworms and literati, to dally with temptation in the shape of choice imported works, rare editions, volumes rich in all the modern wealth of binding and illustration."

The antiquarian aspects of the firm reflected the character and propensities of the proprietor. He was "a hard student all his life, not only of the interior of books, but of their exterior. He has not only been a successful bibliopole, but a cyclopedia on bibliography." His catalogues of *Bibliotheca Americana* became sourcebooks for the scholar; his shop became a treasure house for the collector who lingered there as "a pious antiquarian might haunt an ancient abbey." Importing books from Europe to the Ohio Valley, the Clarke firm specialized in bibliography, American history and archeology. At one time it was described as occupying eleven floors and employing about twenty people. Robert Clarke & Co. included a wholesale department, a book bindery and a book printing office as well as a retail store "crowded with goods . . . arranged with perfect taste."

In 1894, reorganized as a corporation and renamed the Robert Clarke Co., the business continued, an expression of its founder's scholarly interests. It was said,

There is nothing in the way of books, professional or miscellaneous, or of stationery, that can not be had on call at the Robert Clarke Company. But it is not because of their loaded shelves of miscellaneous books, not because of their law libraries and medical volumes, or their stationery and game supplies that the Robert Clarke Company has become famous, but rather because they outrank every other dealer in the world in the extent of their collection and knowledge of Americana.

The historian of the United States, John Fiske, advised readers "to apply to the Robert Clarke Company . . . who keep by far the largest collection of books on America that can be found on sale in this country." Theodore Roosevelt consulted with Robert Clarke while he was writing *The Winning of the West,* and Arthur Conan Doyle paid the bibliopole a glowing tribute when he visited America. Justin Winsor described the firm's *Americana* Catalogues as "the completest booksellers' lists of that kind which are published in America."

As early as 1878, in a catalogue of *Bibliotheca Americana,* Clarke could write: "This Catalogue represents perhaps the largest and most varied collection of books of this class, in booksellers hands, in this country or Europe. . . . It exhibits . . . the character and variety of our usual stock. . . . Libraries, private buyers, and the trade, will find it to their advantage to send to us their list of books wanted . . . as we have especial advantages for the collection of rare books in this class." The rare books assembled by Clarke ranged from works on Alabama to works on the Wyoming Territory, and included studies of pre-Columbian America, Indians and antiquities, genealogy and heraldry, slavery and blacks, and the Arctic. His 1878 catalogue comprised 6,887 items at prices starting at 35 cents for E. P. Davis' *Minnesota* (Minneapolis 1871) in paper, and rising to $35 for a ten-volume set of Bancroft's *History of the United States.*

The Clarke Company was obviously a product of Robert Clarke. He was one who "did not merely make books and sell them, but he knew what was in them and remembered them." A "constant reader," connoisseur and bibliophile, Clarke was not only a bookseller but a scholarly editor and a distinguished collector. In 1868 the prospectus of what would become his Ohio Valley Historical Series was issued, a series for which he edited George Rogers Clark's *Campaign in Illinois* and Captain James Smith's *Captivity with the Indians.* But it was in his own personal library that Robert Clarke exhibited most strikingly the traits of character and the collecting mania that made him also Cincinnati's greatest antiquarian bookseller.

Robert Clarke never married; his books were his family. His home in Glendale was described as "one huge library," for his collections filled the house. When he died it would be said that "the joy of his life was his library." From American suppliers as well as from his travels, which eventually extended to Alaska and Mexico, Europe, India, China, and Egypt, the indefatigable collector amassed his holdings. His tastes embraced archeology, Scottish books, and especially Americana. It was from his library holdings that he drew for the reprints he issued, beginning in 1868 with four rare pamphlets. At one time the rarities in the Clarke library were "in danger of being ruined by rats, which gnawed the morocco bindings." Resourceful even in such an extremity, the collector offered a premium of five cents a rat to the boys employed in his bindery!

Clarke's custom—since he was also a bookseller—was occasionally to dispose of some of his collections when "his library became too cumbrous to be manageable." And so, besides presenting the lyceum with many books, he sold some 4,000 volumes of Americana to Rutherford B. Hayes in 1874, a collection that became the nucleus of the Hayes Memorial Library in Fremont. Another collection of Clarke acquisitions on fishing went to the Newberry Library and was later transferred to the Field Museum. Nearly 7,000 volumes of Americana and Scottiana were sold to William A. Procter who subsequently presented them to the University of Cincinnati.

By that time Robert Clarke was approaching the end of a life devoted to books. In 1894 he confessed that "he had not been above Fourth street for five years, going direct from the depot to his store" and back again to his library. Four years later, reacting to an erroneous announcement of his retirement, he wrote to A. H. Leypoldt: "You are premature in supposing that I have retired from business. At our annual meeting in July, I resigned the Presidency of the Board of Directors. . . . I retain all my stock and am still a member of the Board & hope to stave off an obituary notice . . . for some years yet." That hope was not realized. On 27 August 1899, Robert Clarke died suddenly, precisely where a good book collector should die, in his library.

After his death many of the Clarke papers went to the Historical and Philosophical Society of Ohio—manuscripts and letters of Symmes, Short, Ludlow and their families; papers relating to early Cincinnati; documents pertaining to John Filson and his family; copies of early newspapers, maps, engravings—a treasury of regional history that traced the development of the Queen City of the West and reflected the achievements of the bookseller-collector who had helped transform "Porkopolis" into a cultural Cosmopolis.

Clarke's firm outlived its founder. Years before it had proliferated at least one other firm when Peter G. Thomson, a Clarke assistant in the importing department, set up an independent business on Vine Street. After Clarke's death, in 1903, the Robert Clarke Company sustained a serious fire in the course of which the house presses dropped to the basement "like a thunderbolt." As one observer commented, "The place was known from Boston to San Diego simply as 'Robert Clarke's' and equally well in the British and European capitals; and if that historical place does not rise from its ashes, Cincinnati will have met with a loss which no modern architectural achievement can make good." The Clarke Company did indeed rise almost immediately from the ashes, opening an office opposite the burned-out building the day after the fire. In 1905 the firm established a new retail store on Government Square, "very attractive and well-equipped." It had long since boasted a London office on Henrietta Street, Covent Garden, and as publishers, booksellers, stationers, importers, printers and binders the Clarke Company was "prepared, as heretofore, to receive and supply orders for all American books, and to import, by post or in their semi-monthly parcels, books from London, Paris, and Leipzig."

In 1909 the nature and personnel of the firm underwent a major transformation. In August of that year, after a receiver's sale, the property was divided between two bidders. W. K. Stewart and John G. Kidd became partners in the new company on 1 January 1910. Stewart hailed from Louisville, Kidd from Frankfort, Indiana. Kidd, who had recently arrived in Cincinnati as trouble-shooter for Doubleday, Page, became a rare book dealer of some consequence. He journeyed frequently to England and Scotland in search of antiquarian books, one of his specialties being Samuel Johnson and his contemporaries. In 1933 Kidd bought out Stewart, and the firm name was changed to John G. Kidd & Son, Inc. Sixteen years later, in 1949, a month after he had opened a new bookstore on Vine Street, John G. Kidd perished in a fire aboard the steamer *Noronic*. The annals of the firm founded a century before by Robert Clarke had ended.

Among the Clarke firm's many varied suppliers had been a young man who would one day be dubbed by his intimates "Rare Bill." Unlike his predecessors in the trade, William Clifton Smith was a native Cincinnatian.[12] Born in 1872, he was the son of Isaac Smith whose "ancestors came to Ohio shortly after Symmes' Purchase." "When he wasn't playing hookey to watch the building of the C&O bridge," he attended Woodward High School for a scant three and three-quarter years, during which he read widely. Periods at business college, in a hardware company, the lumber business and the woolen trade followed. Throughout those episodes, even while he rode on horseback through the hills, Smith remained an omnivorous reader. He was also a faithful bookstore customer. At one secondhand shop on Elm Street he purchased $8 worth of books including some Americana, which he promptly resold to Robert Clarke for $13. Another Cincinnati antiquarian dealer had been born.

In 1898, when he was twenty-six years old, Bill Smith opened his first bookstore at Fourth and Main streets. Stocked with general miscellaneous works, it also boasted some "fine editions and remainders," and it endured until the beginning of World War I. In 1901 he issued his first catalogue—the first of some 456—devoted to miscellanea and Americana, and the same year he purchased the Latham Library, the volumes of which bore the owner's brand. Importing from London through his agents, Cazenova & Company, buying at auction, traveling several times a year to New York, finding a Richard de Bury in the James bookstore, young Smith filled his shelves for the most part with limited editions in sets, "some bound in full morocco," remainders, and subscription sets which he sold on the installment plan.

With the outbreak of war, the dapper, rotund Bill Smith who upheld the trinity of "good beef, beer and books," liquidated his business. Three or four years later, when it was revived, it underwent a sea-change. Now this colorful individualist, this "spiritual descendant of . . . Samuel Johnson, who . . . held an opinion on every subject, from arthritis to Zwingli's religious principles," entered the ranks of the rare book dealers and became a specialist in Americana. From offices on the eighth floor of the Central Trust Building in downtown Cincinnati, Bill Smith "developed a world-wide trade." Dealing mostly in Western Americana up to the Civil War, the Smith Book Company offered rare items in historical Americana, the Middle West and the South, as well as the West.

A young colleague from Colorado recorded his reminiscences of Smith and his Cincinnati bookstore: "The owner . . . was the greatest book-man in the business. . . . His specialty was rare books on southern history and general Americana. . . . Those were prohibition days, but the first thing Smith would say was, 'Hi, Fred, how about a drink?' . . . Each bottle was behind a particular book or set of books." From Smith's cards, collectors could purchase catalogued items; from Smith's cartons, they might unearth uncatalogued items.

Those items, catalogued or uncatalogued, included pamphlets on the gold regions, overland narratives, Kentucky almanacs and newspapers, western railroad material, and Vermont broadsides. At one time Smith "had every western periodical 1815–1840 with . . . one exception." His stock was augmented with "tons of river guides, songsters and paper-back thrillers" from the old stock of the James Book Store. Smith obtained his rarities from a variety of sources. One of his methods of procurement was to advertise for books. The volumes thus turned up in library basements or private trunks and attics he subsequently sold to institutions such as Western Reserve, to collectors such as Thomas Streeter or to his colleagues Eberstadt, Goodspeed and Wessen.

Thanks both to his personality and his stock, Bill Smith developed a powerful reputation. Luther Tucker, at one time director of the Cincinnati Historical Society, claimed that "anyone attempting to write a definitive history of bookselling in America without devoting one chapter to Mr. Smith would do well to reconsider his subject." The distinguished librarian Lawrence S. Thompson crystallized the quintessence of Smith in one or two anecdotes:

I could tell you all sorts of stories about Bill Smith, who signed his catalogues as "FLAXIUS" with the "quote," "Rare books are getting scarcer." When he was past ninety I used to stop in to see him at his home in Fort Thomas, just across the river from Cincinnati. He would be stretched out on a couch reading a catalogue, would sit up and call to me, "Larry Thompson! Come in and have a drink and let me tell you a dirty joke." The dirty joke soon reverted to book talk. . . .
My classic story about Bill is the acquisition of the second ed. of John Smith's General History of Virginia. He wanted a modest $450 for it. The old president of the University in 1950 would not permit me to buy a book, even a periodical set, costing more than $50 without his approval. It took Bill and me an afternoon and a bottle of Jack Daniel to figure out the way: The invoice for the Smith was $45 but he also listed about 50 "cats and dogs" (his phrase) for which he charged $2–$10 each. One of the latter fetched $350 recently.

In 1955, in his eighties, Bill Smith retired. "I had to get out of the rare book business," he complained. "Too many people die and leave their collections to libraries and colleges. That's the end of a rare book. It never changes hands again." But his retirement was merely nominal. "Colleagues in the trade refused to let him out, continued to offer him choice items, and families kept asking him to appraise or dispose of their old books. Until a few years ago," it was reported in 1968, "his mail continued to bring inquiries and requests from all over the world." At eighty-seven, still sporting his bow tie, Smith was dapper and rotund as always, still the lover of "good food, drink, conversation and books," still issuing catalogues from his home, still buying and selling rare books. During his later years he lost much of his sight and took to ordering "Talking Books," to which he would talk back: " 'Speak up!' he would cry. 'That woman can't read worth a damn.' "

As expert a master of the curseword as of the rare pamphlet, Bill Smith "damn well" knew the price he paid and the price he received for every "helluva" book that passed through his hands. He hoped to live to be a hundred, but succumbed at age ninety-six, the Cincinnati reincarnation of Dr. Johnson who was known to his admirers as "Rare Bill."

Cincinnati could boast another Smith in the bookselling ranks who, though no relation to "Rare Bill," shared both his bibliophily and his longevity. Bertram L. Smith, Sr.,[13] was dubbed, not "Rare Bert," but "the booklover's booklover." Born in Whiteland, Indiana, in 1874, two years later than "Rare Bill," he wrote for the *Indianapolis News*, covering incidents on the Theodore Roosevelt and William Jennings Bryan campaign trains. Bert Smith served in the Spanish-American War and during World War I was in charge of the postal section at Pershing headquarters in France. After a period in the Railway Mail Service in Ohio and Indiana he surrendered to what had been a "lifetime passion for books" and in 1924 opened his first bookshop.

It was named the Travelers' Book Shop because it was located at Fourth Street and Central Avenue near Cincinnati's old Grand Central Depot and Grand Hotel. Though the name was a fitting one, Bert Smith's bookstore was more aptly renamed after it moved in 1930 to a five-story building on Main Street. Then it was christened precisely what it was—Acres of Books. There were indeed acres of books under Smith's aegis—"over a half million volumes of all kinds, all neatly classified." Though the turnover was almost immediate, Smith was quick to replenish or even increase his stock. An operator on the grand scale, he established a second Acres of Books in Long Beach, California, in 1934, turning over the Cincinnati bookstore to his son Bertram L. Smith, Jr. The founder's advertisement: "We Buy Bookstores" was not exaggerated. There was nothing small about him. According to that aficionado of booksellers Sol M. Malkin, Bert Smith's "shops were booklover's dreams—freedom to ramble and browse among the 'acres' of floors, shelved from top to bottom, its dimly lighted nooks and book piles." And Malkin wrote of the proprietor: "His passion for books was so great that he would usually come in on Sundays, unwrap the latest shipments, check the invoices or bills of lading, then price the new arrivals. . . . And if there was any time left, he would carefully repair any loose bindings and leaves."

Bert Smith, Sr., journeyed to Britain two or three times a year to keep his cavernous Acres of Books supplied. He took his last foraging voyage at age ninety-one. As he himself put it, "There is no age limit in the antiquarian book business." Only to life is there a limit, and this Bertram L. Smith, Sr., reached in 1965, dying at the age of ninety-two. After his death his colleagues paid to the founder of Acres of Books many poignant tributes. One wrote: "Bert Smith has gone on to where all first editions have proper points and . . . pristine dust wrappers." Another recalled: "When Bert Smith was a mere stripling of 90 he . . . bounced in like a pixie Ariel . . . and taught me more in ten minutes about books . . . than I could garner in years of study." And James T. Hardwick of the Ohio Book Store summed up: "He bought and sold more books than any individual in the history of bookselling. A fine gentleman—a loyal and thoughtful friend."

Bertram L. Smith, Jr., who "never enrolled as a student and acquired his knowledge of English literature entirely on his own," became not only the successor to Cincinnati's Acres of Books, but curator of eighteenth-century English literature at the University of Cincinnati Library. Beginning in the book business in 1930, he retired forty-one years later. The store under his jurisdiction has been described as: "a classic.

. . . An old building at least four stories tall, no elevator, dingy and dusty. One concession to modernity was the installation of fluorescent lights on the first floor. All shelving was of wood.

Bert's specialty was literature and his own love was 18th century English literature. Book dealers and collectors came from all over the country to raid his shelves because once a book was priced that was it. He never updated. Prime 19th and 20th century first editions could be picked up for twenty-five cents.

Bert's main source of stock was the reading libraries of Cincinnati's old families.

And today, after both Smiths are gone, the firm of Acres of Books, Inc., continues on Cincinnati's Main Street.

One mid-western dealer who operated not in Cincinnati but in the town of Mansfield added immeasurably to the lustre of Ohio's antiquarian history. Ernest James Wessen[14] was the bookseller-scholar par excellence. He combined Robert Clarke's editing and cataloguing skills with the acquisitive instincts of "Rare Bill" Smith and Bert Smith, and, like them all, he was ageless.

It was inevitable that Wessen should have become a bookseller. His grandfather was a London bookseller and his great-grandfather William Chalmers was an Edinburgh bookseller. He himself was born in Lewiston, Maine, in 1887, and began collecting at age fifteen "when his father gave him two dollars to buy a pair of shoes . . . in Boston and he spent the money on books instead." Between 1905, when he enlisted in the army, and the 1930s, when he founded the Midland Rare Book Company in Mansfield, Ohio, Wessen lived several lives as officer in the Army Signal Corps, engineer, and investigator in the Department of Justice. In Washington he began his serious book collecting.

The scouting for Americana accelerated when Wessen moved to Mansfield. "He traveled widely in the back roads of Western Pennsylvania, West Virginia, Ohio and Indiana," and, "having acquired several bookshelves of items worthy of sale," he launched his catalogue entitled *Midland Notes*. This "well documented, interesting list of Americana" included "comments, bibliographical and satirical." No. 1, issued in 1938, was a modest production offering fifty-four ephemeral almanacs of the Ohio Country ranging in price from $2 to $50. It sold in its entirety. *Midland Notes* continued, published irregularly, each issue listing works in a special field, and in each "the genius behind the catalog shone through." *Midland Notes* No. 100 made its bow in 1967. At that time the bibliographer Jacob Blanck wrote of *The Wessen Century:* "*Midland Notes* is a uniquity. It is the bookseller-scholar made manifest."

Meanwhile, in the Midland Rare Book Company's large back room the fascinating pamphlet collection accumulated, and the proprietor, who actually played the lead locally in *The Man Who Came to Dinner*, came more and more to resemble Alexander Woollcott. In 1974, at age eighty-seven, he died. Ernest James Wessen had placed Mansfield, Ohio, on the booksellers' map.

In 1855, the Cincinnati periodical *Genius of the West* ran an article on "The Origin and Progress of Printing" in which an optimistic statement was quoted: "Now the book publisher and vender in Cincinnati is the ministering agent to a reading public of ten millions of people, in this interior region, soon to be ten times ten millions."[15] Unfortunately that prophecy—as far as antiquarian bookselling was concerned—was not fulfilled. Although Cincinnati, with a population of over a quarter million, was by 1869 the largest inland city of the United States and the center of trade in the Ohio Valley, and although as late as the 1880s it would still be dubbed in many respects "the central city of the nation,"[16] its preeminence as a book center was on the wane. Caspar's *Directory of the Antiquarian Booksellers and Dealers in Second-Hand Books of the United States*, published in Milwaukee in 1885, listed only a handful of Cincinnatians, including, of course, Uriah P. James and Robert Clarke & Company. Even a chauvinistic observer was forced to conclude that "as far back as 1844 . . . Cincinnati . . . contained more booksellers and stationers . . . than it does to-day."[17]

During the late 1850s the growth of railroad lines across the country resulted in a "shift northward to the lake plains." "Twenty thousand miles of track were laid in a decade," spelling the decline of Cincinnati and the rise of Chicago and St. Louis as important commercial and cultural centers. As the historian of the Western Book Trade commented: "The railroads . . . made it possible for Chicago to usurp Cincinnati's position as a wholesale distributing center for the West."[18] A Cincinnati reporter put it more dramatically: "The railroads came and passed and the mountains moved east."[19] And another observer of Cincinnati's fate concluded with resignation and sagacity: "The booksellers have diminished in numbers and left no successors."[20]

NOTES

1. For Cincinnati background, see William T. Coggeshall, "The Origin and Progress of Printing," *Genius of the West* IV:3 (March 1855), p. 72; Henry A. Ford and Mrs. Kate B. Ford, *History of Cincinnati, Ohio* (Cleveland, Ohio: Williams, 1881), p. 277; "Literary Cincinnati," *The Literary World* XIII (29 July 1882), pp. 249–251; Ralph Leslie Rusk, *The Literature of the Middle West Frontier* (New York: Columbia University Press, 1925), I, 23 f, 29; William C. Smith, *Queen City Yesterdays: Sketches of Cincinnati in the Eighties* (Crawfordsville, Ind.: Banta, 1959), p. [1]; Walter Sutton, "Cincinnati as a Frontier Publishing and Book Trade Center 1796–1830," *The Ohio State Archaeological and Historical Quarterly* 56:2 (April 1947), p. 143; Walter Sutton, *The Western Book Trade: Cincinnati as a Nineteenth-Century Publishing and Book-Trade Center* (Columbus: Ohio Historical Society, 1961), pp. vii–xi, 10, 59, 65, 255 f, 279 f (Any writer on the book trade in Cincinnati remains profoundly indebted to the researches of Walter Sutton); John Tebbel, *A History of Book Publishing in the United States* (New York and London: Bowker, 1972), I, 479 ff. For a copy of William C. Smith's anecdotal and autobiographical paper on early Cincinnati booksellers, the rough draft of an unfinished and unused chapter of his book, *Queen City Yesterdays*, I am indebted to Yeatman Anderson III, Curator of Rare Books and Special Collections, Cincinnati Public Library.

2. Frances Trollope, *Domestic Manners of the Americans* (New York: Knopf, 1949), pp. 74, 88, 92 f.

3. Edward A. Henry, "Cincinnati as a Literary and Publishing Center 1793–1880," *Publishers Weekly* (10 July 1937), p. 110, quoting from the *Western Spy* of 13 August 1799.

4. Sutton, *The Western Book Trade*, p. 42 n. 1, quoting from *Liberty Hall and Cincinnati Gazette* of 6 June 1823.

5. Ibid., p. 35.

6. Ford and Ford, *History of Cincinnati*, pp. 281 f; Henry, "Cincinnati as a Literary and Publishing Center 1793–1880," *Publishers Weekly* (10 July 1937) pp. 110 f; Sutton, "Cincinnati as a Frontier Publishing and Book Trade Center 1796–1830," *The Ohio State Archaeological and Historical Quarterly* (April 1947), p. 139; W. H. Venable, *Beginnings of Literary Culture in the Ohio Valley* (Cincinnati: Robert Clarke & Co., 1891), p. 53.

7. For these, see Coggeshall, "The Origin and Progress of Printing," *Genius of the West* (March 1855), p. 74; D. B. Cooke, "My Memories of the Book Trade," *Publishers Weekly* (11 March 1876), pp. 321 f; Ford and Ford, *History of Cincinnati*, pp. 282 f; Henry, "Cincinnati as a Literary and Publishing Center 1793–1880," *Publishers Weekly* (10 July 1937), p. 111; A. A. Livermore, "Nathan Guilford—A Biographical Sketch," *Genius of the West* IV:3 (March 1855), pp. 65–68; "Our Early Book Supply," *Cincinnati Daily Gazette* (12 June 1880), p. 6; Sutton, "Cincinnati as a Frontier Publishing and Book Trade Center 1796–1830," *The Ohio State Archaeological and Historical Quarterly* (April 1947), pp. 140 f; Sutton, *The Western Book Trade*, pp. 35–40; Tebbel, *A History of Book Publishing in the United States*, I, 487 f; Venable, *Beginnings of Literary Culture in the Ohio Valley*, pp. 54 f.

8. "The Book Trade of Cincinnati," *The Literary World* V (10 November 1849), p. 405.

9. For J. A. and U. P. James and their bookstore, see "The Book Trade of Cincinnati," *The Literary World* (10 November 1849), p. 406; *Cincinnati Enquirer* (25 January 1979); *Cincinnati Post* (16 February 1950) p. 31; Ford and Ford, *History of Cincinnati, Ohio*, p. 283; Adolf Growoll Collection, *American Book Trade History* VII, 138; Henry, "Cincinnati as a Literary and Publishing Center 1793–1880," *Publishers Weekly* (10 July 1937), p. 112; "In Memoriam—U. P. James," *The Journal of the Cincinnati Society of Natural History* XII:1 (April 1889), pp. 5–7; Hellmut Lehmann-Haupt, *The Book in America* (New York: Bowker, 1951), pp. 216, 246; William Smith, Tape Recording (23 September 1965) of interview by Yeatman Anderson III (Courtesy Alfred H. Perrin); Sutton, *The Western Book Trade*, pp. 88, 102; Tebbel, *A History of Book Publishing in the United States*, I, 481 f; Venable, *Beginnings of Literary Culture in the Ohio Valley*, pp. 56 f.

10. For Henry William Derby and his bookstore, see "The Book Trade of Cincinnati," *The Literary World* (10 November 1849), p. 406; D. B. Cooke, "My Memories of the Book Trade," *Publishers Weekly* (11 March 1876), pp. 321 f, and (18 March 1876), pp. 378 f; Madeleine B. Stern, "Keen & Cooke: Prairie Publishers," *Journal of the Illinois State Historical Society* XLII:4 (December 1949), pp. 425 f; Sutton, *The Western Book Trade*, pp. 135, 144 ff; Tebbel, *A History of Book Publishing in the United States*, I, 484 f.

11. For Robert Clarke as bookseller and collector, see *Annual Reports of the Historical and Philosophical Society of Ohio for 1898–1899*, pp. 4 f; *Bibliotheca Americana, 1878. Catalogue of a valuable collection of Books and Pamphlets relating to America* (Cincinnati 1878), passim; *Cincinnati Enquirer* (27 August 1899), p. 8; *Cincinnati Post* (19 September 1949), p. 7; "Robert Clarke," *Dictionary of American Biography* (hereafter, *DAB*); "Robert Clarke 1829–1899," *Ohio Archaeological and Historical Publications* VIII, 487 f; Cooke, "My Memories of the Book Trade," *Publishers Weekly* (18 March 1876), pp. 378 f; William Coyle, ed., *Ohio Authors and Their Books* (Cleveland and New York: World Publishing Co., [1962]), pp. 121 f; Ford and Ford, *History of Cincinnati*, pp. 281, 283; The Rev. Charles Frederic Goss, *Cincinnati: The Queen City 1788–1912* (Chicago and Cincinnati: S. J. Clarke, 1912), II, 482, 510 f; Adolf Growoll Collection, *American Book Trade History*, IV, 68 f, 72; *In Memoriam . . . Robert Clarke* (N.p. 1899), passim; J. David Kidd to Madeleine B. Stern, 19 April 1982; "Literary Cincinnati," *The Literary World* (29 July 1882) p. 251; Charles H. McMullen, "The Publishing Activities of Robert Clarke & Co., of Cincinnati, 1858–1909," *Papers of the Bibliographical Society of America* 34:4 (1940), pp. 315–326; George Mortimer Roe, *Cincinnati: The Queen City of the West* (Cincinnati: Krehbiel, 1895), pp. 212 ff; Sutton, *The Western Book Trade*, pp. 297, 301–304; Tebbel, *A History of Book Publishing in the United States*, I, 488 f; William Henry Venable, "Robert Clarke—In Memoriam," *Publishers Weekly* (16 September 1899), pp. 361 f; Justin Winsor, *Narrative and Critical History of America* (Boston and New York: Houghton, Mifflin, [1884]), IV, Part I, 198.

12. For William C. Smith, see R. E. Banta, *William C. Smith Gentleman Bookseller A Tribute* (Hattiesburg, Miss.: Charles F. Heartman, n.d.), passim; Donald E. Bower, *Fred Rosenstock A Legend in Books & Art* (Flagstaff, Ariz.: Northland Press, 1976), pp. 92 ff; *Cincinnati Enquirer* (4 December 1968), p. 29; *Cincinnati Post & Times-Star* (4 December 1968); William C. Smith, *Queen City Yesterdays*, passim; William Smith, Tape Recording (23 September 1965) of interview by Yeatman Anderson III (Courtesy Alfred H. Perrin); Lawrence S. Thompson to Madeleine B. Stern, 7 May 1982.

13. For Bertram L. Smith, Sr., and his Acres of Books, see *Antiquarian Bookman* (23 May 1960) front cover (The writer is most grateful to Anne McGrath formerly of *AB Bookman's Weekly* for citations and copies of pertinent issues); Information from Terence Cassidy; *Cincinnati Enquirer* (14 November 1965); *Cincinnati Post* (13 November 1965), p. 2; "Mail Box," *Antiquarian Bookman* (28 September 1959); [Sol M. Malkin], "Bertram L. Smith, Sr.—1874–1965," *Antiquarian Bookman* (6 March 1967), p. 939; "Bertram L. Smith, Sr.—In Memoriam," *Antiquarian Bookman* (6 March 1967), pp. 939 f.

Information about Bertram L. Smith, Jr., was kindly supplied by Yeatman Anderson III, Curator of Rare Books and Special Collections, Cincinnati Public Library.

14. For Wessen and the Midland Rare Book Company, see AB *Bookman's Weekly* (6 January 1975), pp. 9–11; Robert R. Crawford, "Ernest James Wessen, 1887–1974," *AB Bookman's Weekly* (3 February 1975), pp. 466 f; "Mail Box," *AB Bookman's Weekly* (17 February 1975).

15. William T. Coggeshall, "The Origin and Progress of Printing," *Genius of the West* (March 1855), p. 73.

16. Adolf Growoll Collection, *American Book Trade History*, IV, 53. See also George E. Stevens, *The City of Cincinnati* (Cincinnati: Blanchard, 1869), p. [iii].

17. Adolf Growoll Collection, *American Book Trade History*, IV, 54.

18. Sutton, *The Western Book Trade*, pp. 279 f, 307. See also Allan Nevins and Henry Steele Commager, *A Pocket History of the United States* (New York: Pocket Books, 1977), p. 247; Tebbel, *A History of Book Publishing in the United States* (New York and London: Bowker, 1975), II, 105, 290.

19. *Cincinnati Enquirer* (25 January 1979).

20. Adolf Growoll Collection, *American Book Trade History*, IV, 54.

5

Chicago

The winds of America, like its frontier, shifted west. The country's transformations from wilderness to metropolis were swift. In 1833, only five years after the last Indian war between Sacs and Foxes, a city was born in the Middle West and named Chicago. Its motto, "Urbs in Horto," was a euphemism for the muddy little town on the low banks of a sluggish bayou. Its streets were unpaved, sprouting the green turf of prairie grass. Its sidewalks were wooden planks. Its water supply came from peddler with his pail. Wolves abounded; bears were occasionally seen; and a deer could be shot within a mile or two of the settlement. Prairie chickens and quail invaded the town, along with horse thieves, and fires broke out continually in the flimsy dwellings.

Even in its unprepossessing beginnings, however, Chicago was invested with a generative force, an élan that would lift it out of wilderness and raise it, phoenix-like, from fire, boom and panic. Work on the Illinois and Michigan Canal began. Hides and grain, beef and pork soon rolled out of the city. The population nearly doubled every four years. In time, Chicago's grain elevators and pork-packing establishments would be rivaled by its railroads and "real estate miracles." Meanwhile schools sprang up. So too did bookstores—those symbols of the "city's growth and prosperity," those proofs that "in their constantly accelerating strides to material and commercial supremacy" Chicagoans "have not neglected the furniture of the mind nor ignored the culture of books."[1]

Against this background of aggression and optimism, brash competitiveness and chauvinism, the first Chicago bookstore set up its stand in 1834, "just east of Philo Carpenter's drug-store" on South Water

Street. Since the antiquarian book business was wherever it flourished an outgrowth of the general book business, it might be said that the short-lived firm formed by Aaron Russell of Boston and Benjamin H. Clift[2] of Philadelphia was the antecedent of Chicago's antiquarian trade. In many ways their "Chicago Book and Stationery Store" set a pattern: its proprietors hailed from the East; its stock of miscellaneous, law and theological books, stationery and paper hangings doubtless also came from eastern sources. It served the needs of the frontier community until the Panic of 1837 ended the short but historic life of the first Chicago bookstore.

Meanwhile another Easterner—Stephen Francis Gale,[3] "a quiet, un-obtrusive citizen" described as "bright as refined gold,"—had followed Russell & Clift into the trade. Gale, possibly thanks to an apprentice-ship with the distinguished Boston house of Hilliard, Gray, fared better than his predecessors. His shop, also on South Water Street, was opened in 1835 and became, as many of its descendants would become, "a favorite resort for artists, professional men, and the best class of citi-zens." In that pioneer establishment, pioneers—or their wives—could find not only sheet music and music books but pianos and musical instruments, teachers could select schoolbooks for the new schools, settlers could purchase blank books, stationery, drafting materials and cutlery. That they did so is attested by the boast that Gale's first-year sales amounted to $25,000. Chicago's first circulating library was an added attraction for browsers.

The firm was marked, as most firms were, by removals and changes in style. As A. H. Burley & Co., successors to Gale, it inaugurated in 1850 "the art-union system in Chicago, with some 20 paintings pur-chased 'during the recent revolution in Paris.' " Moreover, Augustus H. Burley, who had first clerked for Gale, must have had the mentality if not the stock of the antiquarian, for decades later he was able to furnish to the Chicago historian Andreas "the earliest copy of a [play] bill which has come into our possession."[4] When in 1856 the firm sold its stock of books, the buyer would be a dealer not only in miscellaneous but in the "rare and curious."

If Russell & Clift established Chicago's first bookstore, and Stephen F. Gale its first circulating library, still another firm, founded in 1842, issued the city's first substantial extant catalogue of books. Like Ben-jamin Clift, Brautigam & Keen[5] came from Philadelphia before opening their stand on Lake Street. Within a few years Brautigam sold out to the Keens, and by 1856 the firm name had been transmuted into Keen & Lee. But it was as Brautigam & Keen that they published in 1844 their twenty-four page *Catalogue of School, Classical, Theological, Law, Medical, and Miscellaneous Books, For Sale By Brautigam & Keen, Franklin Book Store, No. 146 Lake Street, Chicago, Ill.* The catalogue, like the store, naturally reflected the partners' stock and indicated that, among the "Valuable Books in all the Departments of Literature," there were indeed some items tempting to a contemporary or future antiquarian: Joseph Nancrede's *L'Abeille Françoise*, for example, the first French anthology published in Boston; Laennec on the *Chest*; Catlin's *North American Indians*; a set of Jefferson's *Works* noted as *Scarce*; an intriguing *Vie de Washington*. The scientifically inclined might find a Combe or a Lyell, as well as a Goddard on the *Teeth* with *"Many Plates."* Such books as were not on hand were "ordered from the East with all possible despatch," and "orders from a distance" were "promptly and faithfully attended to."

It was not until 1852 that "distance" became less of a handicap to the Chicago dealer, and "despatch" more feasible, for in that year "the first rail link was established with the East."[6] Moreover, the country surrounding the city was "rapidly being opened up by constantly multiplying roads." Though the streets were still muddy, and dotted with rows of wooden shanties, "fabulous accounts of its sudden and marvellous growth" were attracting "capitalists and business men in all parts of the United States." As one newcomer observed, Chicago was fast becoming one of the largest book markets in the country. The center of midwestern bookselling was shifting from Cincinnati to the city on the shores of Lake Michigan. Those huge wagons known as "Prairie Schooners" carried their wares to the outlying country, and so, books stocked in Chicago reached an ever widening market.

It was the perfect time for a young bookseller, born in Northampton, Massachusetts, trained in the H. W. Derby bookstore in Columbus and Cincinnati, Ohio, to change his background and move farther West. A run over the strap rails of the Little Miami and the Mad River and Lake Erie roads via Sandusky, and thence by lake steamer brought David Brainerd Cooke to his new home.[7]

The westward march was becoming habitual to David B. Cooke. As a boy he had migrated by canal to Columbus, Ohio, working in H. W. Derby's bookstore. With his employer he took a load of surplus stock and traveled into the country to auction books from the tail of a wagon.

Even in the early 1840s the winds were shifting west, and when Derby resettled in Cincinnati, Cooke joined him, traveling by stage over the National Turnpike. Then, after more than ten years with a firm whose stock included flutes and sheet music, penknives and wallpaper, Currier prints and Macassar hair oil—as well as Bibles and a full line of publications from the East—Cooke ventured to Chicago.

The store that David B. Cooke opened at 135 Lake Street was described as an "Elegant Book Establishment," the "Great Western Book Concern," where collectors could find the largest stock of books "at Eastern prices." It was said, in fact, "He had such a stock as was suited to the Eastern cities, but was told that he could not sell such expensive books here. But he did sell them readily, showing that the tastes of Western people were not different from those of Eastern people." Although he emphasized law books, in 1856 it was he who bought the general stock of A. H. Burley & Co., successors to Stephen F. Gale, another instance of the interwoven threads that may be traced in the fabric of bookselling. At that time, when Chicago seemed destined to become the railroad center of the country, Cooke leased the "elegant" white cut-marble building nearby at 112 Lake Street and, as a reporter commented: "Among the improvements here going on you will regard none with more interest and pleasure than the multiplying and enlarging of the bookstores. The old ones grow straight; they are eked out with additions; they become taller, broader and more beautiful, until now Chicago is to have as splendid and capacious bookstores as are to be found in the new world." Although his rent was $8,000 annually, his sales amounted to $200,000 in one year, his books reaching not only Chicago but Michigan and Indiana, Wisconsin and Iowa, Minnesota and Kansas.

Fire—that nemesis of booksellers—burned out the Lake Street establishment in 1857, precipitating a series of changes in Cooke's future bookselling activities. By 1864 he joined the firm of S. C. Griggs & Company in whose "palace of books" he served first as clerk and later as partner. In 1868 that firm's stock was destroyed by fire, and the following year D. B. Cooke united with William B. Keen—once of Brautigam & Keen—as Keen & Cooke on State Street. There both shelves and showcases were crowded and enormous stacks of books rose from every available floor space. After the Great Fire of 1871, the partners resumed trade in the Williams and Ferry Building. Their retail department on the first floor was "beautifully and systematically arranged" with busts of prominent authors, ancient and modern, adorning the separate alcoves and reflectors illuminating the premises. Four years after the Panic of 1873, the firm split, Keen taking on the wholesale jobbing trade, Cooke retaining the retail business. At that time his stock consisted of miscellaneous books including the "rare and curious."

In his "Memories of the Book Trade," D. B. Cooke remarked: "To be an educated bookseller in these latter days is something to be proud of. We are the almoners to the hungry souls who yearn for literary food." His career was indeed the prototype of the careers of many booksellers: his business had been marked by removals and changes in style; its path had crossed the paths of his colleagues, for he had bought the stock of one and worked for another; he had survived fire and, for a time, Panic; finally he had found space, limited though it was, for the "rare and curious" in a general stock that ministered to catholic tastes. In short, his history had prefigured that of the burgeoning antiquarian on the westward march.

In 1859, three years after D. B. Cooke leased an elegant marble building on Lake Street, the following letter was written by an aspiring young man to S. C. Griggs, proprietor of another literary emporium of the prairies:

Dear Sir:
Although you will not in all probability recognize my name you may recollect having known me long ago as a little boy staying for a few months in Hamilton, N.Y., with my uncle, Dr. Trevor. My object in writing you at this time is to say that I am anxious to get into a situation in which I can become acquainted with the book business—I have been studying law since graduating from college, but I am about abandoning it for something else—I would prefer going into the book trade to any other, as I think I am better fitted for it than any other—I have always been very fond of books and from reading them and reviews and book notices have obtained a pretty extensive knowledge of them which I think I could turn to advantage—At present I have no capital, but have reasonable hopes of it in the future.
Have you in your establishment any situation which you could offer me, either as book-keeper or salesman—I would accept a low salary merely sufficient to support me and feel confident I could render myself useful to you—I have had considerable experience in business affairs am over twenty-three years of age, a member of the Baptist Ch. and can give the best of references as to capacity and character—...[8]

That letter, variations of which are deposited in the files of all booksellers the world over, was written by Alexander Caldwell Mc-

Clurg. Unlike the writers of most such letters, McClurg was destined to create in Chicago an enduring mecca for rare books.

The firm of S. C. Griggs,[9] to which he applied for employment, traced its history back to 1844 when Mark H. Newman of New York sent an agent, W. W. Barlow, to Chicago to establish a branch house. "In four years the agent was up to his eyes in real estate speculations, and during a little panic he became frightened, and took to his heels" to journey to California. The store he had abandoned was managed for a time by William Bross who eventually sold his interest to S. C. Griggs, son of a Connecticut farmer, whose stock of "school, medical, theological, and miscellaneous books" was estimated at $40,000. Among them were "new and expensive books, many . . . imported direct from Europe." By 1859, when McClurg applied for a clerkship, Griggs and his partner E. L. Jansen were on the way to operating what would become "the largest book-store west of New York, containing a stock of over $300,000, comprising many rare and costly illustrated works in the richest bindings."

McClurg had chosen his target wisely.[10] Born in Philadelphia in 1832, educated at Miami University, Oxford, Ohio, he had, as he had written to Griggs, abandoned the law to serve in the book business. His timing left something to be desired, for with the outbreak of the Civil War, McClurg left his newfound employment at Griggs to become captain of the Crosby Guard, colonel and brigadier-general. Having survived Chickamauga and Chattanooga, he returned at war's end to Chicago, and in 1866 this developing bibliophile, short in stature, long in memory, was admitted to partnership.

Chicago rallied from the war, entering a period of growth and change, stir and excitement, of expansion not only in pork and rails but in books. As one commentator put it in 1866: "Time was, and that too within the memory of living men . . . when the book business of Chicago hardly rivalled . . . an ordinary apple stand of the present day. But as Chicago emerged from . . . a frontier military post to . . . a sprightly trading village, the book business increased, and it has kept steady pace with the unexampled progress of the . . . region."[11] By the decade's end, fast trains brought Chicagoans—and the books they collected—"From Metropolis to Metropolis in 30 Hours!" As testimony to the boast that "The people of the North-West . . . are ravenous readers" and that Chicago's "book-trade . . . is exceedingly heavy," stood a five-story marble block on State Street known as Booksellers' Row. There the Western News Company, Keen & Cooke, and S. C. Griggs plied their trade, and, as early as 1869 in Chicago, that trade included the old and rare. According to an observer of the Chicago book business, writing for the *New-York Tribune*: "Two things are noteworthy. 1. The relative demand for fine bindings, for full and half calf and morocco editions of all standard works, is apparently greater in Chicago than in any other book market in the world. 2. So is the special demand for old, rare, and choice books. It is not uncommon to have $30,000 worth on hand— many of them imported direct from Europe. . . . The [Griggs] store is a paradise for bibliomaniacs."[12]

General A. C. McClurg had much to do with the advancement of bibliomania at the State Street premises. There an observer noted a "folio volume of 63 artist's-proof . . . engravings from Turner, with accompanying text, on large paper, marked at $250; five folio volumes of the 'Musee Royal' and 'Musee Francais' at $600"; an extra-illustrated ten-volume large paper set of Irving's *Washington* at $1,500, and an assortment of treasures "from old missals on vellum to 'Dore's Bible,' from black letter and hand illuminations to the latest triumph of chromolithography." "Not many persons ask for these works in cold blood," the reporter commented. "The demand for them is chiefly kindled by the sight of them." Nonetheless, the demand came, not only from Chicago but from outlying towns—Quincy and Keokuk, Springfield and Omaha. A judge of Carlinville, Illinois, sometimes ordered for his private library "$2,500 worth of rare books in a single bill," and "men in all pursuits; professional, commercial, mechanical, and agricultural," indulged modestly in these "luxuries of literature."[13] If Griggs obtained those treasures abroad, his partner McClurg displayed them with pride at home in a Chicago that had come of age.

On 8 and 9 October 1871, that Chicago was all but obliterated by the Great Fire.[14] Almost every building was wiped out; over 2,100 acres of land were destroyed; 100,000 people were made homeless. Many of the largest bookstores fell in smoking ruin, among them the great houses on Booksellers' Row, the loss in books alone being estimated at $864,000. In the heart of Chicago, as in the core of all great cities, fluttered a phoenix. The city on the shores of Lake Michigan rose from its ashes. So too did many of its bookstores.

After the fire, S. C. Griggs concentrated upon publishing and sold his interest in bookselling to his partners. Jansen, McClurg & Company were more than phoenixes. In their new building erected on the old site, with its galleries of shelving, they rather resembled birds of paradise. Having risen from the fire, they weathered the Panic of 1873 and the years of depression that followed. Indeed, the fire seemed to have stimulated in Chicagoans a sense of the past and a desire to preserve it. Now more than ever McClurg's became a mecca for bibliomaniacs, and one particular area of McClurg's especially attracted the city's developing collectors.

The "Saints and Sinners Corner" of A. C. McClurg's[15] was an outgrowth, partly of this general postfire historical awareness, partly of McClurg's own bibliophilic interests, and partly—cause intermingling with effect—of the habitués who clustered there. The "Saints and Sinners" area in the southwest corner of the building was named by Eugene Field, supervised by the expert antiquarian George Millard, and frequented by men who "feasted our eyes on beautiful books, on old manuscripts, and chatted . . . after the usual fashion of book fiends. . . . Everybody carried some treasures about with him. . . . There was an old cot in the place which Field lugged in one day, and it used to be the custom to hide things in that cot." It was a "most interesting group of liars" who "talked of rare editions, . . . curious editions, . . . fine libraries." Its "Saints" were three divines: Frank W. Gunsaulus who would donate to Harper Memorial Library a collection of incunables including a 1470 St. Augustine and a 1483 St. Albans Chronicle; Dr. M. Woolsey Stryker; and Dr. Frank M. Bristol. The "Sinners" were headed by Eugene Field, journalist, poet, collector who "although he had very little money to expend himself, . . . succeeded in picking up some first editions which are extremely valuable." In one book, coveted but not yet acquired, he audaciously wrote:

> Gude frend, for Iesus sake forbeare
> To buy ye booke thou seest here;
> For I have gone to earne the pelf,
> I mean to buy ye booke myselfe.

Later on, the column "Sharps and Flats," contributed by Field to the Chicago Morning News, would reflect his bibliophily, as would his Love Affairs of a Bibliomaniac. Now, as the late 1870s rolled into the new decade, he vied with his rival "Sinners" at McClurg's: Ben T. Cable, George A. Armour, Charles J. Barnes and James M. Ellsworth of whom it was said: "He would pay more money for a book . . . he wanted than any man in the world, and he would never rest until he got it."

While most Chicago collectors turned to Joseph Sabin of New York or to Europe to amass their collections,[16] the "Saints and Sinners" turned frequently to A. C. McClurg. In their corner, under George Millard's management, could be found "stately old folios, broad-beamed quartos and gems of duodecimos." At one time the corner's collection, valued at $50,000, boasted a manuscript poem of Charles Lamb, a presentation copy of Selden's *Titles of Honour* from Pepys, a first Beaumont and Fletcher, a complete run of Thackeray's *Christmas Books*, inscribed Ruskins and Lambs, at prices ranging from $24 to $450.

In 1883 the firm removed to a palatial building on the corner of Wabash Avenue and Madison Street, a building "admitted to be the largest, best appointed, and most beautiful bookstore in America."[17] The first of its six floors was devoted to the retail trade—"a model of a light, airy, and convenient salesroom," the "central resort of . . . scholars and readers, the wealth and culture of the northwest." Indeed, according to Charles Dudley Warner, "there is more love of books in Chicago than in New York society, and less of the critical *nil admirari* spirit than in Boston. . . . in view of the impressions . . . that the whole population is imbued with porcine proclivities. . . . but . . . the general intelligence which sustains a retail department of the dimensions and variety of . . . the McClurg store . . . is a standing refutation." And so, as the century neared its end, A. C. McClurg's, with its "frescoed ceilings," its "show tables . . . covered with books of varied binding . . . illustrated treasures, splendid quartos, atlas folios . . . on either side a solid wall of books," its costly imports from Europe and the East, stood as a monument for the chauvinistic Chicagoan in defense of Midwest culture. One had only to visit and browse there to be confident that Chicago was "the coming literary rival to the Empire City" and that "notwithstanding all that has been said and written about its ability to kill . . . so many pigs per minute," it "contains and mainly supports the largest book . . . house in America."

The Morris Book Shop[18] established in the mid-1880s was less imposing than McClurg's but it too attracted its faithful, its own variety of Chicago "Saints and Sinners." Francis Marion Morris, it would be said, was "himself . . . a great deal like a book. . . . He is easy to take up, all that he has is yours, you may visit with him today and then leave him alone for years if you wish, and when you come back you find him unchanged." Born in Manchester, Ohio, graduated from Butler University in Indianapolis, he had ventured to Chicago in 1885 and set up a little bookshop in a small room on West Madison Street. Plump, genial, a "Rare 'Old Book' Man," Frank Morris would soon attract McClurg's patrons, Eugene Field and Dr. Gunsaulus, as well as a variety of devotees who would make of his stand "the center of the very select among artists and literati." Fires and urban changes triggered several removals, but the faithful remained. In the Pullman Building at the corner of Adams Street and Michigan Avenue Morris installed a circulating library in a balcony. Wherever he operated, his shop was "packed from floor to ceiling with books old enough to command respect and with private histories augmenting their value." His stock boasted "rare tomes bound by Maroli or David or Trautz-Bauzonnet," and, thanks to his "frequent purchases of private libraries" and his "constant buying at London and Eastern sales," he could offer in his "catalogues issued at intervals" Americana and Shakespeareana, autograph letters and private presses, early printing and first editions, angling and ornithology, association books and extra-illustrated books.

The diminutive General A. C. McClurg may have cast a long shadow, but the cordial Frank Morris typified the collecting passions of the 1890s and early twentieth century during which he flourished. A member of the Caxton Club, he developed a private collection that included black letter volumes, author's presentation books, and autograph letters and manuscripts. He owned the original manuscript of *Dibdin's Ghost* by Eugene Field, along with poems in praise of his shop by that bibliophilic poet and by others:

> Frank Morris has books
>   Both new and antique—
> Editions de luxe—
>   Frank Morris has books
> In the cosiest nooks,
>   Which book-lovers seek—
> Frank Morris has books
>   Both new and antique!

As McClurg was assisted by the indispensable George Millard, Frank Morris availed himself of the services of Anton I. Janski before the latter set out on his own in the manner of most able apprentices.[19]

Morris, however, insisted upon discreet and unaggressive assistance. For at least two decades the following notice hung in his shop: "To make you feel perfectly at ease in examining our stock, employes are instructed not to offer assistance without being asked. This, we hope, will not be considered as inattention on our part. If you seek information, ask all the questions you want without feeling under any obligations to purchase."[20]

The Columbian Exposition of 1893 which turned the attention of the world upon the Queen City of the Northwest doubtless also tended to stimulate the already strong bookish interests of Chicago. During the early 1890s there was a kind of assertion or reassertion of the culture of the Middle Border. Few natives appreciated the story that circulated to the effect that when a Chicago capitalist died the appointments of his library were assessed at $36,000, and his books at $300. With the growth of such clubs as the Caxton, the Chicago Literary, the Dofobs, taste was maturing and bibliophily spreading. There was a market for all varieties of bookselling—for the imported treasures of McClurg, the fine bindings of Morris, and for the sleepers that lay beneath mountains of books in the crowded premises of one of Chicago's most colorful and eccentric antiquarians.

Julius Doerner was "Spartan by nature, German in sentimentality, a Yankee in shrewdness."[21] He was also "an enemy of hypocrisy," "a friend of outcasts," and a man who knew his books. He had come to books by a strange route. Early in life he had been a civil engineer, but the loss of wife and child in one year "turned him against his profession." At that time he inherited some twenty acres of Chicago land, and while awaiting the settlement of the estate, wandered about the city bookshops, buying there and at auction. Having bid more than he could pay for a rare collection of early printed books, he gave the mortgage on his legacy as security, and lost it. The mortgage was foreclosed, Doerner was without his acreage, but he continued to purchase books. One day, after the sudden death of a Chicago dealer, Doerner was requested to catalogue and appraise his stock in return for $3 a day. At the end of six months, the cataloguing still not completed, the bookseller's heirs suggested that he accept the books in lieu of payment. Julius Doerner had become an antiquarian bookseller.

In effect, he had always had antiquarian interests. For his old mother in Pennsylvania he had created and manufactured a book completely on his own—written it, set it up on an old Washington hand press, distributed the type from a single impression, illuminated it and bound it. Now, as a bookseller in Chicago, Julius Doerner "bought constantly, sold little and read much." He resembled an anchorite with his long beard, his hair to his shoulders, his sparkling eyes and melodious voice. Winter and summer he wore an alpaca coat, a panama hat, and celluloid collar. His habits were spartan. He lived on 7 cents a day, cooking vegetable soup in a huge tin kettle once a week and drinking it cold until the kettle was empty.

Doerner's shop on Chicago's Wells Street was as eccentric as its proprietor. "There was just enough space to open the door, to squeeze in: piles of books from the floor to the very high ceiling, drawings, paintings, carvings, leaned against the dusty backgrounds of old tomes." Somewhere there was a piano upon which Doerner—"an excellent musician"—would play Beethoven, Bach or Mozart. Everywhere there were cats, stray cats named after the days of the week upon which Doerner had found them. And in the back of the shop was a Morris chair in which the proprietor would often spend the night.

It was an experience for a collector to purchase a book from Julius Doerner. As one visitor observed, he was "courteous but not inviting or solicitous. . . . If a book is asked for, he will fish it out from among his five hundred thousand books with an almost miraculous quickness, name the price, and then it is up to the customer to say 'Yes' or 'No,' and the interview is ended."

Doerner found many of his half million books in "junk shops, . . . garrets of old mansions, . . . unpromising trunks of storage houses." That his prowls were successful was testified by his stock, his collection of pamphlets, early newspapers and periodicals, of "foreign journals, books and chronicles" relating to American history.

Doerner died, precisely where he should have died, seated in his Morris chair, a book on his knees. After his death, Gordon A. Ramsay, administrator of his estate, sold "a large mass of pamphlets and unbound materials . . . as scrap paper." However, in 1918 he also arranged for the sale of over 50,000 Doerner books. Since these were catalogued—however briefly and inadequately—it is possible to reconstruct a few of the treasures that had lain hidden in the crowded Wells Street bookshop. Of the mass of books assorted, classified and advertised as "probably the greatest collection . . . ever offered in the west to book lovers," some 600 were described as "Rare . . . and Exceptional." Among them were Persian manuscripts, Germantown and Ephrata imprints, the "first

Greek Testament printed in America," the first Hebrew Concordance, a 1611 King James Bible, works ranging from an Aquinas incunable of 1483 to Baudelaire's translation of Edgar Allan Poe, from a Priestley *On Vision, Light and Colours* to Swinburne's *Unpublished Verses*. As the estate administrator declared, "Chicagoans should feel especially privileged that this opportunity is in the Loop. The great number of rare books, separately lotted, will appeal to the individual collector. Libraries and dealers will find the collection valuable." In April 1918 the president of the University of Illinois (Urbana) offered $5,000 for an *en bloc* purchase, and the Doerner collection, amassed from an eccentric antiquarian's prowls through junk shop and garret, came to rest in that institution.

By the turn of the century, a collector unable to find his desiderata at McClurg's, inadequate to cope with the idiosyncrasies of Julius Doerner, could seek for treasure elsewhere. It was appropriate that for the new century a new antiquarian bookstore should emerge. In the southeast portion of Marshall Field Square, two floors above the newly opened John Crerar Library, a man in his early thirties, equipped with a small stock of first editions and Kelmscotts, opened a house that would be "hospitable to all friends of the literary arts for nearly fifty years." Walter M. Hill had bought a cannon to "start a war of his own."[22]

Hill had been born in Bristol, England, in 1868. As the distinguished librarian J. Christian Bay would say of him: "A Roman Britisher, he retained throughout life the cool individualism of his national group, colored by the Puritan integrity of the Victorian age. Aloof but dependable, remote . . . yet with a heart of wax, he . . . considered books in a large way." Indeed he had been trained to do so. In the course of a four-year apprenticeship with the Bristol bookseller Jefferies he had been exposed to innumerable titles which he had memorized. He emigrated to the United States at seventeen, and after bookish employment in New York and Boston he was engaged by A.C. McClurg of Chicago. In 1899, his apprenticeship and journeyman years over, Hill issued Catalogue No. 1 and entered upon the period of his mastery.

His equipment consisted of his small stock, $500 in cash—his wife's savings—and "an instinct for books as infallible as any absolute knowledge—an instinct that creates a relation between us and our wares, or leaves us cold." The equipment was more than adequate for the adventures that would follow during the next half century. Among his feats Hill would number in time his successful auction race against

George D. Smith for a unique Caxton on vellum; his "original, comparative collation" of "a perfect Pickwick" which he bought for 180 pounds, sold for $850, and watched rise to $4,600. Hill's special field was "literature in the English language," and he favored Kelmscotts, Kipling, Stevenson, Keats, Lamb, Fitzgerald and early printed books, many of which he obtained during summer months in England, or at auction. Yet he insisted, "From the very beginning we pinned our faith to books of proven merit in every field, whether common or rare, whether expensive or not." Condition was paramount, but, other things being equal, "the cheap book was as important to us as the high-priced treasure."

Despite that avowal, he was said to "pretend forgetfulness about dates, prices, values, and names, in order to have time to recall . . . what he knew." In time he gained the reputation of catering "to the extravagant wishes of Western millionaires." Certainly there had been and there were in Chicago a goodly number of grand-scale collectors from Edward Everett Ayer to William Brooks Greenlee, from George Manierre to George Paullin, from Dr. Gunsaulus to Cyrus Hall McCormick. The group that assembled at Hill's—for he too had his special coterie—included Vincent Starrett and Roswell Field, Lessing Rosenwald and Austin J. Cross, a "book-mending wizard, who once split a sheet of tissue paper."

Walter Hill liked to insist that the bibliomania which characterized the days of "great universal personal collections" had been succeeded by "the more rational and sympathetic spirit of bibliophilia. We now live," he explained in the early 1920s, "in the era of the carefully organized, logically circumscribed special collection, . . . The bibliophile nowadays insists that his collection indicate in a measure his efforts in life, his work, or his calling." The special collections proposed by Hill included local collections or state groups of authors and topics of national importance, folklore or drama, first issues of authors' first books, association copies, the fugitive poetry of America. "Not in vain," he wrote, "have we had in mind for some years to create a collection of works of intrinsic merit comprising books scarcely known; works of hidden beauty and scant recognition; literary efforts which deserve to rank with the long recognized treasures." The amassing of specialized collections, he perceived, "has been most fruitful in bringing unknown material into deserved esteem. It also has led to a great deal of useful work in bibliography." Surely this was the voice of modernity. In the realms of the Chicago antiquarian a fresh wind was blowing.

The wind more resembled a whirlwind on Saturdays during the early 1920s at Powner's Book Shop on the corner of Clark Street opposite the City Hall.[23] "Saturday," an onlooker observed, "is the great book day. In the back room upon empty book boxes men of all walks of life sit around, prosperous business men, millionaires, . . . students, newspaper men . . . all . . . linked by a common love. They are all ardent book collectors." But it was a "scrambling mass" of bookhunters who bombarded the stalls in front of Powner's shop where Roman antiquities vied with books on sports or "old poetry." Indeed, on Powner's "quarter counter" one Chicago prince of serendipity found "a first edition of Rousseau's 'Emile' with Rousseau's autograph presentation inscription to the King and the royal coat of arms on the binding." In exchange for 75 cents he pocketed the treasure. The reaction of the proprietor was almost as unique as the volume. "Such things may happen," said Powner, "I am glad he got it."

Charles Tracy Powner of Indiana was a fifty-five-year-old Hoosier schoolmaster when he decided to give up his life work and become a bookseller. A quiet man, scholarly looking, he had long been exposed to books and documentary collections. In 1889, when the Decatur County courthouse was remodeled, many valuable local records were destroyed. Despite Powner's protest, the documents were abandoned or sold as junk. In 1901 Powner was appointed official collector of the Indiana State Library, combining his tasks with teaching in Greensburg, Indiana. Two years later he moved to Chicago, but it was not until 1908, in his mid-fifties, that he set up the first Powner bookstore in the old Methodist Church Block on North Clark Street. It would be followed by other stores—the Antiquarian Book Store on East Van Buren, another on West Madison, and still another back on North Clark Street where Powner's operated in a three-story neo-Gothic brick building with book stalls in the front and a rare book room on the second floor. Indeed, in the twelve years that Charles T. Powner devoted to bookselling he built up a chain of stores in four cities.

The Chicago store boasted a varied stock of Americana, occult and metaphysical, rare and curious. It might yield a sleeper like the inscribed Rousseau *Emile* or a first American *Laus Veneris* of Swinburne. Powner's partiality for association copies, rare and first editions, Mark Twain firsts with variants, was reflected in his holdings. In 1915 he acquired the bulk of the stock of the Morris Book Shop—another example of the interconnections traceable in the history of the antiquarian trade. Powner's was "The House of a Million Books," but among the million were always a few rare gems. Perhaps the rarest was Charles T. Powner himself, a man who came late to the trade he loved, who viewed with equanimity the sale of a unique sleeper, and who died, in 1920, as all bookmen should die, "in bed with a volume of Mark Twain propped up before him."

Chicago bookstores have always been less numerous than they were varied. And so, while the collector was limited in the number of local dealers he could patronize, those dealers yielded a broad enough scope to satisfy different tastes. They also presented a colorful panorama of personalities. Frank Morris was no Julius Doerner; Walter Hill was no Powner; Charles Powner was no Adolph Kroch.

Adolph Kroch, who set up shop in Chicago around the same period as Powner, had an altogether different background.[24] He hailed, not from Indiana, but from Germany, and, as he would recall,

In my home town, as a student, I spent most of my leisure time in reading and browsing around in bookshops. My small allowance, augmented by tutoring, I spent freely on books. . . . Next to reading books and pestering booksellers with innumerable questions, the reading of book catalogs was my chief hobby. . . .

My father was a banker, and when he tried to force me to follow his profession, I rebelled . . . sold the library I had so lovingly assembled and . . . bought a third-class ticket to America.

Even that early in life, Kroch was endowed with the requirements of an antiquarian bookseller. He knew his native tongue and could translate Greek into Latin. He had clerked in a foreign bookstore, and so had learned to exercise what he would call "the first duty of a bookseller," namely, the "proper wielding of a duster." As he explained, "It helps him to keep his stock neat and clean, to keep his thoughts on books he affectionately dusts and arranges, and to remember titles." More significantly, Adolph Kroch had mastered what he would describe as the "three fundamentals of a successful bookseller": "(1) to know your books, (2) to become enthusiastic over them, and (3) to transmit this enthusiasm to your clients."

After clerking for three years, Kroch set up shop in "a little hole in the wall" on Chicago's Monroe Street, stocking such books "as appealed personally to my literary taste." In time, Kroch's "literary taste" extended to "the beauties of fine printing," the "work of master-binders," "a noble page from the Gutenberg Bible," "the Kelmscott Chaucer." It also extended to the moderns, and Kroch would play a role in the recognition of James Branch Cabell, Rémy de Gourmont, Edna St. Vincent Millay and Willa Cather.

From that "little hole in the wall" on Monroe Street would develop "the famous international bookstore of A. Kroch" which "rapidly became a significant outlet through the Middle West." Kroch's establishment on Michigan Avenue was the meeting place of a new generation of Chicago's intellectuals: Burton Rascoe and Harry Hansen, Vincent Starrett, Sterling North, Ben Hecht. In his remodeled store he added many departments including of course one devoted to the old and rare. He issued a monthly book bulletin, *Rest and Read*; he inaugurated a book-a-month service. Wearing his toupee along with his "broad kindly smile," Adolph Kroch "kept pace with his success." This "interesting little man" who knew that "bookselling is more than the business of selling books" eventually headed an international bookstore which became to the West what Brentano's was to the East.

The variety of Chicago antiquarian bookstores in the 1920s is reflected in a single issue of the *Evening Post Literary Review*. Under date of 16 November 1928, it contains brief articles on a Walter Hill catalogue, the Argus Book Shop, Targ's Bookstore, and "a new venture in the first edition and fine binding field."[25] William Targ was distributing his holiday list from North Clark Street, and announcing that among books just arrived were "a beautiful edition of the Canterbury Tales and rare copy of the Heptameron in a Sangorski Sutcliffe binding."

As for the Argus Book Shop,[26] it had been founded by Ben Abramson who had come from "a large, old-world, orthodox Lithuanian family," had grown up in the "teeming . . . west side of Chicago at the turn of the century," and had spent his young manhood "reading and schooling at the heels of experience." His father had been a horse-and-buggy "junk peddler," and in return for cleaning the stable his son was permitted to keep the old books picked up on the prowl. So, according to Ben Abramson's daughter, "his love affair with books began." After working in the grain fields of Kansas and wandering the streets of New Orleans, he found employment—as so many Chicago booksellers had—

at A. C. McClurg's. Then the inevitable occurred. With a fellow bibliophile, Jerry Nedwick, Abramson rented a barber shop and converted it into a bookshop. Subsequently, on his own, Abramson moved to South Dearborn and issued his multi-sectioned catalogue *Along the North Wall*.

Like his shop, it reflected his catholic taste. Abramson dealt in pornography as well as in fore-edge paintings and color plate books, in manuscripts, press books and modern firsts. He was a publisher as well as a bookseller, his imprint appearing on the *Baker Street Journal*. He "talked a great book," too, and his talk attracted as many collectors as did his copies of Cabell and Anderson, Millay and Frost. After the 1929 crash, Abramson had been able to increase his stock by grandscale buying. Toward the end of World War II, in 1944, he moved to New York. Wherever he operated he was "a man pursued by demons of his own making." He was also a man who knew that "A book read is an experience won; a book unread is a future experience guaranteed." For a generation he had offered those experiences to Chicago.

Although the *Evening Post Literary Review* of 16 November 1928 made no mention of Wright Howes, he had been issuing his distinguished Americana catalogues from Chicago since 1925 and would continue issuing them for a quarter century. Then, in 1954, Howes produced the "first large-scale attempt at a bibliography exclusively devoted to books relating to human activities throughout the whole continental portion of the United States." *U.S. Iana (1650–1950) A Selective Bibliography In Which Are Described 11,620 Uncommon and Significant Books Relating to the Continental Portion of the United States* stands as one of the indispensable reference tools for collectors, librarians and booksellers in the field of Americana, and as a monument to the productivity of a great Chicago bookseller.

The "new venture in the first edition and fine binding field" written up by the *Evening Post Literary Review* in 1928 was the firm of Frances Hamill and Margery Barker, a firm that still flourishes today.[27] The partners met during their employment in Fanny Butcher's bookshop, and in 1928 when that business was sold they set out their shingle together, Barker providing—according to Hamill—"the imagination" and Hamill providing "the practical approach."

As Frances Hamill put it:

After working in a new bookshop together Margery and I decided to go into the antiquarian book business as partners. Between us we had saved $5000 and we set out for Europe in February 1928. We landed in Sicily and worked our way up through Italy, Switzerland, Germany, Belgium and France and then crossed over to England, Scotland, Wales and Ireland.

We were abroad about eight months visiting every antiquarian bookseller we could find and came home with quite a lot of books and many long lasting bookseller friends. Our first catalogue was issued in the fall of 1928 when we opened up shop at 912 N. Michigan Avenue. From that time on, except for the war years, [when they worked as tool grinders for a General Motors plant] we went abroad every summer.

The shop at 912 North Michigan Avenue where Hamill and Barker began their career was "the well-known antique shop of Mrs. Somerset Maugham." Hence they were able to place their wares against appropriate backgrounds—their eighteenth-century bindings on an eighteenth-century Italian secretary, their small decorative books on a Chinese Chippendale table. They opened with a stock that included first editions of Surtees Sporting Novels, a Barrie presentation copy, a signed set of first editions by A. A. Milne, along with a display of bindings done for the partners in London and "a number of small books . . . bound in Florentine hand-blocked papers."

By the time Hamill & Barker reached their twenty-fifth anniversary, Frances Hamill had been elected president of the Antiquarian Booksellers Association of America—the first woman and the first Midwesterner so elected. Their firm had recently made its most important sale, a set of Signers' letters, and their stock boasted a "manuscript fragment of a poem by John Keats, a magnificently bound 'Rubaiyat,' . . . a presentation copy of a Willa Cather novel." Currier and Ives prints adorned their "skyscraper shop" on North Michigan Avenue, and both partners were on an ascending course.

Like the firm of Hamill & Barker, the Abraham Lincoln Book Shop was a contributing force that lent distinction to Chicago antiquarian bookselling.[28] With a capital of 500 borrowed dollars and so profound an interest in Lincoln and the Great Rebellion that his wife grieved she had "lost him in the Civil War," Ralph G. Newman founded "a small book shop in Chicago" that was destined to become headquarters of "The Abraham Lincoln Industry." Its proprietor was to buy and sell the "major portion of the Oliver Barrett collection" and the collection of the great Lincoln scholar George P. Hambrecht. His shop, whether located on Michigan Avenue or in his own building on Chestnut Street, was "the book shop that everybody runs," the mecca for "a club of

customers" including Carl Sandburg and Alfred Whital Stern, Allan
Nevins and Carl W. Schaefer, Newton C. Farr and Ted Borucki, "a
Chicago streetcar conductor who . . . spent a dollar a month" there. At
Newman's establishment, mail was held for distinguished clients such
as Carl Sandburg, and a kitchen, a bar and a shower were at their
disposal. As Ralph G. Newman declared in the mid-twentieth century,
"We have a refuge for a man who wants to escape the 20th century.
He can go back to the 19th century."

Chicago has yielded several such refuges to collectors who would
retreat to the past. From the 1840s when Brautigam & Keen catalogued
their Jefferson or Laennec, to the 1950s when Hamill & Barker offered
their set of Signers, the history of bookselling in that Midwestern city
has been enriched by the lives and careers of antiquarian dealers. Some,
like the pioneers Russell & Clift, flourished briefly; others, like A. C.
McClurg's which celebrated its one hundredth anniversary in 1944,
endured. All, whether their antiquarian stock was a major or a minor
portion of their holdings, helped transform a muddy little town on the
banks of a bayou into a world metropolis, a cultural link between the
cities of two coasts.

NOTES

1. For Chicago's beginnings and early changes, see "Book Business in the
Northwest," *American Literary Gazette and Publishers' Circular* V:4 (15 June
1865), p. 72; "Chicago's Book Trade," *Chicago Times* (Supplement) (14 June
1884); [Albert D. Richardson], "Western Bibliography. The Book Trade of
the North-West. . . . The Private Libraries of Chicago," *New-York Tribune* (16
October 1869), p. 1; Madeleine B. Stern, *Imprints on History: Book Publishers
and American Frontiers* (Bloomington: Indiana University Press, 1956), p. 104;
Madeleine B. Stern, "Keen & Cooke: Prairie Publishers," *Journal of the Illinois
State Historical Society* XLII:4 (December 1949), p. 428.

2. A. T. Andreas, *History of Chicago from the Earliest Period to the Present
Time* (Chicago: Andreas, 1884–1886), I, 414; Jacob L. Chernofsky, "The Book
Trade in the Chicago Area," *AB Bookman's Weekly* (19 June 1978), pp. 4408–
4409; "Chicago's Book Trade," *Publishers Weekly* (5 July 1884), p. 9; Adolf
Growoll Collection, *American Book Trade History*, IV, 40. (For the use of these
scrapbooks, as well as for innumerable courtesies and generous cooperation,
the writer wishes to thank Jean Peters, former librarian of the Frederic G.
Melcher Library of R. R. Bowker Company.)

3. Andreas, *History of Chicago*, I, 414; II, 488; "Chicago's Book Trade,"

Chicago Times (Supplement) (14 June 1884); "Chicago's Book Trade," *Publishers Weekly* (5 July 1884), pp. 9–10.

4. Andreas, *History of Chicago*, I, 488.

5. *Catalogue of School, Classical, Theological, Law, Medical, and Miscellaneous Books, For Sale by Brautigam & Keen* (Chicago: Press of the Western Citizen, 1844), courtesy Chicago Historical Society; "Chicago's Book Trade," *Publishers Weekly* (5 July 1884), p. 12.

6. For mid-century Chicago, see Chernofsky, "The Book Trade in the Chicago Area," *AB Bookman's Weekly* (19 June 1978), p. 4408; D. B. Cooke, "My Memories of the Book Trade," *Publishers Weekly* (18 March 1876), p. 379; Stern, "Keen & Cooke," *Journal of the Illinois State Historical Society* (December 1949), p. 424.

7. "The Book Trade in Chicago," *American Publishers' Circular and Literary Gazette* (4 October 1856), p. 603; "Chicago's Book Trade," *Publishers Weekly* (5 July 1884), p. 12; Stern, "Keen & Cooke," *Journal of the Illinois State Historical Society* (December 1949), pp. 424–445.

8. John Drury, *A. C. McClurg & Co. Centennial 1844–1944* (Chicago: A. C. McClurg & Co., [1944]), unpaged.

9. "Chicago's Book Trade," *Publishers Weekly* (5 July 1884), pp. 10–11; Growoll Collection, *American Book Trade History*, VI, 98; [Richardson], "Western Bibliography. ... The Private Libraries of Chicago," *New-York Tribune* (16 October 1869), p. 1; "Wabash Avenue, Chicago," *Publishers Weekly* (12 May 1883), pp. 561–563. See also Jack Cassius Morris, *The Publishing Activities of S. C. Griggs and Company*, M.S. thesis, University of Illinois, Urbana, 1941.

10. "Chicago's Book Trade," *Chicago Times* (Supplement) (14 June 1884); "Chicago's Book Trade," *Publishers Weekly* (5 July 1884), pp. 10–11; "Alexander Caldwell McClurg," *DAB*; *Publishers Weekly* (20 April 1901), pp. 1022–1023.

11. "The House of S. C. Griggs & Co.," *American Literary Gazette and Publishers' Circular* (1 May 1866), pp. 4–5. For Chicago in the 1860s, see also [Richardson], "Western Bibliography. ... The Private Libraries of Chicago," *New-York Tribune* (16 October 1869), p. 1.

12. [Richardson], "Western Bibliography. The Book Trade of the North-West. ... The Private Libraries of Chicago," *New-York Tribune* (16 October 1869), p. 1.

13. Ibid.

14. Stern, *Imprints on History*, p. 112.

15. Drury, *A. C. McClurg & Co. Centennial*, unpaged; Growoll Collection, *American Book Trade History*, IV, 40; IX, 9; "McClurg Has Completed Its First Hundred Years," *Publishers Weekly* (2 September 1944), pp. 816 f. I am indebted to Bob Lee Mowry, Director of University Libraries, Wittenberg Uni-

versity, for information about Ben T. Cable, whose books including Washington's copy of the New York 1788 edition of Burns, were auctioned at the Parke-Bernet Galleries in 1942. Mowry has "a theory that he may have been the model for John Buchan's John T. Blenkiron in the Richard Hanney stories."

16. Robert Rosenthal, "If Dibdin Came to Chicago: From Pork to Plantin on the Prairie," Typescript courtesy Robert Rosenthal, Curator, Special Collections, Joseph Regenstein Library, University of Chicago. Robert Rosenthal is preparing a major work on "Books and the City: How Rare Books Came to Chicago (to 1911)." For collectors, see also J. Christian Bay, *The Bookman Is A Hummingbird Book Collecting in the Middle West and the House of Walter M. Hill* (Cedar Rapids, Iowa: Torch Press, 1952), pp. 22–26; *New-York Tribune* (16 October 1869), p. 1.

17. "Chicago's Book Trade," *Chicago Times* (Supplement) (14 June 1884); "Chicago's Book Trade," *Publishers Weekly* (5 July 1884), p. 11; Growoll Collection, *American Book Trade History*, IX, 8, 10; "Wabash Avenue, Chicago," *Publishers Weekly* (12 May 1883), pp. 561–562.

18. Guido Bruno, *Adventures in American Bookshops, Antique Stores and Auction Rooms* (Detroit: Douglas Book Shop, 1922), pp. 92, 97, 98; Growoll Collection, *American Book Trade History*, IX, 92; *The Morris Book Shop Impressions of Some Old Friends in celebration of the XXVth Anniversary* (Chicago 1912), unpaged.

19. Similarly, McClurg's fathered many bookshops, e.g., that of Chandler, "a sort of a George D. Smith of Chicago." See Bruno, *Adventures in American Bookshops*, p. 98.

20. *The Morris Book Shop Impressions of Some Old Friends*, unpaged.

21. *Administrator's Sale of Rare Book Collection* [Chicago 1918] and *Catalogue of Doerner Collection* (Courtesy N. Frederick Nash, Rare Book Room, University of Illinois); Bruno, *Adventures in American Bookshops*, pp. 87–91, 95–97.

22. Bay, *The Bookman Is A Hummingbird*; Bruno, *Adventures in American Bookshops*, p. 94; Walter M. Hill, *Reminiscences and Results of A Quarter Century* (N.p. 1923).

23. Bruno, *Adventures in American Bookshops*, pp. 93–94; Samuel Putnam, *Powner's "The House of a Million Books" A Retrospect 1908–1925* (Chicago 1925).

24. Bruno, *Adventures in American Bookshops*, p. 97; Adolph Kroch, *A Great Bookstore in Action* (Chicago: University of Chicago Press, 1940); Hellmut Lehmann-Haupt, *The Book in America* (New York: Bowker, 1951), p. 247.

25. *Evening Post Literary Review* (16 November 1928), courtesy Frances Hamill.

26. D. B. Covington, *The Argus Book Shop: A Memoir* (West Cornwall, Conn.: Tarrydiddle Press, 1977); Mercer Sullivan, "Ben Abramson Bookseller

1898–1955," *Amateur Book Collector* (October 1955), p. 19. According to Covington, Abramson worked for the Economy Book Store; Sullivan mentions only McClurg.

27. Clipping from *Chicago Tribune*, ca. 1953, courtesy Frances Hamill; *Evening Post Literary Review* (16 November 1928); Frances Hamill to Madeleine B. Stern, 19 April 1981. Margery Barker died in 1980.

28. Ralph G. Newman, "The Abraham Lincoln Industry . . . Address at Annual Meeting of Lincoln Fellowship of Wisconsin Madison February 12, 1954," *Historical Bulletin* No. 13 (1955).

6

St. Louis and Kansas City

"The Territory of Missouri—may it become the Nursery of Literature"[1] was an unlikely toast to have been made in 1817. The territory's principal city, St. Louis, had had its beginnings in the 1760s, a little French village in a wilderness on the bend of the Mississippi, named after the Crusader King of France, and owing its existence to the fur trade. Even then, however, it had boasted a library, belonging to its principal citizen Pierre LeClède, and so, on America's farthest frontier could be found copies of Rousseau and Corneille, Bacon, Descartes and Locke. By 1800, of its 669 white inhabitants, at least 56 owned books. It was noted that one could go up the Missouri River hearing the cries of the wild Arrapahoes while one read *Don Quixote*. Indeed, although St. Louis never became a great antiquarian book center, at no time in its history were books not available. As in other frontier towns they could be bought before there were bookstores to sell them, and by 1823 a pseudonymous writer could send the following high-minded bibliophilic letter to a Missouri newspaper:

There is no species of trade or business which may not receive benefit from the experience of past ages as recorded in books, and there is no man, however low his condition, who is not humanized and civilized and raised in the scale of being by an acquaintance with books.[2]

St. Louis, though it generated only one truly distinguished antiquarian dealer, was always acquainted with books and was long acquainted with booksellers.

The Louisiana Purchase changed the face of French St. Louis. Thou-

sands of Americans streamed across the Mississippi into the village—
settlers and lawyers, clergymen and doctors, "adventurers, gamblers,
and freethinkers," and, in time, the Irishman Joseph Charless who
came with "a few cases of type," and, having ordered a press from
Pennsylvania, established it in a "house of standing-up posts" and on
12 July 1808 issued the first number of the *Missouri Gazette*, the first
newspaper west of the Mississippi. Although the levee might be no-
torious for its street brawls, St. Louis was on the way to becoming "the
Memphis of the American Nile." As a result of the Louisiana Purchase,
the town was transformed into "the crossroads of westward expansion."
One observer would soon note: "Instead of the old-fashioned French
village, it was now a rising city of five or six thousand inhabitants,
with many fine buildings of brick and wood, and carrying on an extensive trade on the noble Rivers Mississippi and Missouri."[3]

Those noble rivers carried not only furs but books. Before bookstores
existed, it has been said, "everybody sold books in early St. Louis."[4]
In fact, in its astounding availability of books frontier St. Louis outdid
Cincinnati and every other outpost in the westward expansion. The
Missouri Gazette became the medium through which an army major,
departing the territory, could advertise that he wished to dispose of "a
small collection of valuable books and pamphlets on religion, law,
physic, science, politics, history, military art, works of genius, &c."
At auction collectors could obtain a wide range of literature from family
Bibles to Walker's *Dictionary*, from the *Works* of Josephus to the *Arabian
Nights*, from *Don Quixote* to Alexander Pope. If the auctioneer was
"the most enterprising of frontier merchants," he had many competitors. A firm of "confectioners and cordial distillers" could announce
that they had "Books to be Raffled For" and those books included a
Johnson's *Dictionary* as well as "several other much admired works."

If collectors could not satisfy their needs through newspaper advertisements, at auction or by raffle, they could certainly find books in
stores that dealt in general merchandise. Such books, often shipped
from New York via New Orleans up the Mississippi River, appeared in
houses devoted to drygoods and groceries, drugs and medicines. One
such establishment—Paul and Ingram—offered a "large assortment of
Rose Blankets" along with many "Valuable Books" including a set of
Fielding "superbly bound," a *Life of Buonaparte*, several children's books,
and the complete works of Mme. de Genlis. Another—Wilt and Her-
zog—seems to have laid in an oversupply of William Shakespeare, for

Wilt informed his uncle, "I have more Loves labour lost than I shall sell for 50 years in this place." Bibles and hymn books, spellers and schoolbooks were among the staples stocked by St. Louis' pioneer merchants. By 1818 a "Reading Room & Punch House" was opened next door to the *Gazette* office on the corner of Main and Second Streets, and a few years later, when the Englishman William Blane visited St. Louis he expressed astonishment at the rapidity with which "literary knowledge spreads itself in America."

In 1820 the spread of such knowledge was facilitated by the establishment of St. Louis' first bookstore. At the "Sign of the Ledger, Main-Street, next door to Mr. Savage's store," Thomas Essex and Charles E. Beynroth offered to a town of under 5,000 inhabitants "binding work, blank books, forms and stationery" and the "anticipated early arrival of a stock of books from Philadelphia." The firm survived the usual changes in partnership and style and, as Essex & Hough, could supply books "in the various branches of literature and science." With the customary chauvinism of frontier settlers they claimed to be able to furnish "any book that can be had in Philadelphia," tagged, more-over, "at Philadelphia prices, with the addition of carriage." In truth, a wide variety of literature was available at the Essex establishment, from Sully and Gibbon to Shakespeare and Scott, from Madame de Stael to Byron, from Adam Smith and Hume to Dugald Stewart and John Quincy Adams. The St. Louis Bookstore founded by Thomas Essex was continued after his death in 1827 by a partner. Its distinction lay entirely in its priority. It had been the first of many that would follow.[5]

By the 1830s, St. Louis received its city charter and established its university. The population was rapidly increasing; "caravans of settlers, sometimes 30 to 50 wagons a day, crossed the Mississippi at St. Louis on their way to the West." Loaded with locally grown produce, the flatboats of Missouri farmers headed toward New Orleans. In 1836 Jay Cooke noted that the citizenry consisted of "part French (almost Savages), Spaniards, Italians, Mexicans, Polish (all noblemen!!!), Indians, a set of gambling Southerners, and a few skinflint Yankees. There is but few respectable persons in St. Louis. . . . The old French people and the Spaniards look more like cut-throats than men." The biased Jay Cooke had overlooked a different array of characters—the traveling book agent; the Methodist circuit rider who "placed books in thousands of homes over the country"; and the Germans—"professional men and scholars, skilled tradesmen, and cheap labor"—who had begun what would become a heavy migration into Missouri. Against such a background, and for such a citizenry, there was a strong market for books.[6]

The market was supplied by several dealers who set up their shingles in the 1830s and offered stock shipped from Baltimore and Pittsburgh, New York and Philadelphia.[7] Freighted to Wheeling or Pittsburgh from Philadelphia and then shipped by river, or sent via New Orleans, the books accumulated on the shelves of newly established dealers in new and secondhand. In 1832, Thomas Essex's son, James C. Essex, specialized in schoolbooks on N. Main Street but offered sufficient variety to survive several removals as well as the Panic of 1837 and to endure into the 1840s.

He had competitors of course, one of them the firm of B. L. Turnbull who opened his wholesale and retail store and bindery in 1834 "in Mr. Chouteau's new brick building, situated on the west side of Main street, nearly opposite the office of the American Fur Company." There he offered miscellaneous books, history and literature to the settlers of St. Louis, including any literate fur traders he might entice into "Mr. Chouteau's new brick building."

Of all St. Louis' pioneer booksellers Stephen W. Meech, proprietor of the Franklin Book and Stationery Store established in 1832, seems to have been most active. Like his competitors he sustained several partnership changes and, as Meech & Dinnies and later as Meech & Loring, he added dimensions to the book trade of early St. Louis. Meech hailed from Norwich, Connecticut, and, having migrated west, in the summer of 1828 set up as a stationer at 8 Main Street, St. Louis. By 1832 he had expanded into books—law books and textbooks, novels and almanacs, along with American and English periodicals. Meech did not hesitate to advertise his distrust of the auction house as competition to the bookseller. In 1841 he "informed the public that he had a large stock 'which he will sell as low, on the average, as the same editions sold under the hammer, at the last book auction, and some editions even lower. Call . . . and be convinced that auction prices are not always the lowest.' " The same year, Meech announced that he had received "85 cases of books and stationery, comprising a complete stock in every department of his business," and he added the significant statement: "The lot was selected personally, and great pains were taken to suit this market." Stephen Meech was actually scouting in person to bring the right book to the right place. His one-time partner J. C. Dinnies bought from farther afield, advertising that he had "received, direct from Lyons, an invoice of 800 volumes, comprising the works of many of the most popular French authors in History, Biography, Science, Belles Lettres, Voyages & Travels and Theology."

Obviously the market for French books was still substantial. For all the changes in St. Louis, it had not sloughed off its Gallic origins. Dickens, alighting from the wharf in 1842, remarked that "In the old French portion of the town, the thoroughfares are narrow and crooked, and some of the houses are very quaint and picturesque: being built of wood, with tumble-down galleries before the windows, approachable by stairs or rather ladders from the street. There are queer little barbers' shops and drinking-houses too, in this quarter; and abundance of crazy old tenements with blinking casements. . . . Some of these ancient habitations, with high garret gable-windows perking into the roofs, have a kind of French shrug about them; and being lop-sided with age, appear to hold their heads askew . . . as if they were grimacing in astonishment at the American Improvements."[8]

Among the "American Improvements" were assuredly the numerous literary emporiums that rose up during the 1840s—Newberry's Literary Depot, H. A. Turner's Western Literary Depot, E. K. Woodward's Literary Emporium. In 1873 E. K. Woodward would be considered "the oldest bookseller in St. Louis, he having commenced the sale of books, papers and periodicals, at the corner of Third and Chestnut streets, in December, 1843." Woodward, who was to buy out Peter Smith, would eventually boast a stock that "embraces books in all departments of literature—school, miscellaneous, law, medical, scientific and juvenile, as well as blank books and stationery. At his establishment can be found the most varied stock of books in the city." Moreover, it is clear that Woodward's shelves, like those of most of the general booksellers and proprietors of literary emporiums in St. Louis, included a not inconsiderable number of antiquarian items. "The lover of old and rare books," it would be said, "can find here the curious and useful, as well as the old and new, and can find a representative of the art preservative of three centuries."

To a frontier town approaching the mid-nineteenth century, books were still less important than guns and saddles. Nonetheless, emigrants converging upon St. Louis to prepare for the journey to the Far West, "traders . . . making ready their wagons and outfits for Santa Fe," passengers boarding "steamboats . . . leaving the levee and passing up the

Missouri . . . on their way to the frontier"[9] found place for books among their gear. The bookselling activity in St. Louis testifies to a market for books. For such an abundant supply there must have been a strong demand.

It is true that Ralph Waldo Emerson, having made an exhausting journey "down the Ohio and up the Mississippi, with the constant threat of being blocked by ice," did not in 1852 view St. Louis as a promising literary center. "This city," he acknowledged, "is a wonderful growth," but "I believe no thinking or even reading man is here in the 95000 souls. An abstractionist cannot live near the Mississippi River & the Iron Mountain. They have begun the Pacific Rail Road; & the Railroad *from St. Anthony's Falls to New Orleans.* Such projects cannot consist with much literature."[10] Yet, only fourteen years later, in 1866, after the divided sympathies of Missourians had been resolved, after St. Louis had "served as a base of Federal operations," and the Civil War was at last over, another visitor viewed the city with far more roseate glasses. Bronson Alcott, the transcendental New Englander, wrote home to his wife:

I am persuaded that if Philosophy has found a home in modern times, 'tis here in this New New England, and that St. Louis is stealing past Boston and Concord even. The freedom and grasp of Genius, the force and speed of thinking, the practical tact in dealing with men and business transactions, which these students of the pure ideas, have to show, all this is as unexpected as it is convincing. Eastern men, slow to believe in things originating elsewhere, might profit by a visit out here. The possibilities of this wondrous West are infinite. . . . Think of a city that can claim . . . two masters of Hegel and Schelling, one of Swedenborg, . . . another of Goethe.[11]

There is little doubt that Alcott's enthusiasm was fired not only by the presence of such thinkers as Henry C. Brokmeyer, William Torrey Harris, and the members of their newly organized St. Louis Philosophical Society, but by the sight of a private "library of rare mystic books," and by the number of bookstores that were proliferating. For the city's German immigrant population there were German bookstores, such as Conrad Witter's, established in 1850 and continued after Witter's death in 1867 by his nephews. "The stock is principally German books . . . but French, Spanish and Italian books are also for sale. . . . Many of their goods are imported . . . some, however, are purchased in New York, Philadelphia and Baltimore." From their "magnificent store on

Fourth street" the Messrs. Witter supplied St. Louis' German-Americans with books to read and books to collect.

For the local citizenry the bookstores mushroomed. E. P. Gray's "extensive" shop on North Fourth Street "in the elegant marble block between Locust and St. Charles streets," was an outgrowth of Woodward & Co., and afforded to browsers a "very large" stock, "occupying four entire floors of the building and a part of the fifth, and embracing everything in the range of literature, science and art, in the shape of a book." One visitor observed that "In looking through his rooms one can not fail to notice the regularity and order which prevail in the arrangement and classification of books. In one place we see the British Poets comfortably and appropriately quartered by themselves, and not far off, . . . in their own alcove are the less pretentious American Poets. . . . The novelists have their place too, not in cheap covers . . . but in elegant dress as becomes the place."

Gray's shelves were crowded with books, juveniles and English literature, schoolbooks and histories. His operation was wholesale and retail, and although the bulk of his business came from Missouri and Illinois, he received orders from "eleven States and Territories." As one reporter noted in 1873, "His store is just such an one as the great city of St. Louis needs, and judging from the amount of business done by him, our citizens show their appreciation of his efforts to carry on a first-class book store."

E. P. Gray had several colleagues, among them Willie H. Gray of Olive Street who, having fought in the Civil War, returned to establish a store which became "a favorite resort for business men and other habitues of Third street and vicinity." There they could find not only United States daily and weekly papers, but foreign publications along with the customary supply of standard and miscellaneous books. For special interests during the postwar period, there were specialist bookshops. Theologians could find religious books at the establishment of J. W. McIntyre on South Fifth Street; J. H. Cook & Co. was strong in cheap literature, dime novels and song books, many of which were purveyed by train boys on railroads and news vendors.

St. Louis, which had benefited from the westward migration and shared the national prosperity of the 1850s, now profited in the aftermath of the war. As boats had once clustered at her wharf, railroad lines converged upon the city. With the new growth came ever more bookstores. Hendricks, Chittenden, begun in 1866, specialized in schoolbooks imported from Boston, New York and Philadelphia. H. C. Wright on Market Street offered subscription books and a miscellaneous stock that included "fine book-marks" imported from England. The St. Louis Book and News Company, established in 1867, was almost a literary department store. Its premises on North Fourth Street "in the centre of the most popular thoroughfare in the city" included a base-ment for "packing and sorting goods for the country trade," a second story devoted to schoolbooks, a third to stationery, a fourth to "inks, slates, mucilage, etc." On the first floor the books were displayed on "tables . . . so conveniently arranged that customers can see their con-tents at a glance, and make selection of such books as they like." By the end of the 1860s, Soule, Thomas & Winsor began business, sup-plying lawyers with standard law books and collectors with "finely bound" English books.

The little frontier town had become a flourishing city by the 1870s. It had survived the Panics of 1819 and 1837, 1857 and 1873. It had survived the great fire of 1849 and the cholera that followed in its wake. Now it boasted not only book emporiums on the grand scale, but bookstores specializing in the secondhand and the antiquarian. As early as 1858 Charles Clifton had commenced a secondhand book business interrupted by his service in the war and a fortune-seeking journey to "one of the Territories." E. Wiggins, "whose place of business is both outside and inside, at No. 310 North Third street," sold sec-ondhand books in the fields of law and medicine, the classics, poetry, romance, science and art. Even after Peter Smith, "the oldest anti-quarian book seller in the city," sold out to Woodward, he persisted in the book business with a "curious and truly miscellaneous stock." The "largest antiquarian book store in the city" was conducted by John Parker, many of whose books were described as "very rare and valuable." "One of the best antiquarian book stores in the city" was run by Father & Wilson on Olive Street and, according to report, "In the matter of hunting up rare and curious books" Mr. Father is "*au fait*. What he cannot procure for one is not worth getting. In the present place of business we find a large and valuable collection of books, both old and new, in all departments of literature." This array of antiquarian dealers of postwar St. Louis was not complete without the German specialist F. Roeslin of South Fourth Street and Charles F. Hergsell of Franklin Avenue who "keeps second-hand books, many of them rare and costly." Almost, it seemed, that, as everyone in St. Louis had sold books before there were bookstores, now, by the end of the 1870s, almost everyone was selling secondhand books.

One or two such dealers left more than mere names to St. Louis' antiquarian history. Philip Roeder,[12] whose large stock naturally included an assortment of interesting secondhand items, began business in 1879 between Third and Fourth Streets. After the usual number of changes of location, he was to be found by the century's end at 307 North Fourth Street where he occupied a "large store and basement." There, as "bookseller, newsdealer and stationer," he carried on a "general retail business" with "a large line of books"—the "largest stock of miscellaneous books in the West." At his establishment was also to be found a wide variety of "leading papers, magazines and periodicals" which attracted "some of the best people in the city." As publisher of The Illustrated Guide of St. Louis (St. Louis 1896), Philip Roeder doubtless made use of some of the local ephemera that heightened the interest both of his shelves and of his Holiday Catalogs.

Allan J. Crawford[13] was in the secondhand book business by 1887, when he is listed in the St. Louis Directory as A. J. Crawford & Co. at "Olive, ne cor. 7th." He continued in the antiquarian trade at least until 1915, when the directory places him at 322 Chestnut. During that period he issued at least fifty-four catalogues which listed not only the usual staple of remainders from local publishing houses, but a wide assortment of Americana including books of the Civil War, history, biography and travel. The lifetime Crawford devoted to the antiquarian trade wound fittingly to its close. The dealer was found on the floor of the shop where he had fallen.

Allan J. Crawford lived into the twentieth century when St. Louis and its antiquarian trade underwent some metamorphoses. By 1904, when the Louisiana Purchase Exposition commemorated the growth of St. Louis and the Middle West, the city's population had grown to over half a million. As it shared in the prosperity of those years of peace, it shared also in the "new wave of prosperity" ushered in by "the industrial activity of the First World War." St. Louis, a center of industry, became a center for a few important book collectors.

William Clark Breckenridge,[14] "Historical Research Writer and Bibliographer of Missouriana," was also "a true book lover" who "wanted to possess his treasures." He began his systematic book collecting, especially on the subject of slavery, in 1899, and within a decade had devised a system of "insert slips" on which he typed information about

the author, thus increasing the value of his library for reference purposes. By 1914 Breckenridge abandoned his work as manufacturer and
devoted the remainder of his life to research, bibliography, collecting.

His books were housed in rooms at the Hazard House—Missouriana,
pamphlets, western history, St. Louis history, rare Americana. Tall
and erect, strong and positive, Breckenridge must have raised the spirits
of local dealers when he appeared in their shops to pick up a scarce
item in his chosen field. As for himself, for over twenty-five years he
gathered material for a book which unfortunately never saw the light
of day although it had a title: "Old Time Book Dealers and Old Time
Book Stores and Their Patrons of St. Louis, From the First Book Store
Down to the Present Day."

A tornado destroyed Breckenridge's house in 1927, and many of the
collector's pamphlets were blown away and many of his books ruined,
although his library file cards were saved. Shortly after, he died, the
scholar who "knew every phase of St. Louis history," the collector who
knew most of its "old time book dealers."

An even more distinguished St. Louis bibliophile, William K. Bixby,[15]
collected not Missouriana but such rarities as original manuscripts of
Byron's poems and letters and Thomas Jefferson's correspondence. Upon
occasion he printed privately from the manuscripts and rarities in his
collection, issuing, for example, in 1922, *Benjamin Franklin on balloons;
a letter written from Passy . . . January sixteenth, MDCCLXXXIV*. In 1911
Bixby invested in the Anderson Auction Company, and as a result,
his brother-in-law William H. Samson became the firm's vice-president.
Some years later, and over a long period of time, duplicates and selections from the libraries of Henry E. Huntington of New York and
William K. Bixby of St. Louis were auctioned by the Anderson Galleries.

A third collector whose activity impinged upon the city of St. Louis
was the eminent librarian J. Christian Bay.[16] Bay arrived in St. Louis
from Denmark in 1892 and helped catalogue the Edward L. Sturtevant
collection of early botanical works in the Missouri Botanical Garden.
Grateful for the hospitality shown him by Missouri in his youth, he
arranged for his collection of Middle Western Americana to be purchased at cost by the State Historical Society of Missouri in 1941. For
nearly fifty years he had assembled that collection on "the history and
literature of the five states of the old Northwest Territory and the five
states of Kentucky, Minnesota, Iowa, Missouri, and Kansas." As J.
Christian Bay wrote, "The collector's views grow with his acquisitions."

Of his own collection he wrote, "The collection forms a unit. It is a library, not a chance aggregation, because it was formed around the idea that our pioneer spirit, our western life, is worth preserving in record and by way of emulation. . . . It still is true that this region, the Middle Border, is our country's heart."

One St. Louis dealer in particular assuredly agreed with such views. Of all the booksellers who traded in antiquarian materials in that city, the leading spirit was William Harvey Miner.[17] Born in New Haven in 1877, a graduate of Yale and George Washington universities, Miner was trained by Luther S. Livingston in the rare book department of Dodd, Mead & Company. Subsequently he headed the rare book department of Burrows Brothers in Cleveland, making "annual trips to Europe in search of fine and rare books." Moving to Cedar Rapids, Iowa, he joined the staff of Luther Albertus Brewer's Torch Press. Finally, in 1917, he moved to St. Louis. He brought with him the background of a man who had served an apprenticeship in rare books and, as author of The American Indians, north of Mexico, the authority of his scholarship.

A visit to the bookstore established on Franklin Avenue by this trained bibliopole was recorded by a St. Louis observer: "You dropped in as you passed by to discuss rare books with the proprietor. You browsed over the book tables and mounted a ladder to hunt for good volumes long out of print, on top shelves, or you looked in the cellar for rare Americana. The proprietor knew where coveted editions could be had in other cities. If you particularly desired an early American biography which not even some large public libraries could boast, he found it for you from some mysterious source.

Talking with William Harvey Miner you felt that books were persons. They were friends he introduced to you and sometimes led you to adopt when you doubted whether you ought to spend the money, finding later you were glad you did. . . . There are and will be, larger book stores, but none where the business of selling books is less commercialized."

Part of Miner's lure lay in his voice which had, according to the collector-librarian J. Christian Bay, "a haunting quality of reverence and wonder, as if he always was under the influence of some beautiful memory or some great and pleasant surprise." His finds alone might have afforded him many moments of genuinely pleasant surprise—"the finding of a copy of the Burgis engraving of the city of New York; . . .

the location of an exquisite lot of rare Western Americana, including a portion of William Beaumont's correspondence." To the delights of his voice Miner added the strength of his memory. Bay remarked that "those who talked with him again after years had passed would find him ready to continue the old conversation as if neither time nor distance had intervened." "There are few men," he concluded, "with whom I would rather scan a suspicious-looking and dusty bookshelf, than with him."

Fred Rosenstock, visiting St. Louis, concurred with such opinions, finding Miner "a great man in the book business." "There were no steals in Miner's shop," he conceded, "but it was a distinction to be able to go to Miner's and be received by him in a friendly manner, have him show you what he had. . . . William Harvey Miner was one of the men I respected most and considered it a special pleasure to know."

The choice items of Miner's stock appeared in a succession of catalogues—works on the Middle West and the Mississippi Valley, the Far West and the American Indian. The introductions and annotations he included testified to his scholarship though the series ended all too soon. Miner died a sudden and untimely death in 1934 when, at age fifty-six, he was struck down by a drunken driver.

At his death the *St. Louis Star-Times* commented ominously:

When death stole in upon William Harvey Miner . . . it took from St. Louis almost the last reminder of old book store days when selling books was a labor of love and the selection and buying of them a solemn rite for the elect. Like everything else, the book business has gone commercial. You decide your need and order your volumes like meat or sugar. There are used book stores left, to be sure, but William Harvey Miner's . . . was different.

For a while, there were bookstores on the western border of Missouri that made up for the decline of bookstores in St. Louis. Kansas City, Missouri, filled the gap, so to speak, and in the end provided the background for a rare book emporium distinguished, flamboyant, enduring.

On the great bend of the Missouri, Kansas City was the outgrowth of two frontier settlements, the river town of Kansas and the "bull-whacking, feverish town of Westport, four miles to the south on the Santa Fe Trail." By the mid-1820s, western Missouri began to attract settlers, and by the mid-1830s, the opening of the Platte Purchase in the northwest brought immigrants and trade. In 1846 Francis Parkman described Westport as "full of Indians, whose little shaggy ponies were tied by dozens along the houses and fences. . . . Whiskey circulates more freely in Westport than is altogether safe in a place where every man carries a loaded pistol in his pocket." With the growth of the Santa Fe trade, steamboats unloaded at the levee and streets were filled with "the roistering brotherhood of the trail." In 1853 the "City of Kansas" was incorporated, and the little river town's levee was described by journalist Albert D. Richardson as "a confused picture of immense piles of freight, horse, ox, and mule teams receiving merchandise from the steamers, scores of immigrant wagons, and a busy crowd of whites, Indians, half-breeds, Negroes and Mexicans." Clearly, Kansas City was a city of the future, but first the terrible disruption of the Civil War had to be surmounted, the Battle of Westport, the "Gettysburg of the West," fought. Only then, after peace was restored, were new markets opened "as the frontier was pushed into the Far West." "In 1865 the end of the pack train and steamboat era was marked by the coming of the first railroad into the city," and what had spelled decline for Cincinnati spelled "a period of uninterrupted growth" for the city on the great bend of the Missouri. Between the 1870s and the 1890s its population would increase from 30,000 to 300,000. Such a community could and did accommodate dealers in the secondhand and rare book trade.[18]

Of all those who traded in books and stationery, wallpaper and fancy goods in the retail district between Sixth and Ninth streets and uptown after the general movement in that direction during the 1880s, a few gained reputations as antiquarians.[19] B. Glick and J. S. Coburn, for example, were cited as "the leading second-hand and rare book dealers," and "lovers of old, rare editions" were said to "haunt their stores in great numbers." Then there was the colorful Herbert L. Mathews who plied his trade on Wyandotte Street. Born in Coldwater, Michigan, he had moved west with his parents. Young Mathews had apparently been attracted to printer's ink from his boyhood days when he sold newspapers. In 1877 he came to Kansas City on foot from the West where he had been working on the Santa Fe extension. "His earthly possessions consisted of a pair of overalls, a blue shirt and a little lunch done up in a red bandanna. . . . He had a few cents in his pocket, from which he accumulated a stock of books." During the 1880s, Mathews was employed in the bookstore of M. H. Dickinson & Co. before beginning his own business with a hundred books. He himself is reported to have had a "wide knowledge of rare books, first editions and special bindings, and his store was well known to every book lover in his vicinity." In 1893 he planned to enlarge the store and increase the stock, but three years later he died.

His place in Kansas City's antiquarian cast of characters was taken by Patrick McArdle, the city's "old book man." In 1879 McArdle arrived in Kansas City from Ireland. After driving a horse car and serving as conductor on the Rosedale horse car line, he opened a stall in the early 1880s, in the "old Metropolitan building at St. Louis and Union avenues." Its stock attracted a variety of booklovers. "The drays unloaded bundle after bundle of gorgeous-backed dreadfuls on the sidewalk in front of McArdle's. Farmer boys crowded around his windows and, tempted by the colorful Nick Carter and Frank Merriwell titles, entered to buy. Stockmen bought up a winter's reading material.

But McArdle's specialty was Americana. His shop was known to residents as a library of American titles." Years later it was said that "There still are some lawyers and other professional men in Kansas City who got their educational background around the tottering old tables in the back of McArdle's book shop."

In time everyone along Union Avenue came to know Patrick McArdle as the "old book man." From six in the morning until ten at night he attracted "a busy custom." "He dealt in books," his patrons recognized, "for the sake of the books, not for money. His very interest in his work made money for him. Books were his friends; he had thousands of books around him. Some were prized first editions. He fondled them and rescanned them. When he sold one, he was glad of the sale, but the sale was bittersweet with the sadness in parting with a possession he loved."

All too soon there were fewer such sales. The once flourishing thoroughfare where he was established was left desolate when the old Union Depot closed. Still, McArdle hung on, his rent reduced from $50 to $5 a month. "Nobody came." In 1915 he stored his books, paying periodic visits to the storage house to view the stacks. At length he sold his treasures, and in 1926 he died, the " 'old book man' of Union avenue," Kansas City.

During the 1880s when Mathews and McArdle set out their shingles, they met competition from a colleague whose bookstore would long survive theirs. In 1884, Theodore Otis Cramer,[20] age twenty-two, hailing from Ohio, opened a small store at 1321 Grand Avenue with a capital of $117.50. Called "Ye Olde Booke Mane," it had "green board shutters" that were "padlocked at night," and its "book shelves were on the sidewalk." It offered, besides a small stock of books and newspapers, a "frontier inventory of candy, magazines and wallpaper." This was the beginning of a book emporium occupying three stories and basement, devoted to antiquarian and secondhand items in the hundreds of thousands, a strong schoolbook department, a technical division, and a philatelic sideline. Samplings of those tons of books were listed in Cramer catalogues—Americana and fine sets, history and biography, art, fiction offered at $27.50 per hundred copies, along with first editions of a *Last of the Mohicans* or a *Mary Baker Eddy*, each priced at $150. For variety, quantity, and the ever-present possibility of a "sleeper," Cramer's bookstore lured the collector to Grand Avenue.

Then, in 1929, the proprietor was killed as the result of a motor car crash, and his son, Clarke A. Cramer, who had assisted his father in the business, took his place. Clarke Cramer was a devotee of books, and under his aegis Cramer's claimed to be "the largest book store west of the Mississippi river, and one of the five largest in the United States." Despite, or perhaps because of the magnitude of its stock—about 400,000 volumes—Cramer's developed "something of the old-fashioned traditional air characteristic of old English shops."

The bookstore continued to survive its proprietors. In 1943 Clarke Cramer died, and the establishment passed to his son, T. O. Cramer II, who introduced a "trust-the-public self-serve" operation. Books were left in the Cramer bookstore entrance overnight and those who made selections were expected to pay for them by dropping coins through a slit in the door. A sign explained the plan:

> Night shift!
> Here's the drift:
> Choose a book, one or more.
> Drop the money in the door.

And so the Cramer bookstore was relieved of secondhand and antiquarian items ranging in subject matter from palmistry to cattle-raising. For all such innovations, the pioneer touch of the founder was gone, as was the bibliophily of his son. Cramer's bookstore, with its huge stock, was going to seed. The son of T. O. Cramer II had no interest in books, and eventually, in 1967, the business was sold to the "unofficial dean of used books in Kansas City," the bearded Frederick Allen Fry who had worked at Cramer's since 1948. Its four floors of shelves still held several hundred thousand books and the "sidewalk book dispensary" was still in operation. Two or three years later Fry began the Cramer liquidation by selling twenty-five tons of books to Smith's Acres of Books in Long Beach, California. Although it was announced that the T. O. Cramer Bookstore at 1321 Grand Avenue was "going out of business," its history had not yet terminated. Another proprietor, Terence Cassidy, took his place in Cramer annals, and in 1973 he and Fred Fry held a "Dutch auction" of the remaining stock of 50,000 books. As Cassidy put it, "The day of the big, general, multiple-story used bookstore has passed." What was left of the shop opened by Theodore Cramer in 1884 would be, it was said, removed to a book warehouse "where customers can order by phone and appointment."

Around the turn of the century, a Kansas City bookseller altogether different from Theodore Cramer offered items of far greater stature than any to be found at "Ye Olde Booke Mane." From 606 Wyandotte Street, George D. Fearey,[21] corresponding secretary of the Western Historical Society of Kansas City, Missouri, issued A List of First Editions, Rare Imprints and Fine Bindings that included—with prices on application—some truly extraordinary works. Despite the grandeur of his offerings, Fearey is remembered today only from his catalogues, "some old post cards . . . from irate customers" in London and elsewhere, and a scrapbook of letters "from Governors and other bigwigs from western states." Yet his List of First Editions, issued around 1900, included the following eyebrow-raising selections: "The original manuscript of the Mormon Bible from which the 1830 Palmyra Bible was printed, and the table on which it was written"; the "Manuscript vocabulary of the Wyandotte language"; "The manuscript Diary of Governor Walker, the first governor of Kansas"; "The original first edition" of the Boydell Shakespeare; an Audubon in "Atlas and Octavo Editions." Fearey apparently was inclined to boast of his achievements while retaining a sense of humor, for, in describing one item in his catalogue—Whittier's Moll Pitcher of 1832, priced at $40—he wrote: "I bought a bundle of scraps at the Fred[e]rickson sale for 50 cents. This and two Shelley letters were in it—so was G.D.F."

Neither the operations of the elusive George D. Fearey nor the

activities of such a local dealer as Kenneth Sender,[22] specialist in Western Americana who purchased government documents in New Mexico,
could satisfy the expanding bibliophilic interests of twentieth-century
Kansas City. For that a knowledgeable, inventive and productive dealer
was required, one who would not only meet the requirements of Kansas
City but make of that metropolis a book center to be reckoned with.
Like William Harvey Miner in St. Louis, Frank Glenn brought to
Kansas City a knowledge and love of books that would soon make of
him a specialist in the spectacular.

Frank Glenn's brow denoted "a high degree of intelligence" and he
talked "straight from the shoulder." He combined the impulses of the
gambler with the instincts of a Sherlock Holmes and the propensities
of a globe-trotter. In addition he had flair, style, panache which rubbed
off on his multi-faceted Kansas City book establishment.[23]

Glenn was born in 1897 in Bearmouth, Montana. Although he never
completed high school, he was a skillful debater in Walla Walla, Washington, and there he was given access to the library of the last territorial
governor of Washington-Oregon, Miles C. Moore, for whom he worked.
He also had access to The Book of Knowledge that his mother purchased.
The combination was apparently sufficient to instill in him a love of
books undeterred by his air corps service in World War I. It was somehow appropriate that his first major employment was for the Grolier
Society, publishers of The Book of Knowledge, which he began can-
vassing in 1924. At the society's Kansas City headquarters he later
established a Rare Book Department and was sent abroad for its expansion. In 1926, when "England's great libraries were thrown on the
open market because of huge estate taxes," Frank Glenn could find the
"jewelled and inlaid bindings, first editions, handsomely bound sets . . .
incunabula, maps, rare prints, children's books" that appealed not only
to patrons of the Grolier Book Shop but to himself.

In 1933, during the Great Depression, the Grolier manager set out
on his own. At 312 Ward Parkway he opened Frank Glenn Books,
"put an Army cot in the basement and lived on the job." He began
with an "$8,000 stock of rare books which he had accumulated over
a number of years," and he began—and continued—with panache. His
stock was flamboyant and diversified. Catalogue 10, issued in 1935,
featured a California manuscript—the De Nebe Family Patent of No-
bility bound in black velvet at $500, a sixteenth-century Persian man-

uscript with four fine miniatures at $450, a fore-edge painting of "Old Paris" at $50, and a 1611 Spenser at $150. Among Glenn specialties were cited art books and children's books, fine sets for private libraries, gift books and maps, Japanese prints and Orientalia.

In time, through major acquisitions and serendipitous finds, Frank Glenn would extend his stock with even more spectacular and varied items. In 1935 he purchased the Charles McAllister Wilcox Collection which included, *inter alia*, a first edition of *Paradise Lost*, a Swinburne manuscript, Shakespeare quartos, and the Kelmscott Chaucer. The following year the proprietor obtained from Twain's English agent the original manuscript of *Tom Sawyer* which he was eventually able to bring "home to Missouri." In the early 1950s "The Strange Treasure of Professor [Thomas Jefferson] Fitzpatrick" passed to Frank Glenn's hands and on to the University of Kansas and the Kansas City Public Library—a treasure that filled and overflowed "several houses, . . . an astonishing accumulation of botany, taxonomy, Americana, Lincoln, Jefferson, the Mormons, and a great deal more." As the university's Special Collections head described it, "The 15 tons of Fitzpatrick's library which were scientific came to Kansas, along with the 67 boxes containing his manuscript collection and his own archives. (Kansas City Public Library took a slightly lesser quantity—the Lincoln, Mormon, and early American books. Glenn kept the rest—and that was a lot—for stock.)"

In between, there were the finds, the two-page letter written by the Duke of Devonshire to report a battle to the king in 1702, a letter that had been used as a bookmark by an eighteenth-century reader; the first edition of Johnson's *Dictionary* found in an Arkansas attic; a Blaeu *Atlas* discovered in Enid, Oklahoma; a psalter once owned by Lincoln and a Cicero once owned by Nathan Hale, both of which came to Glenn as the result of his article, "Your Attic May Be Your Fortune."

Frank Glenn had all the characteristics of the proselytizer. He lectured on books, exhibited books, shared his catholic bibliophily and brilliant imagination with all who were interested, and helped arouse in Kansas City an awareness and appreciation of the old and the rare. As early as 1938 he announced to a library committee: "I have often reflected on the daring and the courage of the man who transported that printing press from Spain to Vera Cruz and then by pack mule up over the mountains into Mexico City and the artistry of the man who was able to produce such a beautiful book as the *Dialogo Doctrina* [*Doctrina Christiana*] a hundred years before printing had been introduced in the colonies of the United States."

Glenn's bookish kingdom shifted locations several times, his shop moving to the Muehlebach Hotel, thence to 1022 Baltimore, and back to the Muehlebach. The Muehlebach quarters were described as "in Gothic style." The premises at 1022 Baltimore, to which Glenn moved in 1939, were far more spectacular. A lengthy, quotable article in *Publishers Weekly* was devoted to a full-dress account of this full-dress bookstore: "Besides the main room, there are six others. . . . Each room has a color scheme and interior design appropriate to its use. . . . The Rare Book Room is the sanctum sanctorum. . . . A reproduction of a painting from an old Persian manuscript decorates the entrance doors of parchment leather. . . . The walls of a . . . dubonnet color harmonize with the . . . mahogany of the shelves and make a perfect setting for the finely bound books lining them. Two comfortable chairs, upholstered in a dubonnet fabric, a sofa covered with an English Regency print . . . against a background of beige, and a large low table are grouped around the fireplace opposite the entrance doors. Draperies . . . on each side of the fireplace . . . conceal the . . . doors of two room-sized vaults." The Rare Book Room was merely one feature of this elaborate emporium which also boasted a Children's Room, a Used Book Department, a Greeting Card display, and even "a loafing room for the staff." Against this lush background, Frank Glenn supervised an operation unprecedented in Kansas City. As a sharp public relations expert, he could display irresistible "Gift Book Suggestions," from Dürer woodcuts to oriental miniatures, from pressbooks to Dickens firsts. As a knowledgeable bibliophile, he could stock his shelves with rare Americana pamphlets including goldseekers' manuals and immigrants' guides. He had the flair and the charisma to attract such a diversity of patrons as Sally Rand and Arthur Rubinstein, Katharine Hepburn, Ethel Barrymore and Philip D. Sang.

In 1942 the Glenn staff was enlarged by the employment of Peggy Couchman Long, who shortly became Mrs. Frank Glenn and who, as Ardis (Peggy) Glenn would succeed to the business after Frank Glenn's death. Meanwhile, they had twenty years of collaboration ahead of them—years punctuated with Glenn's grandiose projects. In 1946 the Frank Glenn Publishing Company was organized. Five years later the "Magic Carpet on Wheels" was launched, a traveling exhibition on the "History of the Book." In 1957 Hong Kong Imports was added to the Glenn enterprises. Two years later Glenn, who had made some forty trips to Europe, took his fifth journey round the world in search of books and manuscripts, finding in Athens a copy of Eusebius printed on vellum and bound for the Medicis.

In 1960 Frank Glenn moved his treasures for the last time, to 1227 Baltimore. Although he was already desperately ill, he insisted: "I shall continue to buy and sell rare books in all fields and will do everything possible . . . to make the new shop an asset to the city." An assistant recalled that "Glenn . . . was given permission to leave the hospital for a week after the transfer to the new location had been made. In that week he visited the 'new store' daily and was physically carried to the basement so that he could inspect the shelf arrangements in that part of the store." Two days later, on 12 June 1960, he died.

His place was taken by his widow who herself became an adornment to Glenn Books. Under her aegis the Glenn stock continues to be rich and varied, ranging from fourteenth-century illuminated manuscripts to a first edition of *Grapes of Wrath*, from aeronautica to printing history. She herself, according to the local papers, "can usually be found at her desk among the reference material perusing a first edition or chatting with the customers." She is aptly called the Belle of Baltimore and she continues a tradition introduced to Kansas City by its most spectacular bookman. Frank Glenn brought color and flair to all the bibliophiles who "came from Missouri."

NOTES

1. *Missouri A Guide to the "Show Me" State Compiled by Workers of the Writers' Program of the Work Projects Administration in the State of Missouri* (New York: Duell, Sloan and Pearce, [1941]), p. 140.

2. Letter to "Citizens of St. Louis" by "Franklin," quoted from the *Missouri Republican* of 24 December 1823 in John Francis McDermott, "Public Libraries in St. Louis, 1811–39," *The Library Quarterly* XIV:1 (January 1944), p. 11.

For early St. Louis, see Howard Mumford Jones, *America and French Culture 1750–1848* (Chapel Hill: University of North Carolina Press, 1927), p. 164; John Francis McDermott, "Private Libraries in St. Louis," *Papers of the Bibliographical Society of America* 51:1 (1957), pp. 27 f; *Missouri A Guide*, pp. 295–305; J. Thomas Scharf, *History of Saint Louis City and County* (Philadelphia: Everts, 1883), II, 1588.

3. H. M. Brackenridge, *Recollections of Persons and Places in the West* (Phil-

adelphia: Lippincott, 1868), pp. 268 f. See also Eleanora A. Baer, "Books, Newspapers, and Libraries in Pioneer St. Louis, 1808–1842," *Missouri Historical Review* LVI:4 (July 1962), p. 347; *Missouri A Guide*, p. 300; John Tebbel, *A History of Book Publishing in the United States* (New York: Bowker, 1972), I, 470.

4. John Francis McDermott, "Everybody Sold Books in Early St. Louis," *Publishers Weekly* (24 July 1937), pp. 248 ff. For further details regarding the pre-bookstore sale of books in St. Louis, see Eleanora A. Baer, "Books, Newspapers, and Libraries in Pioneer St. Louis (1808–1842)," Library School of the University of Wisconsin (August 1961) Typescript, passim; Harold Holmes Dugger, "Reading Interests and the Book Trade in Frontier Missouri," Ph.D. dissertation, University of Missouri, 1951, pp. 337–371; McDermott, "Private Libraries in Frontier St. Louis," *Papers of the Bibliographical Society of America* (1957), passim; McDermott, "Public Libraries in St. Louis," *Library Quarterly* (January 1944), p. 9; *School and Society* 47 (21 May 1938), p. 673.

5. For St. Louis' first bookstore, see Dugger, "Reading Interests and the Book Trade in Frontier Missouri," pp. 350–354; David Kaser, *A Directory of the St. Louis Book and Printing Trades to 1850* (New York: New York Public Library, 1961), pp. 20, 31; John Francis McDermott, "The First Bookstore in Saint Louis," *Mid-America* 21:3 (July 1939), pp. 206 ff.

6. Dugger, "Reading Interests and the Book Trade in Frontier Missouri," pp. 364 f; Jones, *America and French Culture*, p. 277; *Missouri A Guide*, pp. 301 f.

7. For the pioneer St. Louis book dealers between the 1830s and 1870s, see Baer, "Books, Newspapers, and Libraries in Pioneer St. Louis," Typescript, pp. 27–35; Dugger, "Reading Interests and the Book Trade in Frontier Missouri," pp. 337–371; Kaser, *A Directory of the St. Louis Book and Printing Trades to 1850*, p. 33 and passim; "St. Louis as a Reading City," *The Inland Monthly* III:1 (January 1873), pp. 47–58 (Courtesy R. Dunaway, St. Louis, to whom the writer is indebted for information regarding St. Louis booksellers).

8. Charles Dickens, *American Notes* (Philadelphia: Porter & Coates, n.d.), p. 473.

9. Francis Parkman, quoted in Louis B. Wright, *Life on the American Frontier* (New York: Capricorn Books, 1971), pp. 108 f.

10. Ralph L. Rusk, ed., *The Letters of Ralph Waldo Emerson* (New York: Columbia University Press, 1939), IV, 338 ff. See also Gay Wilson Allen, *Waldo Emerson* (New York: Viking Press, 1981), pp. 566 f.

11. Richard L. Herrnstadt, ed., *The Letters of A. Bronson Alcott* (Ames: Iowa State University Press, 1969), pp. 385, 387.

12. For Philip Roeder, see Adolf Growoll Collection, *American Book Trade History*, X, 152; *St. Louis, Queen City of the West* (St. Louis: Mercantile Advancement Co., 1899), p. 171.

13. For A. J. Crawford, see James Malcolm Breckenridge, *William Clark Breckenridge: Historical Research Writer and Bibliographer of Missouriana* (St. Louis: Author, 1932), p. 111; De Simon Company, *Catalogue Fourteen* (New York [1982]), item 311; St. Louis directory information from Laurel Boeckman, Senior Reference Specialist, State Historical Society of Missouri.

14. J. M. Breckenridge, *William Clark Breckenridge*, passim.

15. George L. McKay, *American Book Auction Catalogues 1713–1934* (New York: New York Public Library, 1937), p. 23, #7670.

16. J. Christian Bay, "Western Life and Western Books," *Missouri Historical Review* XXXVI:4 (July 1942), pp. 403–411; Floyd C. Shoemaker, *The State Historical Society of Missouri A Semicentennial History* (Columbia: The State Historical Society of Missouri, 1948), pp. 126–129.

17. For Miner, see J. Christian Bay, "William Harvey Miner," *The American Book Collector* V (March 1934), pp. 71 f; Donald E. Bower, *Fred Rosenstock A Legend in Books & Art* (Flagstaff, Ariz.: Northland Press, 1976), p. 92; De Simon Company, *Catalogue Fourteen*, item 312; Information from R. Dunaway, St. Louis; *Missouri Historical Review* 28:3 (April 1934), pp. 243 f; *St. Louis Star-Times* (12 February 1934), p. 12.

18. For details of early Kansas City, see Adolf Growoll Collection, *American Book Trade History*, VIII, 2; Henry C. Haskell, Jr., and Richard B. Fowler, *City of the Future: A Narrative History of Kansas City, 1850–1950* (Kansas City: Frank Glenn Publishing Company, [1950]), p. 77; *Missouri A Guide*, pp. 242–247.

19. For Kansas City's early antiquarian dealers, see Adolf Growoll Collection, *American Book Trade History*, VIII, 2 and IX, 51; "The 'Old Book Man' Gone," Kansas City Newspaper Clipping (15 January 1926), Courtesy Katherine Sherman, Special Collections, University of Missouri–Kansas City.

20. For Cramer and his bookstore, see Brian Burnes, "Leafing through the city's used-book stores,"*Kansas City Star* (16 March 1980), pp. 8–17 (Courtesy Philip Tompkins, Associate Director of Libraries, University of Missouri–Kansas City); Information from Terence W. Cassidy in interview with author, 14 May 1982; Terence W. Cassidy, "A Brief History of the Cramer Book Store," unpaged typescript (Courtesy Terence W. Cassidy); Information from Ardis Glenn; *Kansas City Star* (14 February 1943, 11 April 1943, 7 January 1965, 23 February 1973, 25 February 1973), Courtesy Kansas City Public Library Newspaper Clipping File and Katherine Sherman, Special Collections, University of Missouri–Kansas City. The writer is indebted to both sources for numerous clippings and information for this chapter; *Kansas City Times* (9 October 1941, 27 January 1967, 31 January 1970).

21. All my knowledge of George D. Fearey comes from Ardis Glenn of Glenn Books, Kansas City, Mo., who generously sent me his *List of First Editions* and shared her extensive information with me.

22. Ardis Glenn to Madeleine B. Stern, 28 May 1982.

23. For details of Frank Glenn and Frank Glenn Books, see *American Library Association Bulletin* (15 October 1938); Ardis Glenn, "Frank Glenn and the Glenn Bookshop: Pioneer Rare Book Dealer in the Midwest," *AB Bookman's Weekly* (7 September 1981), pp. 1424–1434 (The writer is enormously indebted to Ardis Glenn for clippings, pictures, and information concerning Glenn Books); Frank Glenn, *Catalogue Ten* (June 1935), Courtesy Ardis Glenn; *Kansas City Journal* (6 October 1939); *Kansas City Star* (5 January 1930, 7 March 1958, 19 July 1959, 8 April 1960, 13 October 1961, 26 November 1972, 16 March 1980); *Kansas City Times* (13 June 1960, 24 September 1981); Alexandra Mason, "Collection Building: Rare Books in the Great American Desert," *AB Bookman's Weekly* (1 March 1982) p. 1608; *Publishers Weekly* (11 June 1938), p. 2297, (16 December 1939), pp. 2194 ff, (22 March 1941), p. 1295.

7

San Francisco

In January 1853, San Francisco's first daily newspaper described with pride the growth of the city's book trade. In a brief before-and-after picture, readers were made aware that on the shores of the Pacific a New Atlantis was emerging:

The Book Trade in this city commenced with the peddling of a few cheap, old and ill-assorted publications from a hand-basket, in the open streets, and has, within the short space in which almost every other wonder has been accomplished in California, grown to a highly prosperous and ably-conducted branch of daily business—with splendid sales-rooms, well stocked shelves, and in some instances binderies attached to the stores. . . . The tastes and desires of the reading public have correspondingly improved since 1849. . . . [They] now require not only the highest order of literature, . . . but appropriate styles of printing and binding for drawing-room or library purposes are now consulted. The richest and costliest works find ready sale. . . . By every steamer that arrives with freight from the Atlantic shores, the latest English and American publications are received. Such is the book trade of San Francisco.[1]

It is true that before the gold rush an "unmethodical trade in books" had been carried on in the Mexican colony. Despite earthquakes and revolts, the ravages of smallpox and the American conquest, "intellectual light had ways of filtering in," and boxes of books, including works by Voltaire and Rousseau, arrived by ship.[2] There is no doubt, however, that it was the discovery of gold that revolutionized San Francisco. As Frank Luther Mott put it: "Gold was discovered at Sutter's Mill in January, 1848, and the rush of adventurers reached a great height the next year. San Francisco was suddenly a city."[3] Gold dust from the diggings was exchanged for all the requirements of life, and among those requirements were books—books new and secondhand—books that came from the East in cargoes of clipper ships and steamers. After their nine-month voyage aboard a sailing ship from New York or Boston around South America to the Pacific coast, the cargoes arrived at San Francisco's bustling wharves and the crates were unloaded. Books had a warm reception in the city, for there were customers to buy them and booksellers to sell them.

The typical San Francisco bookseller, if a prototype can be sketched, came, like his wares, from the East or perhaps from Europe—Scotland, Prussia, Bavaria. Lured by the news from Sutter's Mill, he crossed the plains or rounded the Horn and arrived in San Francisco in 1849 or a year or so later, joined the gold seekers at Weaverville or Siskiyou or Shasta, working the rich placers, and sometimes, but not always, struck gold. Drawn to San Francisco, he might try his hand at one or two callings before deciding to deal in books. His stock, imported from the East and from abroad, included secondhand books. If he hailed from France and his name was Ernest de Massey he might specialize in foreign books and add an aristocratic touch to the frontier city. If his name was Pomier he might set up a Cabinet de Lecture Français including bookstore, circulating library and reading room. Whatever he dealt in—popular novels published in the East, law books, portraits of Lola Montez, secondhand works in German or French, Latin or Greek—the gold-rush bookseller of San Francisco was nomadic in nature, changing his location repeatedly, and living through a series of fires major or minor. If he survived, he usually combined bookselling with publishing, and indeed many early San Francisco bibliopoles would be remembered less for their bookselling than for achievements in different though related fields. He set a pattern, the early San Francisco bookseller, and he spread the love of books in the City of the Golden Gate.

There, in 1850, "bookstalls 'were to be found at every corner,' "[4] and the next year the *Alta California* announced that "A live Yankee has adopted the plan of traveling up and down Long Wharf, with a horse and wagon, the latter filled with literature for sale, of every description, from the horrifying yellow covered stories of robbers and murderers up to the classics and histories."[5] There almost seemed to be more books in San Francisco than gold dust, and thanks to the perseverance and industry of these early booksellers, "The reading community of San Francisco are not obliged as formerly to spend their leisure hours in poring over the pages of some old book which has found its way around Cape Horn, or across the Isthmus of Panama. Now we receive by every steamer the latest publications . . . solid bound books, and the yellow covered whilers away of careless hours."[6]

If Boston was born bookish, and New York achieved bookishness, San Francisco had bookishness thrust upon it—by the dealer from the East who wearied of pan and shovel and turned instead to trade in the printed word.

Probably the first such dealer in San Francisco's bibliopolic history was John Hamilton Still.[7] Born in the West Indies of Scottish background, John H. Still arrived at the Golden Gate aboard the *Griffen* in September 1849. Almost immediately, without the usual gold-mining interval that punctuated the lives of most early San Francisco booksellers, the twenty-one-year-old Still opened a shop—the Periodical News Depot—on Pike Street. He moved repeatedly in the course of his career, took on a series of temporary partners, and survived with punning humor San Francisco's frequent fires. One of his advertisements announced: "Still live at No. 6 Pine Street, a few doors below the Post Office, subscriber having been burnt out at late fire, Alta California Building, loss $1200."[8] Except for a brief period during which his wife Jane ran the book business while her husband was in "temporary eclipse," Still was a fairly persistent bookseller. By 1855, "six years and ten locations after his initial venture," he opened at 100 Kearny Street The New York Cheap Bookstore. It was well named, for in between his San Francisco stands, John H. Still set up a shingle on New York's Nassau Street as California Booksellers and News Agents. Nonetheless, until his death in 1876 he was identified with the San Francisco book trade. Although his stock was highly generalized, consisting of novels, magazines and newspapers which he circulated among country merchants, express riders and peddlers, Still also dealt in old books. His very first advertisement of 7 January 1850 announced, "Old books bought or exchanged," and it may be assumed that the man who "prided himself on being the oldest book dealer in San Francisco" handled from time to time books of antiquarian interest. Indeed, one of the leading dealers of San Francisco has recalled, "I have had in my hands many rare pamphlets . . . which contained his [Still's] book-label."

If Still was the pioneer San Francisco bookseller, another firm may lay claim to a different priority. Not long after Still had set up his shingle on Pike Street, two New Yorkers—A. S. Marvin and George

B. Hitchcock—opened their Pioneer Bookstore. Hitchcock left a record of its origins during the gold rush: "I happened upon an old schoolmate of mine who was doing a little stationery business, and went in with him. We had a little store about 20 x 11 feet on Clay St., for which we paid $125 monthly. . . . Cash books we sold for $25 and $30 such as we sell for . . . $6 now. I sold a second hand Webster's Dictionary for $25."[9] Not content with the novels and miscellaneous works shipped from the East, one member of the firm of Marvin and Hitchcock went to New York in 1851 on a book-buying trip, thus making what appears to be the first book hunt by a San Franciscan to the Atlantic coast, a book hunt that apparently aimed not only at new but at antiquarian volumes. Both partners—Marvin, "keen" and "enterprising," Hitchcock, "with a small body, but a heart as big as an ox"—had spent a short stint in the mining region before their joint venture in books.

It was a decade of extravagant growth and change, of highs and lows, that unparalleled period between 1850 and 1860 in San Francisco. By 1851–1852 the mushrooming city offered a few auctions and twelve bookstores. By 1856, for a population of some 40,000, there were forty booksellers, and by 1860 there were sixty-two booksellers for a population that had expanded to 358,000. In addition, there were agents engaged by such eastern houses as Fowler and Wells which consigned stocks of their publications to the "pioneer booksellers" Marvin and Hitchcock, or to the water-cure physician George M. Bourne, who sold not only hydropathic journals but Walt Whitman's Leaves of Grass. Indeed, the 1850s have been called the "Golden Age of the book trade in California." Although antiquarian books certainly did not figure importantly in that description, practically everything else did. A prolific and fearless newspaper press publicized divergent opinions. Between thirty and fifty vessels entered or departed the port each day. At the wharves could be seen clipper masts and steamers as well as great storehouses and commission establishments. Malays and Chinese, Swedes, Yankees and Britons swarmed as white-sailed ships dipped down to the Golden Gate. By 1853, although the city had been six times destroyed by fire, it had become "the fourth if not the third city on the continent." Its schools and churches, its bars and theaters, as well as its bookstores, testified to its extraordinary growth. Its only constant attribute was change. San Francisco's growth, however, was by no means continuous. There were setbacks occasioned by a surfeit of goods, "overtrading, speculation, and extravagance." The bank fail-ures of 1854 precipitated a business crisis the next year with several bankruptcies. The overabundant consignment of books from the East resulted in overstocked bookshops in San Francisco many of which succumbed to failure in the very midst of the Golden Age. Nor did the activity of the Vigilance Committee tend to quell the ups and downs of finance.[10]

Nonetheless, signs of good omen pointed to a San Francisco trade in antiquarian books. The *Alta California* of 8 June 1853 heralded the first such omen under the headline,

SHAKESPEARE EDITION of 1632

A Quarto [sic] Volume of the impression of 1632, (the second published) in excellent preservation, with a curious woodcut of the great poet, is offered for sale.

A copy of the same impression discovered by J. Payne Collier, Esq., led to the publication of that gentleman's edition of Shakespeare, which has attracted so much attention in the world of literature.

It may be seen at   Cooke, Kenney & Co.[11]

And so, apparently a Second Folio Shakespeare was offered for sale in San Francisco in the year 1853. Just how Cooke, Kenney, dealers in "Standard works" and "valuable library books such as every one ought to have," obtained a copy of the Second Folio does not seem to have been recorded. Still, a record of its presence in San Francisco five years after the discovery of gold does exist.

So too does the record of San Francisco's first specialist antiquarian bookstore. Established in 1854 by Epes Ellery and Augustus Doyle, the Antiquarian Book Store was the "first in San Francisco to deal [almost] exclusively in secondhand books."[12] Its stock included "Bound editions" of "liberal works," that is, writings by Thomas Paine and Volney, along with such literary classics as *Don Quixote* and *Gil Blas*, *Robinson Crusoe* and *Tom Brown*, not to mention "*Fancys* [sic] in the French language." The shelves of the Antiquarian Book Store yielded editions of Burton's *Anatomy of Melancholy*, Chesterfield's *Letters*, Aristotle, Shakespeare and Byron. Having purchased "The Spiritual Bookstore" of Valentine & Co., Epes Ellery announced in 1858: "I am the only dealer in spiritual books [i.e., works on spiritualism] in San Francisco." Eighteenth-century deism and nineteenth-century pseudo-science were available at the

Antiquarian Book Store where "New and Second Hand Books" were "bought and sold or exchanged on liberal terms. Always on hand a great variety of books on all subjects—some very rare."

When in 1862 Epes Ellery abandoned bookselling, his place was taken by Isidore Nathan Choynski, a Prussian who added secondhand and "valuable books" as a feature of his shop. A large man who sported a stovepipe hat, Choynski had operated a billiard parlor in San Francisco before he opened a bookshop on Second Street.[13] Specialists in foreign books such as Payot in French and Mendheim in German were joined during the 1860s by the stationers Frank & Co., who sold at their San Francisco branch the Hebrew books published by their father Henry Frank, New York publisher.[14] And so cosmopolitan books, new and antiquarian, were coming to this cosmopolis on the shores of the Pacific.

One of the most notable as well as one of the most fascinating of San Francisco's early booksellers—a survivor like most of them of gold-rush days—was a bearded Bavarian named Anton Roman.[15] In 1849, at age twenty-three, Roman crossed the plains to California, joining the gold seekers on the Trinity River, and at Scott Bar he struck gold. In December 1851 he entered a bookstore on the west side of the Plaza in Brenham Place, San Francisco, and exchanged over a hundred ounces of gold dust for books. The shop where this auspicious transaction took place bore the name of one of John H. Still's numerous partnerships, Burgess, Gilbert and Still. Having peddled his books from camp to camp in the Shasta mining region, the migratory bookseller from Bavaria established his Shasta Book Store opposite the El Dorado Hotel in 1853, exchanging Shakespeare and Byron, Milton and Gray, stationery and musical instruments, for gold from the diggings. Four years later he left the northern counties and set up his stand in San Francisco.

By the end of the decade Roman opened a bookstore on the west side of Montgomery Street, north of California. His was a departmentalized shop with a wide range of offerings, new and old, from guides and manuals to elaborate gift books. In 1860 the San Francisco Directory listed him as "importer and wholesale bookseller," and indeed he did sell books on the grand scale. The same year his seventy-one page *Catalogue of Books* specified under sixteen different headings a stock that catered to the requirements of an expanding community. The following year a 259-page *Catalogue raisonné* of standard authors was issued. Roman naturally offered to California customers—pioneers and settlers, miners and homesteaders—books on minerals and their processing, on peat and grape culture, landscape gardening and farm implements. But his stock was not confined to such essentials. At his bookstore an enormous variety of books new and antiquarian could be found, among them "the finest library bound books, embracing all the standard works in the English language." On the center tables were placed works to attract the bibliophile, "the rarest and most costly editions of the poets and favorite authors of the age, together with the choicest gift-books and other *recherche* publications of the English and American press." By the mid-1860s, his stock was valued at $75 or $85,000.

Some of that stock consisted of his own publications, for Roman was becoming a California publisher of note. Many of his books, however, he imported from the East, and in time he established agents not only in New York but in Paris and London, from whom he received shipments which certainly included some antiquarian items. In 1867, with the succcessful pioneer voyage of the Pacific Mail S.S. *Colorado* to Hong Kong, China was brought closer to California than ever before. As a result, there arose an interest in Orientalia which Roman proceeded to supply with books on Yedo, Peking, and Upper and Lower Amoor. With the completion of the Overland Railway in 1869, the attraction to volumes about the West was stimulated, and once again Roman responded with books that were carried by semi-monthly steamer from San Francisco to the East.

In 1871 Roman moved to 11 Montgomery Street, to a building in the Lick House Block adorned with a frescoed ceiling and described as "a magnificent temple of letters" and "the only exclusive book store on the Pacific Coast." Despite the hyperbole, Roman's self-portrait had a kernel of truth. "Here we are," he boasted, "geographically isolated from the great world's throng, and yet the greatest cities cannot show a more complete establishment than ours." Roman's establishment was certainly "complete" enough to include something for nearly every bibliophilic taste. Unfortunately, the Panic of 1873 threatened that "complete establishment," and by the end of the decade A. Roman & Co. was forced to make an assignment for the benefit of its creditors. The founder subsequently went into the field of subscription books, and died in 1903. He is rightly remembered as publisher of *The Overland Monthly* and of Bret Harte's *Outcroppings* rather than as bookseller. Yet he established a bookstore of stature that answered literary tastes for the new and the antiquarian between the 1850s and the 1870s. His emporium had a vital place in the extravaganza that was San Francisco.

If Roman is recalled as publisher rather than as bookseller, his great colleague and competitor Hubert Howe Bancroft is today better known as historian than as bibliopole.[16] Yet he too was, as he put it, "country boy" turned bookseller before he became an historian and a specialist collector on the grand scale. Born in Granville, Ohio, in 1832, Bancroft could boast not only a New England ancestry but a relationship through marriage with the Buffalo bookseller-publisher George Derby. By the time he reached his teens, Bancroft, who is said to have read the Bible at age three, was ready to work in his brother-in-law's shop. In 1852 G. H. Derby & Co. decided to open a branch book and stationery store in San Francisco. As J. C. Derby recalled, "San Francisco . . . had then just emerged from scarcely more than a Mexican settlement to a thriving young city. . . . it was decided to stock the store with about five thousand dollars worth of merchandise, and the goods were duly shipped, by a sailing vessel, around Cape Horn. At the same time our firm sent to San Francisco to take charge of the business two of their clerks, Hubert H. Bancroft and George L. Kenney, both of whom my brother had trained to the book business in Buffalo."[17] These plans were unfortunately altered by the death of Bancroft's brother-in-law George Derby, and the consequent sale of the San Francisco consignment. Nonetheless, Bancroft's sister—Derby's widow—advanced a loan of some $10,000 to her young brother, and with that sum he built up both credit and stock in the East. In October 1856 he boarded the Panama steamer for San Francisco, rented a storeroom on Montgomery Street, and by December, with his partner George L. Kenney, founded the firm of H. H. Bancroft & Co.

The Bancroft store was stocked with books and stationery which had been despatched by the Cape Horn route to California. Eastern publishers continued to send books on consignment. Some antiquarian books undoubtedly found a place among the firm's early offerings of miscellaneous volumes, standard British classics, contemporary poetry and literary works. As for the proprietor, he slept on a cot behind the counter, swept the shop, and opened the cases. Sales at Bancroft's mounted, and the staff was enlarged.

Then, in 1859, the firm decided to bring out a San Francisco handbook, and another turning point in Bancroft's history was reached. For the compilation of the *Hand Book Almanac*, Bancroft gathered together all the books in his shop relating to California, and almost from the start he formed a philosophy regarding collections. "A collection of books," he would write, " . . . has its history and individuality. . . . they are not found in the market for sale, ready made; there must have been sometime the engendering idea, followed by a long natural development."[18]

That "long natural development" in Bancroft's career now followed. From the nucleus of seventy-five books originally assembled from his shelves, he built in time a library of some 50,000 volumes and provided a building to house them. As the country boy had turned into a bookseller, the bookseller was turning into a collector-bibliophile. As Derby wrote, "Young Bancroft early saw the importance of preserving the prehistorical records of the Pacific States. . . . He began to purchase everything that could be found pertaining to the Pacific Slope, Mexico, and Central America. . . . purchasing every book, map and manuscript printed or written in this territory or Empire relating to it, that could be found in Mexico, Central America, or in the Eastern States, even visiting Europe several times in search of needed material."[19]

From his San Francisco colleagues—from the book stalls of Epes Ellery and others—Bancroft added to his collection on the Pacific States. From European marts, from the stalls and antiquarian warehouses of Paris and London, Madrid, Florence and Rome, from catalogues of dealers, Bancroft acquired not only books but entire libraries. Andrade's Biblioteca Mejicana; Ephraim George Squier's library of Central American sources; José Fernando Ramirez's manuscripts and books relating to Jesuit missions—all became part of the Bancroft holdings. Bancroft himself was no bibliomaniac. As he commented, "Duplicates, fine bindings, and rare editions seemed to me of less importance than the subject-matter of the work."[20] However, when his interest in text was titillated, he reveled in books. "Books! Books!," he exlaimed, "I revelled in books. After buying and selling, after ministering to others all my life, I would now enjoy them."[21]

Actually, the Civil War years had been kind to Bancroft's book business. The state of California remained on the gold standard during that period, and hence, while Bancroft's eastern accounts could be paid in depreciated greenbacks, his receipts from the West were all in gold. The tall, broad-shouldered Argonaut with full beard and mustache, wavy iron-gray hair and large expressive eyes was becoming a man of wealth. He was not intimidated by prices. As he wrote, " . . . in rare books the tendency of prices is upward, the number of collectors increasing, and the difficulty in finding good books also increasing. We have always found it more difficult to obtain a really rare book in good condition than to sell it. To the genuine lover of books it may be said: First find the book you want, then buy it, and if you think you have been extravagant, repent at your leisure, and by the time you have truly repented the book will have increased sufficiently in value to give you full absolution."[22]

Bancroft certainly found "full absolution" for his grandiose purchases. In 1869, in a cow pasture on the south side of San Francisco's Market Street, he erected the Bancroft Building to house what was becoming the "largest bookselling and publishing business west of Chicago."[23] This immense five-story brick building with its gargoyled cornice was, even more impressively than Roman's establishment, departmentalized. On the first floor was placed the firm's retail department, on the second the stationery and music instruments were stocked, on the third and fourth the printing presses and binderies. The top story, the *sanctum sanctorum*, was the depository for Bancroft's library and for the workshop that was turning into a history factory. There, alphabetically arranged, was shelved the library of Pacific Coast books. In time that library became so extensive, and Bancroft's determination to provide the history of a frontier civilization so consuming, that his collection resembled a "vast army of authors, arranged in battalions, regiments, and companies."[24] Bancroft, who had sold antiquarian books along with new publications, now gave himself up to the task of converting his own rare books and pamphlets into a grandiose historical instrument. As his library expanded, the books he authored or commissioned rolled from his presses, from the first volume of *Native Races* which appeared in 1875 to his last volume in 1917. Bancroft, it has been said, "caught the history of a civilization before that civilization disappeared." He was able to do so thanks to the rare and antiquarian works he assembled—this "frontier bookseller who turned historian."[25]

San Francisco of the 1860s overcame not only the "pandemonium of the mines" but the "fire and flood" that alternated "sway over the destinies" of its citizens.[26] While California's gold standard swelled the incomes of many San Francisco dealers during the Civil War years, the completion of the Overland Railway in 1869 proved a not altogether unmixed blessing to them. Once the railroad was completed, prospective purchasers were tempted to buy in the East instead of in San

Francisco, and local prices fell. Nevertheless the San Francisco book-seller survived.

Bancroft's retail department was purchased by another Argonaut from New York State, Horace Hawkins Moore, who had been trained in the old and rare book department of Bartlett and Welford.[27] In 1853 he journeyed to San Francisco, tried mining, went to Arizona where he was attacked by the Apaches, and, having sown his wild oats of adventure, established a book business in San Francisco. Of all the antiquarian books imported into San Francisco between 1870 and 1890, it is said that over half were acquired by Moore. In each of them he placed the cost price in small Greek characters. He journeyed east semi-annually to add to his stock, and his attendance at auctions was faithful. At the sale of Joseph Winans' library, Moore was the heaviest buyer, buying back many of the items he had himself sold to that collector. His shop attracted bibliophiles and scholars, as well as wine experts, one of his customers being George Malter, a vineyardist from Fresno who paid the bookseller in wines and brandies. There is only an ap-parent connection between that circumstance and the fact that on the first of every year Moore dove into the Bay from a height of fifty feet, a practice he continued until he was nearly eighty.

During the 1870s and 1880s the West Coast continued to be enriched by imports from the East Coast and from Europe—imports not only of books but of book expertise. Adolph Bourgoin, born in Paris, came to San Francisco after the Franco-Prussian War and worked as a watch-maker. Having received books instead of cash in payment for a repair job, he displayed them successfully in his window and in the early 1880s set up as a bookseller. Affable, courteous, mercurial, Bourgoin had a taste for large illustrated works, and is said to have been "perhaps the first dealer in San Francisco to import a large number of second-hand books from France."[28]

Shortly after Bourgoin entered the book business, another European emigrant opened an antiquarian shop in San Francisco, and the Parisian watchmaker found a colleague in an Irish shoemaker. Patrick Joseph Healy,[29] born in Ireland, had been a journeyman shoemaker in the United States, driven army wagons near the front during the Civil War, mined in the West, and studied law before he opened his first bookshop in 1883 at 104 O'Farrell Street, San Francisco. Between that time and 1893 when he appeared on Powell Street, Healy developed a reputation as a specialist in Californiana and as one of the first dealers

in the West "to recognize and emphasize the value of pamphlets."
According to his colleague Robert E. Cowan, although Healy was not
a rare book specialist, "many of the rarest of early local imprints . . .
passed through his hands," among them a *Mohawk Primer* which was
sold to Dodd, Mead in New York for what was then the highest price
paid for a single volume in California, $500. Not all of Healy's treasures
went east. The major portion of the consular papers and correspondence
of William A. Leidesdorff which he acquired ended in the Huntington
Library. At one time Healy, who obtained his rarities either at auction
or through the purchase of libraries, is credited with having in stock
"between 7,000 and 10,000 pamphlets of Californiana." Thanks to
dealers like Bancroft and Healy, San Francisco was learning to collect
and record its history even while that history was in the making.

By the 1890s, while there was still no single outstanding bookseller
trading exclusively in rare books in San Francisco, the city's general
and secondhand book business had come of age. For this, four booksellers were largely responsible: William Doxey, Harold Holmes, Robert
E. Cowan and Paul Elder. They all had connections of one sort or
another either among themselves or with earlier colleagues.

William Doxey had had his first exposure to the book business in
the employ of Bancroft and Company.[30] Born in England, he came to
San Francisco in 1878 and was, as his biographer puts it, "nomadic in
the first stages of his San Francisco career." In 1881 he was dealing in
"books, stationery and engraving" on Market Street, and by the 1890s
this "brisk, bright, little Englishman who walked on his toes" had
become what has been described as "San Francisco's most fashionable
book dealer." By that time too he occupied a shop under the Palace
Hotel where he offered fine books imported from England, folio volumes
of colored prints and etchings, works on travel, antiquities and architecture, and fine bindings. When Zaehnsdorf visited San Francisco, he
naturally found his way to Doxey's, and offered to bind a book for the
proprietor when he returned to London. Zaehnsdorf fulfilled his promise; unfortunately Doxey's less than knowledgeable assistant sold the
volume by mistake for $2.50. Along with fine bindings, prints of Dick-
ens were a favorite with Doxey, who also displayed in his windows the
works of Eugene Field and of Robert Louis Stevenson in all editions.
His shop became a social and intellectual center, "a favorite gathering
place of writers" and artists. It was so not merely because of the books
Doxey sold but because of his publications. Between May 1895 and

April 1897 he published *The Lark*, an illustrated monthly issued by Les Jeunes in San Francisco and conducted by Gelett Burgess whose "Purple Cow" first grazed there. In addition, Doxey published the Lark Classics including the *Rubaiyat* of Omar Khayyam as well as works by Kipling, Andrew Lang and others. The flight of *The Lark* was high but not enduring. By the turn of the century, Doxey emerged briefly from bankruptcy and subsequently left San Francisco, spending his last years in the rare book department of A. C. McClurg and Company of Chicago.

During the mauve decade, the witty and jovial William Doxey may have been San Francisco's "most fashionable book dealer." It was re-served for yet another San Franciscan to become proprietor of what would become the "oldest antiquarian book store continuously active in California."[31] In 1894, Robert Holmes started the Holmes Book Company of San Francisco. A year later, at age seventeen, his son Harold entered the firm. Although his formal schooling had ended with graduation from grammar school, Harold Holmes was "a man with a book always in his hand." He developed his father's business so that within ten years the company boasted some 40,000 volumes and issued a first catalogue which included Californian, Mexican and Indian items. In the regional specialization that had begun preserving the records of Western American history, Harold C. Holmes played a vital role. He collected pioneer booksellers' labels—and pioneer booksellers; he amassed early letters of California pioneers and researched pioneer writers. His acquisitions came from barn and attic, ghost town and junk yard, secondhand furniture store and old mining town. He gathered together ephemera relating to early Wells Fargo days; the first and only book bearing the imprint of Coloma, California, site of the discovery of gold; a file of Bret Harte's letters and manuscripts; the diary of a San Francisco pioneer druggist; a broadside—found between the pages of a book—celebrating the completion of the transcontinental railroad. The records of events that his predecessors had lived through, Harold C. Holmes acquired and preserved. Through his hands passed the 1850 State Con-stitution; the only known complete file of the first newspaper published in California; an association copy of Figueroa's *Manifesto*, the first book printed in California.

Thanks to Holmes' efforts, both private and institutional collections of Western Americana were developed. Over the years he scouted the field, rescuing rare Western Americana from oblivion, salvaging local ephemera. The earthquake and fire of 1906 consumed a large percentage of pre-1860 California imprints, along with Harold Holmes' Market Street bookshop. From the "mass of ashes, smoke and bricks" he re-emerged, beginning again the building of store and of collections. Through the years he received at his shop such notables as Carl Sandburg and Joaquin Miller; Charles Howard Shinn, author of *Mining Camps*, and Hubert Howe Bancroft, now "historiographer extraordinary." "For many years dean of California antiquarian book dealers," Harold C. Holmes stimulated El Dorado's interest in the records of its unparalleled history.

Connections exist everywhere, especially in the small world of antiquarian booksellers. In 1897, when Patrick J. Healy decided to operate from his home, much of his stock was purchased by yet another San Francisco dealer, Robert Ernest Cowan.[32] Born in Toronto, Canada, in 1862, Cowan had been brought to the City of the Golden Gate a year after the completion of the transcontinental railroad. After studying medicine and music and developing an interest in philately and Californiana, he opened his first bookshop on Powell Street in 1895— Cowan's Old Book Store. A few years after the Healy purchase, he acquired for $100 the papers of the coast merchant William Heath Davis. By 1902 Cowan decided to house his stock in his home, placing his treasures in the back parlor. Thanks to this decision, he successfully weathered the fire and earthquake of 1906. Once the loosened plaster had been swept away and the bricks of San Francisco cooled, local institutions began rebuilding their lost libraries. And so, with "more than 75% of his stock intact," Cowan was able to supply not only public libraries but private collections as well, among them those of Wagner and Macdonald.

Cowan "seldom took any interest in a book published after about 1870," and he was perhaps more engrossed in bibliography than in bibliopoly. Today he is remembered less as a bookseller than as the bibliographer of the history of California. Of the 4,700 items in the Cowan bibliography, 3,500 had at one time been in his own library. Yet this bibliographer of California who became librarian for William Andrews Clark, Jr., really "never ceased his book buying and selling," often buying back from the heirs of a collector the books he had originally supplied. It was he who in 1916 negotiated the sale of Augustin S. Macdonald's collection of Californiana to Henry E. Huntington for $25,000, and it was he who in 1935 sold the overland narratives in the John L. Hitchcock collection to the University of

California at Los Angeles. A bookseller, whether he makes his bid for immortality as historian or publisher or, as in Cowan's case, as bibliographer, is always a bookseller.

Although the name of Paul Elder is associated with the Tomoyé Press, and he is recalled as publisher rather than as bookseller, he too sold books in California.[33] Moreover, his career epitomizes those connections that are so interwoven in the antiquarian trade. Paul Elder was trained by William Doxey, and would in turn train John Howell. After he left Doxey in 1898, Elder set up as dealer in new and secondhand books and provided threatening competition to his former employer. John Howell recalled the personalities encountered at Elder's shop on Post Street after he joined the staff in 1903: "It was at Paul Elder's that I met many interesting people: Henry Huntington, Ben Greet, Ethel Barrymore and her uncle John Drew, Margaret Anglin, Billie Burke, and Schumann-Heink among them. Ethel Barrymore was young and tall and graceful and quite informal. She thought nothing of sitting on the floor while she examined a pile of books; she spoke of Joseph Conrad and recommended particularly that I read him."[34] The fire of 1906 destroyed the Elder bookshop, and for three years the proprietor transplanted his operations to New York where, with John Henry Nash, he offered the publications of the Tomoyé Press.

By 1912 Paul Elder's manager determined to strike out for himself. John Howell, who had worked on the *San Francisco Call* after his studies at the University of California, and served a long apprenticeship with Paul Elder, opened his first shop on the mezzanine floor of 107 Grant Avenue. As he explained, "Although I had practically no capital, I decided to specialize on old and rare books and to make connections in England and France."[35] His decision was brilliantly implemented. Within a few years the tall and portly Howell had resettled at 434 Post Street where he "could provide an atmosphere in keeping with the business of old and rare books." As one of his employees commented, Howell's books "reflected his own taste," which inclined to seventeenth-century English titles as well as Western Americana.[36]

Annual visits east replenished his stock and brought him into personal contact with collectors of great stature: A. Edward Newton, John Gribbel of Philadelphia, Henry C. Folger for whom he negotiated the sale of the William T. Smedley Shakespeare-Bacon library and to whom he sold for $2,000 Lincoln's copy of Shakespeare. Treasures flowed into John Howell's shop: a presentation Izaak Walton; Dickens' copy of

Pamela; the letters and memoranda written by Sir Walter Scott to John Gibson, these last sold to Hugh Walpole who had been searching for them "since boyhood."[37] Howell could also boast a copy of the *Narrative of adventures* of Zenas Leonard (Clearfield, Pa., 1839)*, the prime source for the Walker expedition to the Yosemite Valley. This had been part of the library purchased from John L. Hitchcock. Hitchcock was the son of that Hitchcock who had been a partner in the firm of Marvin and Hitchcock, San Francisco's pioneer booksellers. Howell in turn sold the Zenas Leonard to Robert E. Cowan, a transaction that certainly linked the San Francisco book world of past and present.

Such links continued. As Howell had served his apprenticeship with Paul Elder, David Magee served his with John Howell. Born in Yorkshire, England, son of a cleric and grandson of the archbishop of York, the sparkling and untheological David Magee was literate from birth and could "scarcely remember the day I could not read."[38] Early in 1925, after an English public school education and a pedestrian period in the office of an export-import firm, he sailed aboard the *Orca* for the new world and crossed the continent by train. Through the good offices of Albert M. Bender, young Magee was employed by John Howell for $75 a month plus $10 worth of books from stock.

In his battle of the books with his employer David Magee was definitely on the side of the moderns, and by the early spring of 1928 he decided to set up for himself. With $5,000 on loan, he opened on Post Street, and after an initial sale of a fore-edge painting to Russell Garton, was on his way. That way was punctuated by frequent book hunts in England where Magee searched principally for nineteenth- and twentieth-century American and English manuscripts and literature, as well as earlier material.

Leona Rostenberg, reviewing his autobiography *Infinite Riches*, commented:

With the development of his stock Magee naturally acquired a variety of customers, among them the Thomas More collector Maurice Harrison whose holdings were augmented by exceedingly rare contemporary translations of *Utopia*; Albert "Mickey" Bender, barely five feet tall with a cleft palate, who, "like many men of small stature . . . loved big books." . . .

* Henry R. Wagner bought a copy of this in Chicago for $75 and sold it to Huntington who disposed of it as a duplicate. See Ruth Frey Axe, *Henry R. Wagner: An Intimate Profile*, 1979 AB Bookman's Yearbook, p. 28.

Publications of the Grabhorn Press long fascinated Magee, and in 1960 he issued a splendid catalogue of five hundred Grabhorn Press items. One of Magee's most important contributions to the antiquarian field—not mentioned in his memoirs—is his comprehensive collection of Victorian literature catalogued in three handsome volumes and sold en bloc to Brigham Young University Library.[39]

By that time the charming and modest David Magee had been joined by younger colleagues who were building the future in San Francisco, among them Robert Haines and Robert L. Rose who opened the Argonaut Book Shop on Kearny Street in 1940, Edward L. Sterne who, after specializing in "air material" in Sacramento, launched a San Francisco antiquarian bookshop in 1951 "with the mezzanine devoted to aeronautica," and John Swingle who began as a book scout in Orange County in 1955.[40] Born in Yorkshire, Ireland, Canada, Ohio or New York State, venturing west overland or by way of Cape Horn or Panama, San Francisco's antiquarian dealers had for over a century brought to the Pacific coast the riches of the East. Now they, or their descendants, were returning those riches to collectors the world over. Thanks in large measure to its antiquarian dealers, the cosmopolitan City of the Golden Gate can still be mined for treasure.

NOTES

1. *Alta* (11 January 1853) quoted in Hugh Sanford Cheney Baker, "A History of the Book Trade in California 1849–1859," *California Historical Society Quarterly* XXX:3 (September 1951), pp. 249 f. This extremely informative three-part article ran in the *California Historical Society Quarterly* as follows: XXX:2 (June 1951), pp. 97–115; XXX:3 (September 1951), pp. 249–267; and XXX:4 (December 1951), pp. 353–367. For the New Atlantis see Franklin Walker, *San Francisco's Literary Frontier* (New York: Knopf, 1939), p. 14. Another informative article on California booksellers and collectors is Warren R. Howell, "Exploring California Book-Trade History," *AB Bookman's Weekly* (8 January 1979), pp. 240–265.

2. Baker, "A History of the Book Trade," XXX:2 (June 1951), p. 98.

3. Frank Luther Mott, *American Journalism* (New York: Macmillan, 1950), p. 290.

4. Baker, "A History of the Book Trade," XXX:2 (June 1951), p. 103.

5. *Alta* (18 June 1851), quoted in Baker, "A History of the Book Trade," XXX:2 (June 1951), pp. 108–109.

6. *Alta* (8 March 1851), quoted in ibid., p. 104.

7. For John Hamilton Still, see Baker, "A History of the Book Trade," XXX:2 (June 1951), pp. 100–101, 113–114, XXX:3 (September 1951), p. 256; Hazel N. Chambers, "John Hamilton Still San Francisco's First Bookseller," *The Book Club of California Quarterly News-Letter* XV:4 (Fall 1950), pp. 75–80; Robert Ernest Cowan, *Booksellers of Early San Francisco* (Los Angeles: Ward Ritchie Press, 1953), pp. 3–4.

8. In the San Francisco *Daily Alta* (6 May 1850), quoted in Chambers, "John Hamilton Still," p. 76. For the remark on rare pamphlets containing the Still book label, see Warren R. Howell, "Exploring California Book-Trade History," *AB* (8 January 1979), p. 240.

9. Baker, "A History of the Book Trade," XXX, 101. For Marvin and Hitchcock, see also pp. 105–106, 113, and Cowan, *Booksellers of Early San Francisco*, p. 75.

10. For details about the decade, see Baker, "A History of the Book Trade," XXX, 109, 249, 254, 352, 364, 367; Eliza W. Farnham, *California In-Doors and Out (1856)* (Nieuwkoop: De Graaf, 1972), p. xxvi; Madeleine B. Stern, *Heads & Headlines: The Phrenological Fowlers* (Norman: University of Oklahoma Press, 1971), pp. 120, 121; Madeleine B. Stern, "Two Letters from the Sophisticates of Santa Cruz," *The Book Club of California Quarterly News-Letter* XXXIII:3 (Summer 1968), pp. 51–62.

11. Quoted in Baker, "A History of the Book Trade," XXX, 250. George Kenney was Bancroft's young companion in the California venture of 1852. See Baker, "A History of the Book Trade," XXX, 108. He became Bancroft's partner.

12. For details regarding Ellery and Doyle, see Baker, "A History of the Book Trade," XXX, 254–255, 354–356, 365; Cowan, *Booksellers of Early San Francisco*, pp. 26, 74.

13. Cowan, *Booksellers of Early San Francisco*, pp. 26–28.

14. Baker, "A History of the Book Trade," XXX, 357; Madeleine B. Stern, *Books and Book People in 19th-Century America* (New York: Bowker, 1978), pp. 235–236.

15. For Anton Roman, see Baker, "A History of the Book Trade," XXX, 356–357; Stern, *Books and Book People*, pp. 210–231.

16. For H. H. Bancroft, see Baker, "A History of the Book Trade," XXX, 108, 354; Hubert Howe Bancroft, *Literary Industries: A Memoir* (New York: Harper, 1891), passim; "Hubert Howe Bancroft," *DAB*; John Walton Caughey, *Hubert Howe Bancroft: Historian of the West* (Berkeley and Los Angeles: University of California Press, 1946), passim; Cowan, *Booksellers of Early San Francisco*, pp. 14–23; J. C. Derby, *Fifty Years Among Authors, Books and Publishers* (New York: Carleton, 1884), pp. 31–33; Walker, *San Francisco's Literary Frontier*, pp. 302–315.

17. Derby, *Fifty Years*, p. 31.
18. Bancroft, *Literary Industries*, pp. 119–120.
19. Derby, *Fifty Years*, pp. 32–33.
20. Bancroft, *Literary Industries*, p. 89.
21. Walker, *San Francisco's Literary Frontier*, p. 306.
22. Bancroft, *Literary Industries*, p. 123.
23. Walker, *San Francisco's Literary Frontier*, p. 302.
24. Bancroft, *Literary Industries*, p. 119.
25. Walker, *San Francisco's Literary Frontier*, p. 315.
26. Bancroft, *Literary Industries*, pp. 57, 58.
27. Cowan, *Booksellers of Early San Francisco*, pp. 29–35.
28. Ibid., pp. 38–42.
29. Ibid., pp. 60–69.
30. For William Doxey, see Cowan, *Booksellers of Early San Francisco*, pp. 51–59; Flodden W. Heron, "The William Doxey Bookshop," *The Book Club of California Quarterly News-Letter* XV:4 (Fall 1950), pp. 83–85; Wallace Kibbee, "William Doxey and 'Les Jeunes,' " *The Book Club of California Quarterly News-Letter* VI:3 (December 1938), pp. 5–8; Robert O'Brien, "The Doxey Story," *The Book Club of California Quarterly News-Letter* XV:2 (Spring 1950), pp. 27–31; John Tebbel, *A History of Book Publishing in the United States* (New York: Bowker, 1975), II, 468.
31. Harold C. Holmes, *Some Random Reminiscences of an Antiquarian Bookseller* (Oakland, Calif.: Holmes, 1967), passim; Leona Rostenberg and Madeleine B. Stern, "Antiquarian Booksellers and Their Memoirs," *AB Bookman's Weekly* (22–29 December 1980), pp. 4190–4192.
32. Cowan, *Booksellers of Early San Francisco*, pp. ix–xiii, 79–100.
33. For Paul Elder, see Marion B. Allen, "The Tomoyé Press," *The Book Club of California Quarterly News-Letter* XVI:4 (Fall 1951), pp. 84–88; Cowan, *Booksellers of Early San Francisco*, p. 74.
34. John Howell, "A California Bookman," *The Book Club of California Quarterly News-Letter* XIX:1 (Winter 1953), p. 4. For a more detailed treatment of Howell, see Warren R. Howell, "Two San Francisco Bookmen: An Interview Conducted by Ruth Teiser," Typescript (Berkeley, Calif.: Bancroft Library, 1967).
35. Howell, "A California Bookman," p. 5 and passim (pp. 3–10).
36. David Magee, *Infinite Riches: The Adventures of a Rare Book Dealer* (New York: Eriksson, 1973), p. 52.
37. Ibid., p. 54. Leona Rostenberg and Madeleine Stern sold to John Howell in 1950 an Estienne Greek Testament of 1550 which they had purchased on their first European book hunt of 1947.
38. Magee, *Infinite Riches*, p. 4 and passim.

39. Rostenberg and Stern, "Antiquarian Booksellers and Their Memoirs,"
pp. 4204 f.

40. Autobiographical sketches of booksellers written in 1962 in reply to an
inquiry from Wilbur J. Smith, Head, Department of Special Collections, University of California at Los Angeles Library.

8

Los Angeles

A titan among West Coast booksellers once suggested that the Rounce and Coffin book club differed from the Zamorano Club in three respects: the former was "not exclusive"; on the other hand it was "very disorderly," and it "never took itself very seriously."[1] Is it possible that it is in precisely that trinity of ways that the city of Los Angeles differs from other parts of the West? Certainly something of the distinctive flavor suggested by those differences has descended upon the booksellers of Southern California. They emerged and flourished against a peculiar background. Their development came later than that of their peers in the North, and perhaps for that very reason their chauvinism and their spirit of competitiveness were sharpened. Surely the exterior climate of the City of the Angels has had some effect upon the interior climate of bibliopolic Angelinos. Similarly, the presence in their midst of that unparalleled cinematic outpost known as Hollywood helped influence if it did not shape some aspect of bookselling history in Southern California. Whatever the reasons—meteorological or geographical, historical or sociological—the booksellers of Los Angeles form a phenomenon within a phenomenon.

In 1850, when gold rush San Francisco was mushrooming into a metropolis with bookstalls at every corner, Los Angeles was a settlement in cattle country, the hub of the ranchos. The sun beat down upon its adobe houses, its plaza, its church. The northern portion of the town was "laid out in streets," while its southern part consisted of "gardens, vineyards, and orchards." The wine produced from its grapes resembled, it was said, "the best Madeira." Game abounded—geese and duck, quail and deer, elk and antelope. Of the inhabitants of the Pueblo de los Angelos an observer noted that they "are of the better and wealthier class of Californians." Some of them slaughtered cattle, some of them danced and fiddled, many of them gambled at monte and billiards. Their future, according to one visitor at least, was bright, for he predicted, "Possessing a climate of unequaled mildness and a soil of great fertility, it must inevitably, ere long, be surrounded by a large population."[2]

The population of Los Angeles had the church for its prayers and the tavern for its roistering, but it was not until the early 1860s, when "Spanish California ownership passed to American-born merchants and settlers,"[3] that it could boast its first bookstore.

Samuel Hellman, who had arrived in the village as early as 1855, naturally did not stock antiquarian items.[4] His wares included books and new music received "by every steamer," along with stationery and cigars, hardware, paints and glass. Whatever the motley nature of his "wholesale and retail" shop, it marked the beginnings of a trade that would in time help reshape the hub of the ranchos into a hub of American culture.

That reshaping was given a strong impetus during the latter part of the nineteenth century. In the Centennial year of 1876 the Southern Pacific Railroad entered the City of the Angels. A decade later—in 1885—the Santa Fe Railroad reached southern California.[5] In the wake of the subsequent real estate boom, pioneer booksellers—some dealing in new books, others in secondhand—set up their shingles.

Frederick D. Jones, born in South China, Maine, in 1855—the year Samuel Hellman arrived in Los Angeles—was educated at Haverford College and spent some time in Kansas City before he opened a bookstore on Los Angeles' South Main Street in 1887.[6] Later, in a "big rambling place" on West First Street, with "balconies and crowded aisles," Jones' Bookstore offered to Angelinos a variety of stationery and ink, a computer patented by the owner, and an array of secondhand books: schoolbooks and medical books, law books, reference books, religious books. A true California cultist, Jones called himself an "Evolutionary Socialist." His presence in Los Angeles, which continued until the 1930s, certainly played a part in the "evolution" of the city's book trade.

Jones was joined in time by several colleagues: J. W. Fowler who hailed from Iowa started Fowler and Colwell on West Second Street in 1888, opening another store a decade later where secondhand books were stocked in the basement. Like the Jones bookstore, Fowler's was gifted with longevity, for in 1938 Fowler Brothers celebrated its golden jubilee in the book business.

Despite the Panic of 1893 and the depression that lingered on, new and secondhand bookstores continued to rise on Los Angeles city streets. C. C. Parker, whose wing collar added to his immaculate style and gentility, gave an aristocratic air to the stand between Olive and Grand.[7] Parker not only taught elocution but specialized in new books that embraced "the more lasting and important works of literature." And as C. C. Parker, with gray hair and white mustache, became Old Parker, his colleagues clustered in the city. "The Eclectic Book Store" opened by James Wallen Smith purveyed not only paperback novels but "scarce and valuable books." According to a younger colleague, Smith was "the first to emphasize Californiana." Such an emphasis, preceding the great San Francisco earthquake which spurred so much regional collecting, was notable at the time. J. W. Smith did not die until after the turn of the century when his widow continued the business with Henry W. Collins as manager. Collins, who had had a long apprenticeship with the London firm of Edwin Parsons and Sons, "was probably the first Los Angeles bookseller . . . trained in the Rare Book Trade"[8]—another significant bibliopolic first.

Angelinos of the mauve decade could buy their books not only at the Jones and Fowler bookstores, C. C. Parker's, and "The Eclectic Book Store," but at Stoll and Thayer's "Big Bookstore" on South Spring Street, a "commodious store with a large balcony," or at the Old and Rare Bookshop of Griest and Bauer on Seventh and Broadway. Indeed during the 1890s there appears to have been an efflorescence of bookstores in the garden city of the West.

Just a few miles northeast of Los Angeles, in the San Gabriel Valley, Pasadena was the background for still another book emporium of the 1890s, one endowed not only with longevity but with a vital generative power. In 1894 Adam Clark Vroman opened a new bookstore devoted to new books—a store that indirectly would have some bearing upon the field of antiquarian book collecting.[9] Vroman has been described as a "combination railroad man and aesthete" whom "Sherwood Anderson might have created . . . if God had not." Born in La Salle, Illinois, in 1856, he had worked as train dispatcher and photographer before he opened the Pasadena emporium of books that was destined to become a "potent cultural force." By 1929, at Vroman's-in-the-

Fields, two young employees were at work, both of whom would in their individual ways help mold the bibliophilic taste of Southern California. Lawrence Clark Powell, future librarian, was one of them. He still recalls "Vroman's sweet-smelling basement, perfumed with pine packing-boxes and paper-and-ink." He recalls too how he and his fellow employee, the future printer Ward Ritchie, drove the Vroman truck to Los Angeles "to pick up special orders" from the city's bookshops. By the time Powell and Ritchie had come to Vroman's, that huge shop "with probably the largest wholesale and retail volume of any bookstore in the West" also boasted a "few shelves of first editions and press books." Whatever its stock, the fact that it trained—even for so brief a period—two Southern California bibliophilic giants entitles Vroman's to a niche in antiquarian history.

By 1900, Norman C. Holmes arrived in Los Angeles from San Francisco and opened on South Main Street "a large new and second hand book store."[10] According to that keen observer Lawrence Clark Powell, Holmes' "second-hand stock contained too large a proportion of 'plugs.' " When, in due course, the Holmes Book Company moved to Sixth Street, the proprietor "set up a little platform on the sidewalk, throwing into the street an occasional free book by Robinson Jeffers to bring him an audience." The largest of Holmes' multiple secondhand bookshops in Los Angeles, the Sixth Street location had shelves running up to high ceilings on all sides as well as a balcony room, and those shelves were jammed with secondhand books which "would today be treasures."

And so, the style of Southern California booksellers began to take tentative form; the phenomenon within the phenomenon was being born—the cultural beginnings that would before long blossom into what has been called a "Small Renaissance: Southern California Style."[11]

In that small renaissance a bookstore launched in the year 1905 played a dominant role. Ernest Dawson, a carpenter's son, was born in 1882 and grew up in the mission town of San Luis Obispo.[12] As a boy, he delivered advertising leaflets for the local bookshop, earning his $3 a week by such collateral labors as selling wallpaper, framing pictures, and cooking glue. In his spare time he read and bought books. When Ernest was in his teens the family moved to Los Angeles, and there the boy was employed part time by the Dickensian bookseller Henry Ward. Ward, who had been born in England, was a specialist in paper-covered novels priced from 10 to 25 cents whose provenance was frequently the Salvation Army. An "energetic merchandiser," he also started a rental library, and when he was not selling dime thrillers, he was spouting Shakespeare and Pope. Certainly he offered a future book-seller a colorful and varied apprenticeship, not to mention the oppor-tunity to accumulate a library, for all that he "must occasionally have let some very good items slip through his hands."

Then, in April 1905, young Dawson struck out on his own. Renting part of a store at 713 South Broadway, he placed his own collection of books upon shelves built by his brother-in-law and adorned the window with his own stamp collection. Dawson's Antique Book Shop—the first specialist antiquarian bookstore in Los Angeles—was open for business. Ernest Dawson cannot properly be said to have been meta-morphosed from collector to bookseller until he made his first real killing. At the Salvation Army, which had provided his former em-ployer Henry Ward with much salable merchandise, young Dawson negotiated the purchase of 2,250 books at a penny each. One of the treasures thus obtained was a copy of *Indian Basketry* by O. T. Mason—a work that one of Ward's customers, Le Compte Davis, had sought in vain. Dawson now had the right book for the right party and was about to blossom forth as a bookseller. As he liked to recall:

I jumped on my bicycle and called at his office. "Remember, Mr. Davis, you wanted a copy of this book." It had a paper cover and I told him he could have it for $2.50, have it bound for $1, and for $3.50 he would own a book worth $5.

...I can still see him ringing out the money—$2.50—on the table. I rode down Broadway with my hands on my pockets instead of on the handle bars, jingling the money. I had bought a book for a penny and sold it for $2.50.

Ernest Dawson had become a bookseller. The saga of his triumphs had begun. For a short time in 1906 he formed a brief partnership with Henry Collins, whose antiquarian training, taste and scholarship com-plemented Dawson's energy and interests. At the end of the following year he published his first rare book catalogue which also happened to be the first rare book catalogue issued in the City of the Angels. That "goodly list, containing a number of California items now quite rare," initiated a series of outstanding catalogues that punctuated the years, catalogues introduced by such notables as A. Edward Newton, Robert E. Cowan and Christopher Morley, catalogues that have become ref-erence books, from *Californiana* to *Frontier Americana*, from *Southwest Books* to *Asiatic Books*.

Meanwhile, Ernest Dawson's stock, bookselling techniques and customers were gradually taking shape. At a succession of locations within
proximity of the booksellers' row that would establish itself along West
Sixth Street, Dawson plied his antiquarian trade. Little diverted him—
except his interest in utopian experiments, and for a brief period between 1913 and 1914 the proprietor turned the business over to an
employee to devote his energies to the Voluntary Coöperative Association of Los Angeles. The experiment was short-lived, Dawson doubtless finding a more attainable utopia within the walls of his own premises.
In 1922 Dawson's Book Shop was moved to 627 South Grand Avenue,
a "long one story building . . . remodeled to provide ample window
display and a balcony at the rear," one wall decorated with a large
mural of the "Bookworm." By the time the firm celebrated its fiftieth
anniversary, it had moved to a two story building on South Figueroa
Street.

Whatever the location of Dawson's Book Shop, the tastes and interests of the founder were reflected in the stock that adorned his
shelves. In 1911 Ernest Dawson made his first book-buying trip abroad,
"skimming the cream" from such shops as those of Francis Edwards and
Henry Collins' former employers, Edwin Parsons and Sons. As a result
of such journeys, and through purchases from local libraries and American book auctions as well as from English dealers whose books were
shipped around the Horn, the Dawson wares were assembled: manuscripts and early printed books, color plate books and Western Americana, examples of fine printing and literature that ranged from a "shilling
calf-bound Ossian" to a Kelmscott Chaucer.

As the stock accumulated, Dawson's techniques were crystallized.
He became "a master at merchandising" who aimed at "keeping his
books in a constant state of fluctuation." The prices of slow sellers were
reduced, and a bargain table was placed at the entrance to the shop.
Certain special privileges were offered to customers and potential
customers.

In the shipping room, from time to time, another set of shelves were filled
with books, too shabby and worn to be offered for sale. . . . School boys and
girls, in need of some standard publication, but lacking funds to buy, would
be directed to these shelves to help themselves. Often, book scouts asked for
permission to scan these shelves hopeful of finding a title that might, at best,
bring 25 to 50 cents, perhaps more. Mr. Dawson took especial delight in any

discoveries they made. He never forgot that the springboard for his entrance into the antiquarian book world was his initial purchase of over 2,000 books for one cent apiece from the Salvation Army.

Along the north wall, at the rear of the shop, were large bins under a long counter which contained the "lay-aways." Here, small collectors, temporarily out of funds, could store their book finds and pay as little as 50 cents a week before claiming their treasures.

Young Dawson was being transformed, as the years passed, into Father Dawson, and Father Dawson was aware not only of what he knew but of what he did not know. He reached the ultimate in bookselling wisdom when, in answer to the query, "how long it takes to learn the rare book business?" he replied, "I really wouldn't know. I've only been in the book business fifty years."

Through those years Dawson's Book Shop attracted a variety of customers, from the regal, white-haired Robert Ernest Cowan to the rotund and cherubic Henry R. Wagner, from that authority on Southwest Indians, Frederick Hodge, who himself resembled a "wrinkled . . . old Indian," to the specialist in great printing, John I. Perkins. For Doc Hanna, Dawson supplied Western Americana. For A. Edward Newton and Hugh Walpole, for Thomas Streeter and Everett Graff, the "caravansery of letters" created by Ernest Dawson was a productive source of supply. As one of his peers summed up: Dawson "brought more books into our region than any other single person."

Thanks to reorganization and new partnerships, the bookshop founded by Ernest Dawson developed and expanded. Thomas Neal, who had trained in C. C. Parker's bookstore, came to Dawson's in 1933 and played a role in the acquisition of the Langstroth Library of nineteenth-century books. A graduate of the University of California at Los Angeles, Father Dawson's older son Glen studied illuminated manuscripts and early printing under the Munich antiquarian Emil Hirsch and turned up "several examples of pre-Gutenberg printing" in the Orient before he was made a partner in 1937. A decade later Father Dawson's younger son Muir, who had studied printing during his attendance at Pomona College, joined his brother as partner. By that time Father Dawson retired from the business he had created, and the skills of his sons were reflected, and continue to be reflected, in the new emphasis upon Orientalia, private press work, and western printing.

A year after his retirement, in 1948, Ernest Dawson died. He had assuredly proved "The Importance of Being Earnest" in his life work. To him "a second-hand bookshop" was "the home of a religion . . . a temple." He himself had been a catalyst, a civilizing agent, in Southern California, and his bookshop had sent forth devoted missionaries to keep the faith.

Los Angeles shared flamboyantly in the financial boom of the 1920s.[13] Hollywood was entering its heyday, and its studios required reference books. In 1926, the William Andrews Clark Library was founded, a library that would become distinguished for its great collections of Robert Boyle, Oscar Wilde, John Dryden. The University of California at Los Angeles, in process of building a huge research library, needed and devoured books. In 1928, the great collector Henry E. Huntington opened the library and art gallery that bear his name in San Marino. And, in the years that followed, the earthquake that almost destroyed Long Beach, the great Montrose flood that occurred on New Year's Eve of 1933/1934, even the depression itself did not entirely obliterate the vitality and constructiveness that had marked the roaring twenties in Southern California. Indeed, the Rounce and Coffin Club—that informal and casual version of the Zamorano—was founded in the early 1930s. By that time the cresting wave of the 1920s had fostered on West Sixth Street a booksellers' row that became the cultural center of Los Angeles. Well into and beyond the 1930s booksellers lined both sides of that street from Grand Avenue almost to Figueroa, a few setting out their shingles on the fringes and around the corners.

As the real estate boom and railroad development of the 1880s had brought booksellers to Los Angeles, so now on the wave of the opulent 1920s they established themselves in the city, scouting and peddling, buying and selling, setting up exhibitions, supplying collector and university, studio research department and gallery with an extraordinary variety of antiquarian books and prints. Who were they, those booksellers who, through boom and bust, plied a trade that illumined a city?

One of the brightest images in the kaleidoscope of Southern California was Alice Millard, wife of George Millard who had been "custodian" of the "Saints and Sinners Corner" of McClurg's in Chicago.[14] In his later years he moved to Southern California, and at his death his widow sold off the standard sets and Sangorski and Sutcliffe bindings in which he had delighted, and set forth on her own. She not only catered to the tastes of the 1920s and 1930s; she epitomized them at their best. She herself "looked as if she had been created by the pencil of Edward Burne-Jones," and her "sense of style" was nothing less than magnificent. Elegantly attired, she drove in a huge black limousine to visit such customers as Mrs. Doheny, and the books she sold matched the elegance of the seller. If necessary she would not hesitate to borrow half a million dollars from the bank to buy books in Europe "because," she decided, "Pasadena needs them." She sold them, of course, not merely to regional collectors but farther afield—to J. P. Morgan, to the McCormicks.

In her house, "La Collina," designed by Frank Lloyd Wright, Alice Millard displayed her wares, many of which had never been seen before in Southern California—illuminated manuscripts and rubricated incunables, original Blake water colors, Rowlandson drawings, early Doves Press proofsheets. Upon occasion she held exhibitions at the "Little museum of La Miniatura" in Pasadena. In 1929 her Kelmscott Collection was loaned to the museum for that purpose and catalogued, and in 1933 she assembled a Doves Press exhibition there. There is no doubt that she set an unprecedented style in Southern California. As one of her younger colleagues commented, "She brought great manuscripts, magnificent incunables, books printed by Jenson and Wynkyn de Worde and Fust and Schoeffer . . . to this part of the world. She . . . educated the rare-book buyers of Southern California to a much higher level of appreciation than they'd ever had before."

They bought from other dealers, too, who flashed their own particular images in Los Angeles' kaleidoscope during the period of boom and bust.[15] A 1924 Los Angeles telephone directory lists many of the old standbys: Dawson's Book Shop and Fowler Brothers, the Holmes Book Company, the Jones Book Store and Parker's, along with Dellquest's Rare Book Shop. Dellquest's claimed existence since 1885, and its permanent desiderata included "Books, pamphlets, maps, letters, documents, and early newspapers relating to CALIFORNIA, WESTERN STATES, LINCOLN, POE, JENNY LIND."

Among later arrivals was the Old Book Chamber of the Unity Pegues Book Shop on Hollywood Boulevard, managed by Paul Jordan-Smith, a firm that specialized in "Rare Books and First Editions, both Ancient and Modern," and aimed "to recreate somewhat the atmosphere of the old English book shops where Johnson, and Lamb used to prowl about."

During this period Hollywood also boasted the Satyr Book Shop which issued its Catalogue No. One in March 1927, announcing: "We want especially modern first editions, standard sets, fine bindings, art, arihitecture [sic], limited editions and old books and pamphlets on California and the West." In addition, the Satyr solicited "Original stories, suitable for motion picture adaptation. . . . We act as brokers for authors and guarantee good prices for suitable material."

From Jenny Lind to Samuel Johnson, from Californiana to screen scripts, an extraordinary assortment of collectibles was available to Angelinos who could patronize as great a variety of booksellers. There was the sensitive Louis Epstein who became identified with a succession of bookstores. After running one in Long Beach, he established the Acadia Book Shop on Los Angeles' West Sixth Street which he sold to Richard and Ralph Howey for a sum variously reputed to be $1,500, $1,600, or $2,250. Louis Epstein would lend books to a colleague even when he was accumulating stock for another shop. On Eighth Street he opened Epstein's Book Shop, a decade later—in 1938—setting up his Pickwick Bookshop in Hollywood. Epstein customers included James Cagney and Marlene Dietrich who, once mistaken for a clerk by another customer, proceeded to act the part to perfection, William Faulkner sending books to Oxford, Mississippi, and Aldous Huxley, searching for a used Bible. Finally, Louis Epstein transferred most of his stock to the Argonaut Book Shop run by his brother Ben on booksellers' row. There too for a time, before moving to Philadelphia, Ralph Howey carried on in his "little English nook" that accommodated only one customer at a time but where every item of his choice stock, from a Cobden-Sanderson binding to a Bodoni, was in its appointed place.

The colored fragments of Los Angeles' antiquarian past reassemble themselves, interrelate one with the other, reflect their early bright-ness. Shake the kaleidoscope and the images flash by: David Kohn's Curio Book Shop on Third Street with its storehouse on Sixth appears again, its books "crammed helter skelter in bins, piled on the floor, stacked in the basement," among them a "marvelous stock of old pa-perbacks in mint condition." The proprietor himself can be reanimated as he stands in the doorway, his hat pulled down to his ears, or sleeps again, as was his custom, on the balcony of his shop.

The cast of characters walks out again on the stage that was Los Angeles' booksellers' row: Warren Rogers, husband of Ernest Dawson's sister, who plied a sizeable secondhand trade; Bunster Creeley, husband of a niece of Norman Holmes, who had been a flyweight boxer before he opened the Abbey Book Shop where he employed the future librarian H. Richard Archer and the future bookseller Philip S. Brown.

Philip Brown had come from Minnesota in the 1930s, and after his stint with Creeley moved to Pasadena where he assisted Charles Yale who had managed Dawson's Book Shop for fourteen years before setting up in business. Later on, Brown would join with Yale's son Charles P. Yale in the firm of Yale and Brown.

Maxwell Hunley, indestructible, destined to endure, was scouting for books in 1926 or 1927, embarking upon the career that would make him an expert specialist in Western Americana.[16] Born in Cameron, Missouri, in 1900, he yielded to the lure of Los Angeles, and in 1930, from his apartment on Laclede Avenue, issued his first *Catalogue of First Editions and Rare Books*—and sold everything in it. A second catalogue of first editions, entitled *Highlights of American Fiction*, was sold en bloc to Mrs. Doheny. Between 1932 and 1950 Hunley operated from "a mousetrap in an arcade on Beverly Drive," a mousetrap which attracted some giant prey, especially from the screen world: Jean Hersholt and Charles Boyer, Ginger Rogers and Robert Montgomery—not to mention Frank Hogan, defender of Mr. Doheny in the Teapot Dome Scandal.

By the 1930s the booksellers' ranks had been joined by such divergent characters as Jean French, who sold art books to the research departments of the studios, Larry Edmunds who catered to the movie industry, Louis Samuel of the Penguin Bookshop, Beverly Hills, who dealt in first editions, and the colorful and flamboyant Stanley Rose. Rose, who hailed from Matador, Texas, had run away to enlist in World War I. Then, for a time, he peddled books in Los Angeles, "primarily risqué items which he hawked in the studios," before opening two Hollywood bookstores, one of which has been described as "spectacular." There such celebrities as John Barrymore, Red Skelton and Jim Tully could find best sellers or art books, while the proprietor, a splendid raconteur who "dressed like a Hollywood swell" and "spoke like a Texas farm boy," played court jester.

Surely there was never a greater range of personality than among the booksellers of Los Angeles in its early heyday. From the elegant Alice Millard to the incorrigible Stanley Rose, they flashed their individual color upon a scene that has not been duplicated. Often interrelated either by marriage or employment, they attracted as varied a clientele as they were themselves varied, a clientele that ranged from a Red Skelton to a Mrs. Doheny. They brought to Southern California an array of books, from incunables to paperbacks in mint condition.

And so, while they enlivened the particular place in which they carried on their business, they also enlightened it.

No one of the personalities who appeared in Los Angeles during the 1920s and 1930s brought more enlightenment to that sphere than a young man "short and slim with thick curly black hair and the face of a young satyr" who "looked like a poet, . . . spoke like a poet, . . . lived like a poet . . . [and] was a poet." He was also, as it turned out, a bookseller. His name, Jacob Israel Zeitlin, was soon to be known to all the bibliophilic world as Jake Zeitlin.[17] Born in Racine, Wisconsin, in 1902, he was taken as a child to Fort Worth, Texas, where his father, an orthodox Jew, carried on the family business, Acme Vinegar Company, and entertained hopes that his son would either follow in his footsteps or join the rabbinate. He showed no inclination for either way of life. Rather, under the influence of his high school teacher, he inclined toward the reading and creating of literature. At that formative period Jake was exposed not only to poetry but to "tales of Chicago's literary renaissance" from the lips of two young vagrants, Ben Abramson and Jerry Nedwick, who worked for a time in the family vinegar works. So too did the young poet, despite his disinclination, serving as sales manager for the company from 1920 to 1925, working in addition for a time for the Fort Worth *Star-Telegram*. By 1925 he had acquired a wife, a daughter, and a strong desire to uproot himself from inherited destiny. It was then that Jake Zeitlin flipped a coin to determine whether his future lay in Chicago or Los Angeles.

Jake carried a packet of books with him when he tramped and hitch-hiked from Fort Worth to Los Angeles, but when he arrived in the City of the Angels his first job was bookish only by indirection. For E. L. Doheny's oil company the young man drove a gardener's truck which he also loaded with fertilizer. Before long he worked in Holmes' bookstore and later in the book departments of May's and Bullock's department stores. Then, with books on commission from Father Dawson, Zeitlin began peddling his wares from a satchel to the bookmen of Los Angeles.

In 1927, a boom time in Southern California, sandwiched between the founding of the Clark Library and the establishment of the Huntington, Jake Zeitlin opened his first bookstore. At 567 Hope Street, near the Bible Institute and the new Public Library, the young man from Texas rented the back doorway of the T. J. Lawrence Real Estate Company for $35 a month. The area, about twelve feet deep and eight feet wide, was dubbed "At the Sign of the Grasshopper," "because like the grasshopper in Aesop's fable, I fiddled and sang in the summertime and froze and starved in the winter." A new era in Southern California's antiquarian history had begun.

Not long after, Zeitlin moved around the corner to 705 1/2 West Sixth Street—to "a little half-store, just big enough for a couple of hundred books and a minimal gallery" designed for such purposes by Lloyd Wright. "Everything about it," according to one observer, was "unusual"—its grasshopper symbol, the orange and black patterned wrapping paper, even the cable address "Jabberwocky." Like the store, the stock was small but interesting and innovative. Jake was attracted to the books of great contemporary printers, books from the Nonesuch and Golden Cockerell presses, books of the San Francisco Grabhorns, of Eric Gill and Francis Meynell. Some of his stock came on credit from Father Dawson; some he imported from the London brokers, William H. Jackson; some he bought from Douglas Cleverdon of Bristol. When, in 1928, Ernest Dawson imported "cases and cases of incunabula" from his London agents, Marks and Company, he sold some to the young proprietor for 10 percent above cost. In the same year another Ernest enriched Zeitlin's wares—Ernest Maggs—who, on a visit from London, left a Shakespeare folio and several outstanding English first editions on commission.

It was at this period too that Jake Zeitlin offered in his shop exhibitions of prints and graphic arts. Filling his window with woodcuts of Eric Gill, he mounted exhibitions of wood engravings by Paul Landacre, early prints of the desert and Big Sur country, prints of Arthur B. Davies. As the proprietor put it, "My wall was about 6 feet x 8 feet, but it was the only wall in which these things were being shown." Naturally Zeitlin's exhibitions, as well as his books, attracted a fervent group of artists and writers. In 1937 or 1938, the poet metamorphosed into bookman would introduce the work of Käthe Kollwitz to Los Angeles at an opening chaired by Melvyn Douglas. As for himself, he liked to collect the prints of Pieter Breughel the Elder, succeeding, as he did not fail to mention, in assembling more of the prints of the Vices than of the Virtues.

Zeitlin climaxed the eventful year of 1928 with publication of his first catalogue, graced with a foreword by Wilbur Needham and adorned with the grasshopper logo. He had published a book of poems the year before and he, his stock, and his style had begun to attract to his shop

a parade of customers. In time Jake Zeitlin knew everyone worth know-
ing in the book world, and at one time or another they beat a path to
his door: Robert E. Cowan and Henry R. Wagner, Frederick Hodge
and Joseph G. Layne, Phil Townsend Hanna and Gregg Anderson,
Frank Hogan and Bern Dibner, Elmer Belt and Paul Jordan-Smith,
Robert Schad and Nathan Van Patten, Jean Hersholt and Edwards
Huntington Metcalf, Dr. A.S.W. Rosenbach, Estelle Getz and Estelle
Doheny. He attracted writers, too, from Saroyan and Morley to Aldous
Huxley and Wytter Bynner. He attracted collectors and browsers with
his books, his prints, his open house talks and poetry readings, his
charisma. Indeed, they found that even the smell of his shop was good,
a blend of the Turkish cigarettes he favored and the paper, ink, and
leather that surrounded him.

As the years passed, the shop underwent changes of location if not
of personality. At the time of one of those moves late in 1934, Ernest
Dawson wrote to "Dear Mr Zeitlin" the following warm note of welcome
which still hangs, framed, on Zeitlin's wall:

> Congratulations on your lovely new Shop.
> Welcome to the Wilshire Grand District.
> May the love of books and Prints be stimulated by your efforts.
> My best wishes for your success.[18]

After several moves on West Sixth Street, Zeitlin left Booksellers'
Row in 1938 for the remodeled carriage house of the Earl estate on
Carondelet Avenue where a grand opening was made grander by a
speech from Aldous Huxley. Then, after a decade there—in 1948—
he transformed himself into Lord of the Red Barn when the firm of
Zeitlin & Ver Brugge occupied the huge Pennsylvania Dutch building
on La Cienega Boulevard. At various times in his long career he was
aided by a number of assistants of whom the most eminent was certainly
Lawrence Clark Powell, who confesses, "It was as his biblio-factotum,
typing letters, wrapping and delivering, dressing the window, and meeting the city's cultural elite . . . [that] I laid the foundations of my career
as librarian and writer." Zeitlin attracted not only the distinguished
but the exotic, counting among his employees Fillmore Silkwood Phipps
and E. Digges Graves.

It was Lawrence Clark Powell who in 1937 catalogued the D. H.

Lawrence manuscripts, which Zeitlin was handling. For that catalogue Aldous Huxley wrote a foreword and the printing was executed by Powell's colleague from Vroman's, Ward Ritchie. Indeed, as early as 1928, Jake Zeitlin had given Ward Ritchie his first printing commission, a few poems by Carl Sandburg, and subsequently the bookseller had published Lawrence Clark Powell's thesis on Robinson Jeffers in an edition illustrated by Rockwell Kent and designed by Ward Ritchie. Fine printing and publishing interested Jake Zeitlin as a collateral career, and his name is associated not only with the Ward Ritchie Press but with the Primavera Press of the 1930s.

The catholicity of Zeitlin's interests is attested by the fact that the author of the poems *Whispers and Chants* became an expert in the history of science. He himself recalls that it was through research on the books owned by Charles Lincoln Edwards that he first developed an eye for early science. At all events, the proximity of the office of Dr. Elmer Belt certainly stimulated Jake's interest not only in supplying him with Vinciana for his Leonardo da Vinci collection but in adding to his collection of medical rarities. In time, Zeitlin numbered among the collectors of his early science Dr. Nathan Van Patten of Stanford University and Dr. Logan Clendening of Kansas City, Dr. Harvey Cushing, Bern Dibner and E. L. De Golyer. In the mid-1950s, with Dibner's backing, Jake Zeitlin acquired the second collection assembled by the discoverer of vitamin E, Dr. Herbert M. Evans, and with it a notable stock of books in the history of science. The Lord of the Red Barn could boast at one time such extraordinary rarities as a copy of Galileo's first publication, the *Compasso Geometrico*, and a Galileo letter of 1635 describing to Peiresc the workings of a magnetic clock and discussing the scientist's difficulties with the Inquisition!

Zeitlin's career had encompassed the highlights of literature and the highlights of science. The hitchhiker from Fort Worth had been transformed from the dark-haired bohemian poet who looked like a young satyr into a "grizzled old humanist." He owed much to the Los Angeles of which he had become a citizen—to the generosity of Ernest Dawson, to the "studios and what they bought," to the collectors. In return, he had helped create in Southern California that "small renaissance" he had perceived and described. He himself had been, and continues to be, a renaissance man who happens to live in Southern California.

Among Jake Zeitlin's many quotable remarks none is more apt in a computerized age than his affirmative statement: "The ideas of men which are worth preserving will still be printed on paper." The antiquarian dealers of Los Angeles have done much to preserve those ideas.

The influx of booksellers into Southern California after the growth of the railroads in the 1880s and after the prosperity of the 1920s was followed by another wave of antiquarian booksellers in the 1940s. The day following Pearl Harbor Day, Bennett and Marshall opened shop; Robert Bennett had been apprenticed in the Holmes Book Shop, and Richard Marshall had worked for Dawson's. Toward the end of the decade, Harry Levinson left his Caxton Bookshop in New York for Southern California. One of the happier offshoots of the war was the migration to the West Coast of Kurt Schwarz, who brought with him his profound knowledge of oriental art after his experience of Anschluss and Japanese-occupied China. All these later arrivals who enriched the "small renaissance" of Southern California with their own special knowledge must form the basis for another history. Meanwhile, continuing the earlier tradition, the Lord of the Red Barn still holds sway on La Cienega and at Dawson's Book Shop Father Dawson's sons carry on. Glen Dawson brings to the partnership his expertise in Californiana, Muir Dawson his expertise in fine printing, paper making and calligraphy.

The sun-baked Pueblo de Los Angeles has suffered the infiltration of smog. The studios of Hollywood have long since passed their heyday. Many of the great collections assembled by giant booksellers have been consigned to institutions. Like every metropolis, Los Angeles has been subject to computerization. And yet, printed on paper, the ideas of men that are worth preserving are still preserved. For this the antiquarian booksellers are largely responsible. To the casual flamboyant City of the Angels they brought a warmth, a color and an appreciation for the best that has been thought and said in the world. The forces that made of Southern California a small renaissance world still persist. Among those forces the antiquarian booksellers stand in the vanguard.

NOTES

1. *Books and the Imagination: Fifty Years of Rare Books Jake Zeitlin Interviewed by Joel Gardner*. Oral History Program (University of California at Los Angeles 1980), pp. 111–112. Without the cooperation of Jake Zeitlin of Zeitlin & Ver Brugge and of Muir Dawson of Dawson's Book Shop this chapter could not have been written. Both gentlemen generously lent to the writer not only

copious source materials but their memories and their knowledge, and she wishes to express to them her deepest gratitude. She is grateful, too, to Betty Rosenberg of Malibu, California, for relevant material.

2. Louis B. Wright, *Life on the American Frontier* (New York: Capricorn Books, 1971), pp. 152–154.

3. *A Bookman's View of Los Angeles* (Los Angeles: Zamorano Club, 1961), pp. 6–7.

4. For Hellman and other pioneer Los Angeles booksellers, see Ernest Dawson, *Los Angeles Booksellers of 1897* (Claremont, Calif.: Saunders Press, 1947), pp. 5 & passim.

5. *A Bookman's View of Los Angeles,* pp. 7–8.

6. Ernest Dawson, *Los Angeles Booksellers of 1897,* pp. 8–9; J. M. Edelstein, ed., *A Garland for Jake Zeitlin* (Los Angeles: Dahlstrom & Marks, 1957), p. 53.

7. E. Dawson, *Los Angeles Booksellers of 1897,* p. 6; Edelstein, ed., *A Garland for Jake Zeitlin,* p. 54; Lawrence Clark Powell, *Vroman's of Pasadena* (Pasadena, Calif., 1953), p. 11.

8. E. Dawson, *Los Angeles Booksellers of 1897,* p. 10.

9. Ibid., p. 12; Lawrence Clark Powell, *Recollections of an Ex-Bookseller . . . Printed to mark the anniversary of the new Bookshop of Zeitlin & Ver Brugge* (Los Angeles 1950), p. 3; Powell, *Vroman's of Pasadena,* passim; Ward Ritchie, *Bookmen & their brothels: Recollections of Los Angeles in the 1930s* (Los Angeles: Zamorano Club, 1970), pp. 17–18.

10. *Books and the Imagination,* p. 126; E. Dawson, *Los Angeles Booksellers of 1897,* pp. 11–12; Edelstein, ed., *A Garland for Jake Zeitlin,* pp. 56–57; Powell, *Vroman's of Pasadena,* p. 11.

11. Jacob Zeitlin, *Small Renaissance: Southern California Style* (Los Angeles 1972).

12. E. Dawson, *Los Angeles Booksellers of 1897,* pp. 11–12; Edelstein, ed., *A Garland for Jake Zeitlin,* p. 51; Anna Marie Hager, "Ernest Dawson and His Wonderful Book Shop: A Reminiscence," *Los Angeles Westerners Corral* (September 1981), pp. 1, 3–7; Ritchie, *Bookmen & their brothels,* pp. 4, 11–12; Russell Arthur Roberts, *Dawson's Book Shop: Publisher of Western Americana and Patron of the Book Arts* (Los Angeles 1964), passim; Fern Dawson Shochat, *The Fiftieth Anniversary of Dawson's Book Shop: 1905–1955* (N.p. [1955]), passim; *Southern California Book Store Series, Thomas A. Neal,* Oral History Program (Claremont, Calif.: Claremont Graduate School, 1972), p. v; Francis J. Weber, *Up 65 Years to Larchmont* (Los Angeles: Bela Blau, 1970), pp. 9–10; Zeitlin, *Small Renaissance: Southern California Style,* pp. 7–8.

13. For the background of the period, see *Books and the Imagination,* pp. viii, 164; Edelstein, ed., *A Garland for Jake Zeitlin,* pp. 50, 53; Carey McWilliams, *The Education of Carey McWilliams* (New York: Simon and Schuster, 1979), p. 42; Ritchie, *Bookmen & their brothels,* pp. 1, 20; Zeitlin, *Small Renaissance: Southern California Style,* pp. 5–6.

14. *Books and the Imagination*, pp. 141–143; Zeitlin, *Small Renaissance: Southern California Style*, p. 7.

15. *Books and the Imagination*, passim; Edelstein, ed., *A Garland for Jake Zeitlin*, passim; Louis Epstein, "West View: Memoirs of Mr. Pickwick, L.A.'s literary godfather," *Los Angeles Times*, undated clipping (Courtesy Jake Zeitlin); McWilliams, *The Education of Carey McWilliams*, pp. 48 f; Powell, *Recollections of an Ex-Bookseller*, passim; Ritchie, *Bookmen & their brothels*, passim; Roberts, *Dawson's Book Shop*, unpaged; Xeroxes of Catalogues and Los Angeles Telephone Directory Listings (Courtesy Muir Dawson).

16. *Books and the Imagination*, p. 360; *A True and Authentick Account of the Life of the Distinguished Bibliophile and Bookseller Maxwell Hunley, Esq. As Heard From His Own Lips By A Sincere Lover of Books* (Typescript, courtesy Muir Dawson).

17. *Books and the Imagination*, passim; Edelstein, ed., *A Garland for Jake Zeitlin*, passim; Lawrence Clark Powell, *From the Heartland: Profiles of People and Places of the Southwest and Beyond* (Flagstaff, Ariz.: Northland Press, [1976]), pp. 131–132, 140; Lawrence Clark Powell, "Mr. Bookseller," *Westways* (July 1974), pp. 27–31, 67; Powell, *Recollections of an Ex-Bookseller*, p. 13; Ritchie, *Bookmen & their brothels*, pp. 3, 38; *Southern California Book Store Series Jacob Zeitlin*, Oral History Program, Claremont Graduate School (Claremont, Calif., 1972), pp. v–vi. The Zeitlin & Ver Brugge Archive is deposited in twenty-seven boxes in the University of California at Los Angeles Library.

18. Ernest Dawson to Jake Zeitlin, 15 December 1934. (Courtesy Muir Dawson, who adds: "Jake has this framed in his office. I love this item. It shows an open spirit that characterized my father and was an influence on many people.")

9

Cities to the South

The South itself might be described as a "peculiar institution," for, despite a strong tradition of literacy, it had, during most of the eighteenth century and much of the nineteenth and twentieth, few notable booksellers. It could boast great libraries—Westover and Monticello housed two of the greatest in the country. But there were few local booksellers to match their stature. While booksellers flourished in the urban centers of the North, their place was taken in the South by general merchants and factors. Direct importation from abroad on the part of collectors accounted for many of the books on Southern bookshelves, and so, while there were many fine books and libraries in the South, there were few booksellers of note. It may have been easy to read and own antiquarian books, but it was less easy to purchase them on the spot.

The ambivalence that emerges from a study of Southern culture in general and bookselling in particular was enunciated by a member of the trade who for a period did settle in the far South. As late as the 1930s, Charles Heartman observed that "The deep South is hungry for books," but at the same time he commented that "One . . . can count on the fingers of one hand the dealers in the South, qualified and responsible, who can properly supply needs or create demand."[1]

The ambivalence is emphasized by the differing interpretations of historians of the South. Richard Beale Davis, author of *Intellectual Life in the Colonial South*, avers that "from the seventeenth century a great number of southern colonists owned and read books; . . . by 1700 there were a few impressive libraries . . . .the titles of books in dated inventories and in letters ordering them prove . . . that there was no cultural lag; . . . there were in some eighteenth-century libraries sixteenth- and earlier seventeenth-century imprints." Citing the libraries of William Byrd II, Thomas Jefferson, John Mercer, Peter Manigault and John Mackenzie, Davis concludes that "there were in the colonial South book collectors in the best sense."[2] On the other hand, referring to a later period, W. J. Cash in *The Mind of the South* discounts those "proofs commonly advanced by apologists—that at the outbreak of the war the section had more colleges and students . . . in proportion to population than the North; that many planters were ready and eager to quote you Cicero or Sallust; that Charleston had a public library before Boston, . . . that these Charlestonians, and . . . older and wealthier residents of Richmond . . . and New Orleans, regularly imported the latest books from London." Cash concludes that the South "far outran the American average for (white) illiteracy" and that its "intellectual and aesthetic culture" was "a superficial and jejune thing."[3] William Charvat astutely put it:

The rich South was the despair of the book trade. There was money there for the luxury trade, and it was a happy hunting ground for peddlers of Carey's expensive Bibles and atlases, and for richly bound special editions. But as a staple-crop region, it was hit hard by all depressions, which meant bankrupt booksellers and bad debts. Moreover, its retailers were sluggish; . . . "Your booksellers," wrote Carey to [John Pendleton] Kennedy in 1833, "are the most inert people on earth. They complain that business is bad and take good care that it shall not be otherwise, . . . "[4]

The banking panic of 1837, which hit the entire nation, hit the South especially, heralding a depression period that lasted until 1841. The devastating effects of the Civil War upon the agrarian South included the destruction not only of book stocks but of records of book stocks. The hostilities and conflicts of the Reconstruction period exacerbated the difficulties of conducting bookstores in the South.

An attempt to study the bookselling scene in "Uncle Sam's other province"[5] may help, to some extent, to understand the anomaly of a region that fostered readers and collectors who were qualitatively and quantitatively superior to most of its booksellers.

ANNAPOLIS/BALTIMORE

A day or two on horseback could carry a colonial Baltimore collector to Philadelphia, one factor that made the presence of local booksellers almost superfluous.[6] Moreover, in the tobacco trade that prevailed between Maryland and England, books were often exchanged for the weed, and collectors could stock their shelves directly without reference to an intermediary. According to Maryland inventories between 1700 and 1776, "nearly sixty percent of the free white population possessed books," some of which were described as "Very old." Among these were, for example, a "parcel of owld Sermons," seventeenth- and eighteenth-century law manuals, a 1686 edition of Sir John Chardin's *Travels in Persia and India*, and various editions of Seneca. If parochial libraries in Maryland reflected the desire "to strengthen the religion of the established church," there were enough secular books scattered about in private libraries to substantiate a growing interest in the humanities.

Some of those books were indeed purchased on the spot from factors and merchants who operated general stores where imports from abroad were available. One order from a supplier requested: "Second Hand Books will be far more acceptable provided they be Sound & not of the oldest & Obslete [sic] Editions, but if such are not Conveniently to be Mr Johnson is desired to purchase them new." Antiquarian books, in short, were obtained in colonial Maryland from an urban center such as Philadelphia, or directly from England, or through general merchants as distinguished from specialist booksellers. As the tobacco business diminished in importance in Maryland's economy, direct trade with London booksellers decreased and the incentive grew for the development of Baltimore bookstores.

Who were those early dealers who helped supply Marylanders with books? Probably "the earliest recorded Maryland bookseller" was Evan Jones who plied his trade in Annapolis in 1700, who is remembered as "a Sober Person" active in colonial public life, and who died in 1722. Jones's name survives in an interesting imprint. Thomas Bray's sermon, *The Necessity of an Early Religion*, was printed in Annapolis "by order of the Assembly by Tho: Reading, for Evan Jones Bookseller," and according to Evans (904): "This is supposed to be the first book printed in Maryland. It is, however, hard to reconcile this single publication at this time with other known facts regarding the introduction of printing into the Province over a quarter of a century later."

A quarter of a century later, the colonial printer William Parks combined his activities as printer-publisher with those of bookseller and binder. In 1729 he advertised for sale "A parcel of very curious

Metzotinto Prints." He sold books imported from London to Maryland customers, at times importing the sheets which were later folded and sewed at his Annapolis premises. But, like most of the early booksellers who are remembered for their printing, Parks was better known as public printer of Maryland and Virginia than as a bibliopole.

It was the printer William Rind who in 1758 opened what has been called "the first significant bookstore in the colony." In his house on West Street, Annapolis, where "the late Mrs. M'Leod formerly kept tavern," Rind kept the books he imported and established a circulating library. In partnership with Jonas Green to whom he had been apprenticed, Rind issued a broadside in 1764 announcing an unusual method of "Disposing of a Large and Valuable Collection of BOOKS, MAPS, &c"—by lottery. The scheme was probably less than successful, and the following year he moved to Virginia.

By the next decade, one or two printer-booksellers were operating in Maryland. William Aikman, a Scot, arrived in Annapolis with a supply of books and stationery in 1773, and set up his bookstore-circulating library on West Street. His stock consisted of "above 12 hundred volumes on the most useful sciences, history, poetry, agriculture, voyages, travels," and his imports from London included "the *English* classicks, miscellanies, voyages, novels, plays, &c. to be sold at the *London* prices for cash only." Hume and Blackstone, Locke and Montesquieu were all available at Aikman's shop, which shortly became a social center for Annapolis citizens who could browse among the books, taste the "wet goods," and exchange loyalist sympathies with the proprietor. As a result, no doubt, of those loyalist sympathies, William Aikman left Maryland for Jamaica, West Indies, in 1775, where he died nine years later.

While Aikman was still plying his trade in Annapolis, in 1773, William Goddard set up a printing office in Baltimore "on the capital of a single guinea." Goddard, who hailed from Connecticut, had already proved himself "a good printer, and an able editor," having been "the first printer in Providence, Rhode Island; and . . . publisher of the *Pennsylvania Chronicle* in Philadelphia." Now, at the corner of South and Baltimore Streets, with the aid of his sister Mary Katherine Goddard, he issued his *Maryland Journal*, the first newspaper in Baltimore. Six years later he entered into partnership with Eleazar Oswald, an Englishman who would serve as captain under Arnold at Ticonderoga.

Their partnership was formed for bookselling as well as printing, but it was William's sister Mary Katherine, "a woman of extraordinary judgment, energy, nerve and strong good sense," who performed many of the labors of the establishment while her brother was otherwise engaged. In 1803 she moved the shop from Baltimore Street to smaller quarters on Chatham Street, retiring toward the end of the decade.

After the Revolution, the Maryland bookselling center—if it could be described as such—shifted from Annapolis to Baltimore. When the Hartford wit Joel Barlow contemplated a bookselling career in 1784, he bethought himself not of his native town but of Baltimore. By 1790 the community boasted at least three circulating libraries, and during the first quarter of the nineteenth century the growth in population, the increasing importance of Baltimore as a port city, and the briskness of trade made it a promising background for booksellers. Northern firms, such as that of Mathew Carey, set up branch offices in Baltimore, and for a time the city seemed a likely rival of Philadelphia.[7]

One dealer who flourished during this period was Fielding Lucas, Jr., bookseller, stationer and publisher of "fine books and maps."[8] Born in 1781 in Fredericksburg, Virginia, he trained in Philadelphia until 1804 when he moved to Baltimore and signed a petition—along with his colleagues—"against allowing book auctions by a competitor." The Philadelphia firm of M. and J. Conrad and Company, booksellers and publishers, had, like Mathew Carey, set up a branch office in Baltimore, which Lucas appears to have managed. In 1807 the firm was styled Conrad, Lucas and Company and, as importers from the Northern centers of New York, Philadelphia and Boston as well as from abroad, they helped supply Baltimoreans with literary needs in new and secondhand books as well as with stationery and artists' supplies. In 1810 the partnership was dissolved, and Fielding Lucas, Jr., took over the book stock on Baltimore Street near Calvert in the heart of the business district. As publisher of maps and atlases, drawing books and children's books, he gained a reputation, and at his death in 1854 the Baltimore printer-booksellers passed a resolution of respect to their late colleague. During the 1850s the Lucas building was remodeled on the plan of a London library and the four-story colonial structure continued to house the bookstore to which Lucas's son, William F. Lucas, succeeded. Subsequently, as Lucas Brothers, it was carried on by the third generation: William F. Lucas, Jr., J. Carroll Lucas, and their sister. As

"America's Oldest Office Products and Furniture Firm" Lucas Brothers, Inc., survives today.

Despite the survival of the Lucas firm, Baltimore's promise as a book-selling center was not fulfilled. The struggle over the Bank of the United States led to feverish speculation in the city between 1810 and 1820. The War of 1812 cast its shadow over Chesapeake Bay, and the sacking and burning threatened Baltimore as well as Washington. In the trade battle over control of the Susquehanna, Baltimore lost to Philadelphia, never sustaining the position as bookselling center that had once seemed within its reach.

WASHINGTON

One factor which contributed to the development of bookselling in Washington was the outcome of its status as the national capital. As *Publishers Weekly* noted in an article on Washington bookstores: "The private libraries to be found here and the governmental patronage have made the fortunes of several of our booksellers."[9] Perhaps the most famous such library was that of Peter Force, whose collection of books and manuscripts was purchased by Congress in 1867 for $100,000. Both Peter Force and the Library of Congress assuredly helped make of Wash-ington, D.C., a bookish if not a bookselling center.

Although there were booksellers along the Potomac before and during Force's lifetime, most of the booksellers of the area plied their trade after his demise. It is true that John Randolph of Roanoke had book receipts from such a firm as Thompson and Howard in Washington, and that one of Thomas Jefferson's favorite agents was George Milligam of Georgetown, who bound and procured books for him. The stationer-booksellers Gray and Ballantyne, later known as William Ballantyne & Sons, went into business in 1852, and John C. Parker, who began as a newsboy in Baltimore, opened a stand on F Street in 1862 that developed into a stationery and book business that became "one of the largest" in Washington. Several of Washington's bookselling establish-ments, however, either originated or expanded after the Civil War.

At C. C. Pursell's, which started on Ninth Street in 1870, visitors might find "amid its air of refinement . . . all the requirements of a cultivated taste, both in stationery and books." On the same street, Lewis S. Hayden opened an establishment in 1876 which offered "books whose rarity and antiquity command the admiration and the respect of the scholar, antiquarian, and man of letters." Hayden, a native of Baltimore, and a man of "courteous manners and strict integrity," offered to his rarified clientele a rarified stock including "rare gems of classical and historical literature." In addition, at his premises browsers might leaf through 50,000 pamphlets from sermons to essays on sewerage, not to mention 10,000 engravings.

In 1872 Robert Beall succeeded to an older bookstore that became a landmark of the national capital. The Waverley Bookstore on Pennsylvania Avenue, begun by Pishey or Piskey Thompson, passed under the aegis of Frank Taylor and was known as "a favorite . . . lounging place for the public men" of the day who, between "discussing books and current affairs," would tell anecdotes or "joke with the clerks." One visitor, having borrowed $300 from the proprietor, went next door to the "faro-bank of Goode & Prindle," won $1,000 and returned to spend his winnings on books. Thus the Waverley cast its bread upon the waters.

Robert Beall, a native Washingtonian, clerked for Taylor until 1872, when he succeeded to the business. He was heartened to a life of bookselling after Secretary of the Treasury John Sherman, who had a $1,000 appropriation for books on finance, singled out Beall to fill his order. Beall inherited not only a varied stock, which he augmented, but a roster of distinguished patrons. Through the years the Waverley Bookstore catered to the literary tastes of Washington's illustrissimi. Some were lured there by the "very many rare and interesting volumes, not to be found in Washington outside the Congressional Library." Some were lured by those "close and intimate associations which grow between the bookbuyer and the bookseller." They ranged from Osceola, chief of the Seminoles, to Daniel Webster, from Charles Sumner to Judah P. Benjamin. Count Bertinatti, Italian minister, made frequent appearances at the Waverley Bookstore, entering with a courtly bow and offering his jeweled snuffbox to proprietor and clerks. Committees of Congress were especially welcome, since they frequently came to add to the "reference-books or other literary resources of the Government." Because of illness, Robert Beall was forced to retire from the business he had enhanced, and in 1896 most of the stock went under the auctioneer's hammer. As the press put it, "The closing of Beall's store removes one of the city's landmarks." Less than two years later, the proprietor, "one of the best-known Washington booksellers," died.

Another Washington bookstore, destined to longer life than Beall's, began the same year Beall took over the Waverley Bookstore—in 1872. A few years later W. H. Lowdermilk bought into the business that would survive almost a century. A colleague visiting Lowdermilk's when it was nearing the end of its life described it aptly:

In Washington, D.C., Lowdermilk's was the outstanding dealer in history-related books, and perhaps the oldest. At that time, they'd been in business seventy-five or eighty years. They were especially strong in out-of-print government publications in every field—geology, anthropology, archaeology. You could find in their storeroom reports and documents published way back in the 1810s, 1820s, 1830s. Some were in the original envelopes that the government intended to mail them in. Lowdermilk bought remainders from the U.S. Printing Office.

You could find the original reports of Fremont, Powell, the surveys of the Colorado River, and the thirteen-volume set of the surveys the government issued in the 1850s with a view to establishing a cross-country railroad. They had hired the best surveyors and the greatest artists of that day to plan the route and to sketch and make paintings of the scenery. . . .

Lowdermilk's . . . was one of the last great general bookstores in the United States.[10]

William H. Lowdermilk, founder of the establishment, had been born in 1839 in Cumberland, Maryland, had moved to Louisville, Kentucky, where he had learned the art of printing and had enlisted in a Kentucky regiment in the Civil War, rising to the rank of colonel. After eight months in Libby Prison he was exchanged and proceeded to serve at Shiloh and Chickamauga. By the 1870s, in Washington, D.C., the colonel proceeded to establish what would become "one of the largest book-stores in the country." Its F Street premises were enlarged in 1888 when an adjoining store, connected with the original by archways, was taken over and shelved from floor to ceiling to accommodate the "immense stock." In the cellars of Lowdermilk's were stored the vast numbers of government publications, along with some 25,000 pamphlets, duplicates, and "works infrequently wanted." A branch house was opened in London's Chancery Lane, "through which a quick supply of English publications and weekly consignments of rare works from the London sales and stores" were received. Between 1889 and 1899 the firm issued *The Washington Book Chronicle and Bulletin of Government Publications*, a quarterly journal "with one or two brief original articles on some topic of interest to collectors . . . and . . . 'the general reader,' " and with a list of government publications for sale by Lowdermilk.

Colonel Lowdermilk's death in 1897 did not end the firm. W. H. Lowdermilk & Company continued as specialists in rare books, Americana, and government publications, and as a "favorite resort for the public men of the capital." In the end, when its owners were Arthur and Betsey McShane and William Thompson, its strength proved its weakness. And this factor, together with twentieth-century "progress" spelled its doom. The building on 12th Street which it occupied in 1969 was scheduled for razing to make way for an expanded subway system. As the Washington *Evening Star* put it: "The stock itself was one reason for the decision to close rather than move when progress and the subway struck. The weight involved was just too much to make a move financially feasible." In February 1970, the Lowdermilk books, prints and office furnishings were sold at auction. Among the 150,000 volumes, 60,000 out-of-print government publications, and 1,200 paintings and prints that came under the hammer were the McKenney and Hall *History of the Indian Tribes*, fifty-two original glass negatives of Mathew Brady photographs, Civil War broadsides, and presidential proclamations.

There were other bookshops in Washington that attracted the browser—Luther Cornwall's general antiquarian bookstore, or Whyte's with its early printed books in contemporary bindings, especially in the field of English literature. But when Lowdermilk's was razed, something in the way of a national landmark disappeared. Progress was not altogether compatible with the advancement of the printed word.

RICHMOND

Washington was occasionally on the route of the first American book agent, a traveling salesman who had settled in Dumfries, Virginia. Much has been written about Parson Mason Weems, but Lawrence Wroth has captured his essence most colorfully in a few sentences: "For thirty years there was no more familiar figure on the roads of the Southern States than this book peddler and author who, provided gypsy-like with horse and wagon, his wares and his fiddle, travelled his long route year after year, sleeping in wayside inn, farmhouse or forest, fiddling, writing, selling books. . . . He makes a bit of color in an often-times dreary landscape."[11]

Born in Anne Arundel County, Maryland, in 1759, Weems was ordained at age twenty-five, and so earned his title of "Parson." In 1794, however, he traded the ministry for bookselling, having commenced a business relationship with Mathew Carey during a visit to Philadelphia. Between 1795 and 1825 when he died, Parson Weems covered the Atlantic seaboard, dispensing books. With headquarters in Dumfries, he took orders and subscriptions from North to South, but nearly every one of his journeys included forays in Virginia. In his hob-nailed boots he strode along the roads of Virginia, through James River country, selling books from a cart or displaying his wares in taverns—wares that usually included his own compositions. His advice to Mathew Carey was that, to sell to Virginians, books must be "attractively bound." In general, he believed that the South was "a Country . . . where the passion for Reading is rising with a flood beyond all former notice of Man."

As far as the South in general, and Virginia in particular, were concerned, views about the susceptibility to books were conflicting.[12] According to some scholars, Virginia cavaliers and gentlemen "accumulated important collections of books" and "Private libraries were more common in colonial Virginia than in the North." Sons of Southern gentry, sent abroad for their education, returned with book collections, which they later augmented through purchasing agents in London. At the end of the eighteenth century, La Rochefoucauld-Liancourt noted that in Virginia "the taste for reading is commoner among men of the first class than in any other part of America."

On the other hand, some historians conclude that the private libraries of colonial Virginia were smaller than was commonly thought. Nonetheless, there is no doubt that there were great libraries in Virginia and that they included early printed books. Jefferson, for example, owned a 1589 Hakluyt, a 1609 Johnson *Nova Britannia* and Williams' *Virginia* of 1650. George Sandys' verses of 1626 adorned the shelves of William Byrd and Thomas Jefferson.

Obviously such books never appeared on Parson Weems' peripatetic cart. Whether they could be found upon the shelves of local booksellers is debatable.[13] Indeed, when Weems described the contents of a typical Southern bookstore he cited Bibles or Testaments, Chesterfield's *Principles of Politeness*, Webster's *American Spelling Book*, Jedidiah Morse's

American Geography, along with *Pilgrim's Progress*, *Robinson Crusoe* and *Charlotte Temple*. Between 1790 and the mid-1830s there were many Richmond dealers who advertised such wares in local newspapers: Frederick A. Mayo; Fitzwhylsonn and Potter (later William Fitzwhylsonn); Samuel Pleasants who supplied John Randolph of Roanoke upon occasion; Timothy Brundige, neighbor of Parson Weems in Dumfries. Some combined their bookselling with printing and publishing, while Brundige served also as Dumfries postmaster.

It has been calculated that, between 1811 and 1837, in and around Poe's Richmond, there were some twenty-two dealers in books, among them Thomas Ritchie, also proprietor of the *Enquirer*; Peter Cottom who in 1815 opened a circulating library "at his bookstore the second door above the Eagle Tavern"; William A. Bartow, who in 1822 started the earliest juvenile library in the United States at his bookstore, the Richmond Juvenile Library. One dealer, Richard D. Sanxay, who had been associated with Fitzwhylsonn, continued the latter's business, and his bookstore became "one of Poe's favorite haunts during his editorship of the *Messenger*."

Later, around the mid-century, Thomas J. Starke founded a firm destined to survive several decades in Richmond. When its stock was destroyed in the burning of the city on 3 April 1865, the invincible proprietor, in partnership with Josiah Ryland, formed the firm of Starke & Ryland, which continued until 1877. Three years later, Thomas Starke, with two of his sons, returned to the book business under the style of Thomas J. Starke & Sons, and after Starke, Sr.'s death in 1889, one of those sons bought out the business, conducting it under the name of H. M. Starke & Co. Young Starke, who had spent "all his spare hours . . . in his father's bookstore," specialized in religious literature. By 1893 his firm, now H. M. Starke & Estes, opened new premises on Richmond's Main Street in what was described as "the most striking edifice" in the area. Its second floor housed "a fully equipped printing office," while its third floor was devoted to a large stock of stationery and books—Bibles and prayerbooks, hymnals and miscellaneous books. "So that the bookseller will be something more than a shopkeeper," H. M. Starke attempted to unite the divergent elements of the Virginia book trade, becoming secretary of the Virginia Booksellers' Association. Only a few months after the firm's removal to new quarters, however, it was forced to make an assignment. "Slow collections and the tightness of money" during the panic of 1893 were causal factors. The panic of 1893 affected the book trade of the entire nation. The devastation that followed in the wake of the Civil War was, however, a Southern phenomenon. Its effects were felt not only in the capital of the Confederacy but throughout the South.

CHARLESTON

If Richmond was the capital of the Confederacy, Charleston, South Carolina, was the intellectual capital of the South. Despite that status, its local booksellers were few in number, and only one of them became truly memorable. Isaiah Thomas mentions among booksellers of eighteenth-century Charleston three gentlemen who hailed from Scotland: Robert Wells, " 'at the Great Stationery and Bookstore, on the Bay,' " dealer in "imported books" who "printed a newspaper"; one Woods, a binder and bookseller; and James Taylor, "binder, and an inconsiderable dealer in books." Robert Bell of Philadelphia held auctions as far South as Charleston, where he transported "collections of books, new and old."[14]

Not until the mid-nineteenth century did a Charleston dealer emerge compatible in stature with the intellectual capital that formed his backdrop. John Russell was born in Charleston in 1812 shortly before the outbreak of war with England.[15] He learned the rudiments of the book trade early in life at the establishment of John P. Beile, predecessor of Samuel Hart, and so, as the Southern poet Paul Hamilton Hayne remarked, "educated in the book-trade," he "mastered, at a comparatively early age, its requisitions and technicalities." In 1840, a member of the firm of Russell and Sass, he was active as auctioneer and commercial merchant. Later in the decade, on Charleston's King Street, he opened his literary emporium that was to serve for a time as the intellectual center of the South's intellectual capital.

In 1847 the proprietor journeyed to Philadelphia, doubtless to buy books; two years later, when he visited New York, he carried with him a letter of introduction from the poet William Gilmore Simms to Evert A. Duyckinck. He traveled at least once to Europe, and it was on the Channel packet that, mistaken for Lord John Russell, he acquired the sobriquet of "Lord John" that was to cling to him for the rest of his life.

"Lord John" boasted a bright, quick mind, native shrewdness, generosity and clever and witty conversation. He could also boast a knowledge of new and antiquarian books which was to make of him one of the most successful booksellers of the South. Indeed, Augustus Flagg of Little, Brown stated that John Russell sold more fine books in proportion to the population than almost any other dealer, and Trübner of London declared him one of the most accomplished bibliopoles in the United States.

His name was inscribed in prominent gilt letters above the main door of 251 King Street where he presided over a large store with handsome plateglass windows. Brisk and confident, he eagerly showed to his customers a pocket Elzevir or a black-letter work imported from abroad. Both counters and shelves were heavily laden with books identifiable through a single extant Russell catalogue. "Lord John" stocked an array of medicine, science and theology, philosophy, history and military works, travel books, numismatics, juveniles, art and literature. Among his highlights were a Bodoni *Iliad* in three royal folio volumes which he priced at $50, the brilliantly illustrated four-volume *Galerie de Florence*, tagged at $125, and Lemaire's *Collection of the Latin Classics* in 144 calf volumes at $250. By 1860 the stock was valued at $20,000. It included, of course, works of interest to Southerners and works that bore Russell's own imprint for, besides being a bookseller, he was a publisher both of *Russell's Magazine* (April 1857–March 1860) and of many fine individual volumes.

Many of the authors published by Russell were habitués of his bookshop. The proprietor's sanctum at the rear of the store became a salon for the most eminent Southern literati. There, around a comfortable stove in winter, would flock William Gilmore Simms who played Johnson to a group of Boswells who included the poets Paul Hamilton Hayne and Henry Timrod, James Petigru, Nestor of the Charleston bar, the planter William J. Grayson, many of the illuminati of the antebellum South. As they discussed the latest in Southern literature or the earliest in European imports, Lord John wore, as Simms described it, "a most triumphant aspect, in consequence of a recent discovery of huge masses of valuable antique matter in literature, such as a passionate Bibliop is apt to go into exstacies [sic] over; crying, with Dominie Sampson, Prodigious!" Prodigious indeed were the books and the collectors who trooped into Charleston's King Street bookstore.

In 1857 Russell's half-brother James C. Jones, who had clerked in the bookstore, became a partner, the firm style changing to Russell and Jones. But few years were left for the flourishing of an emporium that displayed a superb collection of beautifully bound books. Just before the outbreak of the Civil War, James C. Jones was drowned. When war began, it became all but impossible to import Northern and European publications into the Confederate states. The proprietor became adjutant of a battalion of reserves and, to save his stock from the effects of bombardment, stored it in Camden.

As it turned out, Camden lay in the direct line of Sherman's march. Sherman's soldiers broke open the Russell cases, scattering or destroying their contents. Charleston had become a vista of vacant houses, rotting wharves, grass-grown streets, yawning walls and shattered windows. The once beautiful bookstore on King Street was empty of shelves, a place of ghosts. The defeated South did not rally during the years of Reconstruction. Indeed, the Reconstruction Acts stripped it, abolished its state governments, and placed it under military rule. Only at the point of the bayonet did the South accept the Fourteenth and Fifteenth Amendments, and troops still paraded its streets. With the meagre stock left to him, "Lord John" set up business again at 285 King Street, but part of the remnants of that stock was sold at a sacrifice, and on 21 November 1871 he died. According to the inventory of goods and chattels after his death his once valuable holdings were appraised at $2,500.

NEW ORLEANS

While Charleston merited the title of intellectual capital of the South, New Orleans has been styled "the Confederacy's largest and wealthiest city."[16] Its size and its wealth were outcomes of its early history.

The city that arose on the Lower Mississippi, founded by Bienville and named after Philippe d'Orléans, was a place of Indians and mosquitoes, river life and fever, rather than of libraries. However, even in the first part of the eighteenth century there were books in some homes.[17] The inventory of the Kolly estate, for example, dated 1730, included, besides a backgammon board, sixty octavo volumes, eleven quartos, fourteen folios, and "several antiquarian books." By 1769, three hundred volumes were cited in the inventory of the Prevost estate, and they included works of Locke and Montesquieu, Rousseau and Voltaire. The Louisiana Purchase in 1803 brought Americans from New York and Massachusetts, Virginia and Kentucky to New Orleans, and the small frontier town of about 8,000 population that was a "trading post and shipping point" was on its way to becoming the emporium of the South, the "Mistress of the Mississippi." Even in 1803, however, at the time of the Purchase, it was observed that there were "no booksellers" in New Orleans, "and for a good reason, that a bookseller would perish of hunger there in the midst of his books." Despite the absence of specialist dealers, books were sold in New Orleans, as they were in many towns of the West, by merchants, importers, and newspaper proprietors. Along with parasols, an assortment of religious books might be displayed, and, through the general merchant, Condorcet and Boileau, Crébillon and Corneille filtered into the town.

The first self-styled New Orleans bookseller has been identified as Mermet, "marchand libraire," who began his operation in 1808 and three years later was located on Chartres Street. Between 1804 and 1824 it has been estimated that New Orleans accommodated "at least fifty-six different persons or firms . . . concerned with bookselling," and as the city was becoming bilingual, so too were the stocks which featured new and secondhand books in English as well as in French. Many of those books were unloaded on the crowded levee, and one observer, Benjamin Latrobe, noted in 1819 among the buyers and sellers who thronged the levee, "on the margin of a heap of bricks . . . a bookseller whose stock of books, English and French, cut no mean appearance" and included a ten-volume collection of pamphlets about the "American War."

By 1809 the pioneer New Orleans bookseller Mermet had a competitor in Pierre Roche, who brought from Philadelphia "a complete assortment of French books, including, 'editions and Parisian bindings which leave nothing to be desired.' " The Roche family appears to have carried on as booksellers on Royal Street at least until 1824, first under the aegis of the widow Roche who printed funeral tickets and advertised an assortment of wines along with "hand tooled books," and then as Roche Brothers, "libraires et papetiers." Whether or not Mermet and Roche had any dealings with the collector J. B. Castillon is conjectural, but Castillon's library was announced for sale in 1809 as "une Bibliothèque assez volumineuse," consisting of eight or nine hundred volumes forming "une collection précieuse et rare en ce pays," and including both seventeenth- and eighteenth-century French works. Bookselling activity was certainly accelerating. Books were imported from Paris, London and New York; reading rooms were opened; books were sold by lotteries. The tribe of booksellers was increasing. Very early in the nineteenth century, J. F. Lelievre claimed to have begun a business that combined the sale of religious articles, fancy goods and books. Lelievre survived to publish the "first book printed in French on the subject of gardening in Louisiana"—the *Nouveau Jardinier de la Louisiane*—and in his "boutique de livres" he continued to offer, along with books, garden seeds, art materials, toys and office furniture. The firm continued under the style of V. O. Lelievre, and later Mrs. V. O. Lelievre, until about 1870.

Meanwhile, in 1811, not a Frenchman but an American—the "third-generation descendant of an immigrant from London"—arrived in New Orleans from his native New York and became the "best bookseller" in his adopted city. The *Louisiana Gazette* announced that B. Levy had "opened a Book and Stationery store in Chartres street opposite Mrs. Fourage's boarding house" and would "always have on hand a large and general assortment of Stationery . . . together with an extensive assortment of Law and Miscellaneous books." Benjamin Levy, born in 1786, had begun his career as a bookbinder, later becoming a partner of James Olmstead in a New York stationery business. A year after his establishment in New Orleans, Levy took on as partner Michael Reynolds, but the partnership of Reynolds and Levy was short-lived, ending in bankruptcy. Undeterred, Benjamin Levy & Co. in 1815 opened a book and stationery store where a broad range of literature was available along with the law books in which the proprietor specialized. The stock was augmented with a variety of "fancy stationery" that included not only pens, slates and portfolios, but dirks, thermometers and billiard balls. Benjamin Levy has been styled "the first important Jewish printer-publisher not only in the South, but probably in the entire country." As publisher he issued New Orleans's first business journal, the *New-Orleans Price-Current and Commercial Intelligencer*. In 1825 he moved to a new brick building on the corner of Chartres and Bienville streets, where his store occupied the ground floor and his presses the third. There he remained until 1840, printer, publisher, and seller of books by Adam Smith and Johnson, Bacon and Franklin. Three years later his career ended in bankruptcy. Deeply affected by the banking panic of 1837, and involved in unsuccessful real estate transactions, Levy terminated his book business, though it was still solvent, in 1843 when his stock was auctioned. The name of Levy, however, was not absent from the roster of New Orleans booksellers. Benjamin's son carried on as Alexander Levy and Company, "bookseller and stationer," and later "law booksellers and stationers," until 1866.

The New Orleans levee was becoming a bustle and babble of tongues where Indians and blacks peddled their wares and bales of cotton, hogsheads of tobacco and sometimes crates of books lay on the quay. The South's great city boasted not only oyster shops and gambling rooms but several bookstores. In 1824 William M'Kean entered the lists of English booksellers, and a year later one of New Orleans' most scholarly booksellers began operations.

A. L. Boimare, who has been acclaimed Louisiana's first bibliographer, was born in France, educated at the Sorbonne, and came to America in 1825, opening a bookshop and "Cabinet de Lecture" on New Orleans' Chartres Street. There he offered a variety of legal and medical works, histories, novels, and school texts in French and Spanish. Like his confreres, he also sold stationery and patent medicines, wallpapers, champagne and burgundy. Boimare was, however, not only a bookseller and the proprietor of a circulating library, but an indefatigable collector of books on the early history of Louisiana which he refused to sell unless he owned duplicate copies. Those books—and his knowledge of them—attracted to his shop a host of learned New Orleans scholars and antiquarians from Charles Gayarré to Judge Xavier Martin. Boimare's stock was diversified after his journey to France in 1828 when he imported mathematical instruments and thermometers, plaster statues and "a very rare miniature of Napoleon," not to mention such mundane articles as ladies' stockings and fine truffles. In 1829 he added a printing establishment to his premises and took on a partner, Benjamin Buisson, veteran of the Napoleonic Wars, in the firm of Buisson et Boimare. Not long after, Boimare had printed one of his rarest finds, offering copies for sale in the New Orleans shop. Thus Bernard de la Harpe's *Journal Historique de l'Establissement des Français à la Louisiane*, printed from the manuscript discovered by Boimare, was preserved from the fires and rat holes that destroyed so much of Louisiana's written and printed heritage. Boimare's bibliopolic career as transmitter and preserver ended, to all intents and purposes, around 1840 when he returned to France.

Like Benjamin Levy, however, he had a successor in his son Francis who in 1851 opened a short-lived bookstore on Royal Street for which he engaged his father's assistance. By 1853, the bookstore was closed, and Boimare père returned again to his native country. Subsequently,

Francis Boimare undertook the sale of lawbooks along with "old works on Louisiana and Mexico, etc." possibly inherited from his father. Before his death, A. L. Boimare, "ancien libraire à la N[ouve]lle-Orléans," published his *Notes Bibliographiques et raisonnées sur les principaux ouvrages publiés Sur La Floride et l'ancienne Louisiane*, a work that entitles him to the rank of Louisiana's first bibliographer. Toward the end of his life, Boimare père worked for the Paris specialist in rare Americana, Charles Chadenet. And so the scholar-bookseller who had brought his skills from France to the New World carried back to France his vast knowledge of Americana.

Along Royal Street and Exchange Alley, Chartres Street and Camp Street, the bookseller-printers of New Orleans set up their shingles. By the mid-century, a Spanish bookstore provided an outlet for the La Patria press on Exchange Alley and Victor Hébert had established his French Librairie on Chartres Street. Later in the century, William Muhl offered secondhand books in English and French to the growing bilingual Creole population of the city. During the 1870s, F. F. Hansell started business on Camp Street. Unlike many of his predecessors, Hansell was a native of New Orleans, and "in the elegant St. Charles avenue home of his parents he had fitted up one of the most complete private printing establishments ever possessed by an 'amateur printer.' " Hansell, who began modestly, eventually took over two buildings for an enterprise that included printing and publishing, bookselling and stationery. By 1903 he was ensconced on Canal Street, one of the largest wholesale and retail book firms in the South, a center of attraction to the people of New Orleans.

New Orleans dealers in books somehow survived the catastrophes that punctuated the second half of the nineteenth century. Out of the ruin caused by Civil War, out of the devastation caused by the Great Yellow Jack epidemic of 1878, the city emerged, and by the mid-1880s it could play host to the World's Cotton Industrial Exposition.

During the twentieth century, the great city on the lower Mississippi was the home of several noted book collectors. Simon J. Shwartz concentrated, somewhat as Boimare had done, on the history of Louisiana, and much of his "magnificent collection" was eventually acquired by yet another distinguished New Orleans collector. Edward Alexander Parsons began collecting before he attended school.[18] He continued collecting until "the history of his library" became "the history of his mind." Parsons, who regarded Francesco Petrarca as "The Perfect

Scholar," was partial to Aldine editions, especially Aldine incunables and first editions in original bindings with distinguished provenances. As he described the growth of his holdings: "The collection grew apace . . . and spread like the waters of my native Mississippi in floodtime. . . . It was accepted in a city not bookish, among a people cultured but not over-given to letters, as perhaps an incurable malady, to be hoped not contagious . . . and to be tolerated in a community where one man could devote his life to the Carnival, one to chess, many to the pursuit of the Goddess of Chance, in the high way in Cotton, in the popular ways in cards, keno, roulette and lotteries."

Although Parsons' collection was housed in the city of New Orleans, it did not originate there. Parsons bought in London from "princely dealers like Quaritch, the Maggs brothers and old Mr. Sotheran," in Paris from M. Auguste Blaizot on the Boulevard Haussmann, from Sotheby's, from the Paris quays and New York's Fourth Avenue. He visited Europe every three years to acquire books. If he ever patronized the booksellers of his native New Orleans, he makes no mention of such transactions in his bibliophilic autobiography.

Actually, there were few if any New Orleans booksellers who could have provided Parsons with "the vintage of the first Aldines" for which he thirsted. Indeed, in all the South there were few if any such booksellers. Charles Heartman's observations, made in the 1930s, are substantiated by an investigation of the origins and development of antiquarian bookselling in the cities to the South. The South, hungry for books as some of its denizens might have been, satisfied that hunger in Europe or the book marts of the North. And so the South, rich in its varied, often tragic history, distinguished by a scattering of fine libraries, was comparatively barren of noteworthy antiquarian booksellers. The lack seems to bear out the conclusions of scholars like W. J. Cash and William Charvat, that the "intellectual and aesthetic culture" of the South was "superficial," and that "the rich South was the despair of the book trade." Apparently the collecting of books in the South was never widespread, never democratized. Rather, it was confined to the few—to the elite among planters and merchants—who could afford to travel abroad to fill the lacunae of their shelves with rarities. As a result, though there were some splendid collections in the South, there were few notable local bibliopoles who found a fertile field there. This strange anomaly seems to have been peculiar to "Uncle Sam's other province."

NOTES

1. Charles F. Heartman, *Twenty-Five Years in The Auction Business And What Now? Reminiscences and Opinions* ([Chicago] 1938), unpaged.

2. Richard Beale Davis, *Intellectual Life in the Colonial South 1585–1763* (Knoxville: University of Tennessee Press, 1978), II, 626.

3. W. J. Cash, *The Mind of the South* (New York: Knopf, 1941), pp. 91 f, 94.

4. William Charvat, *The Profession of Authorship in America, 1800–1870* (Columbus: Ohio State Press, 1968), pp. 37 f.

5. Cash, *The Mind of the South*, p. vii, quoting Allen Tate.

6. For the Maryland book trade, see William Charvat, *Literary Publishing in America 1790–1850* (Philadelphia: University of Pennsylvania Press, 1959), pp. 19, 28; Adolf Growoll Collection, *American Book Trade History*, VI, 74; Leona M. Hudak, *Early American Women Printers and Publishers 1639–1820* (Metuchen, N.J.: Scarecrow Press, 1978), pp. 321–338; Thomas E. Keys, "The Colonial Library and the Development of Sectional Differences in the American Colonies," *Library Quarterly* 8 (1938), pp. 373–390; Rollo G. Silver, *The Baltimore Book Trade 1800–1825* (New York: New York Public Library, 1953), passim; Isaiah Thomas, *The History of Printing in America* (New York: Weathervane Books, 1970), pp. 532–540; Joseph Towne Wheeler, "Books Owned by Marylanders, 1700–1776," *Maryland Historical Magazine* XXXV:4 (December 1940), pp. 337–353; Joseph Towne Wheeler, "Booksellers and Circulating Libraries in Colonial Maryland," *Maryland Historical Magazine* XXXIV:2 (June 1939), pp. 111–137; Joseph Towne Wheeler, "Literary Culture in Eighteenth-Century Maryland, 1700–1776," *Maryland Historical Magazine* (undated summary); Lawrence C. Wroth, *A History of Printing in Colonial Maryland 1686–1776* (Baltimore: Typothetae, 1922), passim.

7. See James Weston Livingood, *The Philadelphia-Baltimore Trade Rivalry 1780–1860* (Harrisburg: Pennsylvania Historical and Museum Commission, 1947), passim.

8. For Lucas and his firm, see James W. Foster, "Fielding Lucas, Jr., Early 19th Century Publisher of Fine Books and Maps," *Proceedings of the American Antiquarian Society . . . October 19, 1955* (Worcester, Mass.: American Antiquarian Society, 1956), pp. 161–212; Adolf Growoll Collection, *American Book Trade History*, VIII, 129. According to a current Lucas Bros. news release, the firm traces its history to 1780 when Campbell, Conrad & Company, stationers, was founded in Baltimore. In 1804 it was acquired by a Philadelphian, Fielding Lucas, Jr., and began trading under his name. According to the release, Lucas came to Baltimore in 1800 from Philadelphia, where he had been engaged in the printing business.

9. John F. Coyle, "Memories of Washington Bookstores," *Publishers Weekly*

(21 May 1892), pp. 769 f. For further details of the Washington book trade, see "Robert Beall," *Publishers Weekly* (3 March 1887), p. 346; Adolf Growoll Collection, *American Book Trade History*, II, 65; XIII, 16 f.

10. Donald E. Bower, *Fred Rosenstock: A Legend in Books & Art* (Flagstaff, Ariz.: Northland Press, 1976), p. 94. For Lowdermilk, see also *AB Bookman's Weekly* (26 January 1970), p. 248, (23 March 1970), quoting an editorial in *The Evening Star*, Washington, D.C. (6 February 1970); Adolf Growoll Collection, *American Book Trade History*, VIII, 126; *Publishers Weekly* (23 March 1970), pp. 54 f; *New York Times* (30 December 1897) (According to this obituary of Lowdermilk, he went to Washington in 1878 "and built up a large bookstore."); *Washington Post* (10 February 1970); *Washington Star* (10 February 1970). I am deeply indebted to Greg Anderson, reference librarian of the Library of Congress, for information regarding the Lowdermilk firm.

11. Lawrence C. Wroth, *Parson Weems: A Biographical and Critical Study* (Baltimore, Md.: Eichelberger Book Company, 1911) p. 7 and passim. For Weems, see also Charvat, *The Profession of Authorship in America*, p. 39; Richard Beale Davis, *Intellectual Life in Jefferson's Virginia 1790–1830* (Chapel Hill: University of North Carolina Press, 1964), p. 80; James Gilreath, "Mason Weems, Mathew Carey and the Southern Booktrade, 1794–1810," *Publishing History* X (1981), pp. 27–49; Lewis Leary, *The Book-Peddling Parson: An Account of the Life and Works of Mason Locke Weems* (Chapel Hill, N.C.: Algonquin Books, 1984); Emily Ellsworth Ford Skeel, ed., *Mason Locke Weems: His Works and Ways* (New York 1929), 2 vols., II, xiii–xxiv and passim.

12. For these conflicting views, see Davis, *Intellectual Life in the Colonial South*, II, 623; Richard Beale Davis, *Literature and Society in Early Virginia 1608–1840* (Baton Rouge: Louisiana State University Press, 1973), passim; Keys, "The Colonial Library and the Development of Sectional Differences in the American Colonies," *Library Quarterly* (1938), p. 383; George K. Smart, "Private Libraries in Colonial Virginia," *American Literature* X (1938), pp. 24–52.

13. For Richmond booksellers, see Agnes M. Bondurant, *Poe's Richmond* (Richmond, Va.: Garrett & Massie, 1942), pp. 98 f, 115 ff; Davis, *Intellectual Life in Jefferson's Virginia*, pp. 77–85, 111; Adolf Growoll Collection, *American Book Trade History*, XI, 100; James Napier, "Some Book Sales in Dumfries, Virginia, 1794–1796," *William and Mary Quarterly*, Third Series X:3 (July 1953), pp. 441–445; *Publishers Weekly* (14 May 1892), pp. 739 f; (11 March 1893), pp. 424 f.

14. Hellmut Lehmann-Haupt, *The Book in America* (New York: R. R. Bowker, 1951), p. 58; Thomas, *The History of Printing in America*, p. 578.

15. For John Russell, see Madeleine B. Stern, *Imprints on History: Book Publishers and American Frontiers* (Bloomington: Indiana University Press, 1956), pp. 60–75, 405–409.

16. Allan Nevins and Henry Steele Commager, *A Pocket History of the United States* (New York: Pocket Books, 1977), p. 220.

17. For books and booksellers in New Orleans, see John M. Goudeau, "Booksellers and Printers in New Orleans, 1764–1885," *The Journal of Library History* V:1 (January 1970), pp. 5–19; Adolf Growoll Collection, *American Book Trade History*, VII, 12; Bertram W. Korn, "Benjamin Levy: New Orleans Printer and Publisher," *The Papers of the Bibliographical Society of America* 54:4 (1960), pp. 221–241; Roger Philip McCutcheon, "Books and Booksellers in New Orleans," *Louisiana Historical Quarterly* 20:3 (July 1937), pp. 606–618; John Tebbel, *A History of Book Publishing in the United States* (New York: R. R. Bowker, 1972, 1975), I, 467 f; II, 454; Edward Larocque Tinker, "Boimare First and Still Foremost Bibliographer of Louisiana," *The Papers of the Bibliographical Society of America* 24 (1930), pp. 34–42.

18. Edward Alexander Parsons, *The Wonder and The Glory: Confessions of a Southern Bibliophile* (New York: Thistle Press, 1962), passim.

10

Lone Stars

The art of selling rare books often depends less upon the state of geography than upon the state of mind. It can, as has frequently been noted, be practised anywhere. And so, although most antiquarian dealers tend to cluster in large and lively metropolitan centers, some conduct their business in remote or lonely sections of the country. They are, so to speak, the geographical mavericks or anomalies among antiquarian dealers. Some of them, tucked away in distant places, have led enormously productive and fascinating lives. Others, whose roots were planted in soil far removed from the great American book enclaves, have climbed to greatness in their profession. One handful of these "lone stars"—and other handfuls could be selected by other historians—forms the subject of this chapter. Texas and Colorado, Mississippi and Vermont have never been the background of great and thriving antiquarian book centers. Yet they have generated individual dealers whose lives have enormously enriched the antiquarian trade. Indeed, the history of that trade could not even aim at completeness without their stories.

HENRY STEVENS OF VERMONT

One of them came from the Green Mountain State and called himself throughout his amazing life, G.M.B., Green Mountain Boy. If he was not the greatest of all nineteenth-century American antiquarian booksellers, he closely approached that height. Henry Stevens of Vermont may not have selected a thriving metropolitan book center for his place of birth, but he certainly selected the right time in which to buy and sell books—a time when a multitude of great books and manuscripts was available and when great collections were being formed by individuals and institutions in the United States, when there was, as he put it, "a great rage for splendid private libraries."[1] As a result, the richness of the books that passed through his hands has scarcely since been equaled. It is comparable with the richness of his life and the rich stores of his mind. The Green Mountain Boy became Bookman of the World.

Henry Stevens was born in Barnet, Vermont, in 1819, and he was born to books. His father, Henry Stevens, Sr., farmer, innkeeper and millowner, was a forager for books and pamphlets. "In his historical mousings in garrets, among sequestered hen-coops and old barrels, he chanced . . . upon . . . a bushel of old Continental and State money. . . . This he called his 'Antiquarian Currency,' and with it bought in his travels through the country vast numbers of old books, papers, tracts, etc." When Father Stevens died at age seventy-five, he left "his house full of books and historical manuscripts, the delight of his youth, the companions of his manhood, and the solace of his old age."[2]

Those delights and companions, that solace, were part of Henry Stevens's birthright. Studies in the district schools, Peacham Academy and Newbury Seminary and a year of teaching preceded his attendance at Middlebury College. In 1840 a clerkship in a congressional committee in Washington led to a relationship with Peter Force which became a decisive factor in his life. When the young man continued his education at Yale, he took with him "a commission from Force 'to collect books, pamphlets, and MSS. in aid of the American Archives,' " the "monumental project" for reprinting United States historical documents. In the course of his studies at Yale and later at Harvard Law School, Stevens was "all the while dabbling in books and manuscripts." As he recalled, "During vacations and holidays I . . . for five years scouted through the New England and Middle States prospecting in out-of-the-way places for historical nuggets, mousing through public and private libraries and old homestead garrets, chiefly on behalf of Peter Force and his American Archives." Having "beat the bush" in New England towns and hamlets, he "gathered up the fruit"—Revolutionary pamphlets, Connecticut election sermons, ephemera on the French and Indian Wars. He attended auctions in New York, at one of which he met "his first great client," John Carter Brown. By 1844, a law student at Harvard, he was "all the while sifting and digesting the treasures of

Harvard Library" even as he was "reading passively with legal [Joseph] Story, and actively with historical [Jared] Sparks." This was the time when the great New England historians Sparks, Bancroft and Parkman were becoming acquaintances of the Green Mountain Boy. And this was the time when Henry Stevens was becoming a bookseller, a Yankee trader in books, or, as he would have preferred, "a seller of books," not a dealer in merchandise.[3]

He was also developing the bookselling techniques that would distinguish his career. In January 1844, age twenty-five, he compiled a catalogue of 500 works on America which he submitted to Peter Force with the cautionary statement: "Bartlet [sic] & Welford [booksellers], [and] Bancroft & Sparks have each & all applied to me for some of them, but I have uniformly refused to part with one until I had presented you with a catalogue. I would on no consideration part with them, but to get out of debt. I must have money, and soon too & my last resort shall be to sell my library."[4] Stevens was doomed to suffering financial predicaments, for his love of books frequently outran his wherewithal for them. He was a man of many facets. As Richard Garnett observed, he was on the one hand "shrewd and crafty" and on the other "open and candid." Tending toward plumpness, he was on his way to becoming the "jolly red-faced" bookseller who "prided himself more upon having made another man's library than he would have done upon having made his own fortune."[5]

Books were already becoming not merely his "wealth of gold and silver" but his "stores of golden thoughts"[6] when, in July 1845, he boarded the steamer *Caledonia* in Boston for his first book-hunting expedition abroad.[7] He was armed with forty gold sovereigns ($400) borrowed from friends and letters of introduction from Francis Parkman, and from Jared Sparks to Antonio Panizzi, librarian of the British Museum. He was armed also with his love of books, his knowledge of books, and his connections with those who would build libraries and had commissioned him to forage. His destiny was upon him. He was about to become the bibliopolic liaison between England and the United States. In future, as his biographer would put it, Henry Stevens would work "in two currencies: pounds and dollars."

Stevens himself in the 1880s wrote a succinct account of this first portentous journey:

In July, 1845, a young man from Vermont, at the age of twenty-six, I found myself in London, a self-appointed missionary, on an antiquarian and historical book-hunting expedition, at my own expense and on my own responsibility, with a few Yankee notions in head and an ample fortune of nearly forty sovereigns in pocket. . . . Those were indeed happy days, when on a July morning one might run down a hundred brace of rare old books on America in London at as many shillings a volume as must now be paid in pounds. The shops of Rich, Rodd, Thorpe, Pickering and others were looked through the first fortnight, and books to the amount of more than £1000 "turned down" and reported to American clients. They were scrambled for in Boston and New York like hot buckwheat cakes at a college breakfast. It was hardly possible to sweep them together fast enough.

Between 1845 and 1847, during his first sojourn in London, Henry Stevens acted as purchasing agent for the Library of Congress, the Smithsonian Institution, for Peter Force, John Carter Brown 'and—at the suggestion of George P. Putnam—for James Lenox. In addition he became special agent for Antonio Panizzi of the British Museum. As he explained in a letter to James Lenox written in 1846:

I came to England as a student of American History and Literature. After pursuing my researches for some six months in Her Majesty's State Paper Office and the Library of the British Museum, I was applied to by Mr. Panizzi, the Librarian of the Museum, to undertake the task of ascertaining the deficiencies of the Library, both in books relating to America in all languages, and in American Literature generally, and as far as lay in my power to supply such deficiencies as I might find. . . . I have now also a similar arrangement with the Bodleian Library at Oxford.

Given free access to the British Museum Library stacks, Stevens succeeded in compiling a desiderata list of 10,000 items which Panizzi promptly asked him to supply. As the librarian would later advise his trustees when eyebrows were raised at some of Stevens's prices, "It may be more advisable to accept than to reject Mr. Stevens' offer." The two men would negotiate together for decades. "By 1865," according to Stevens' biographer, the bookseller "had placed over 100,000 American books in the British Museum, thereby making that collection the most complete in Americana of the century." He had foraged for those books at dealers' shops, and he had fought for them at auction. The Green Mountain Boy advised James Lenox of the availability of the Gutenberg Bible at auction in 1847—the first Gutenberg to cross the ocean. "As quick on the trigger after an American book as a cat is after a mouse," Henry Stevens would send many firsts to his native land as the years passed.

Most of those years were spent by the great bookseller in London. His connections with America were sustained by periodic visits home and by his continued relationship with his clients. Stevens' associations with his customers[8] were as effective as his techniques in obtaining the rarities with which he supplied them. Between the Scylla and Charybdis of "the two 'old bachelors' " James Lenox and John Carter Brown, he steered a safe course. Brown had given him "a *general order*, for *all* rare old books relating to Am^a. which he had not already,—and will pay *'fair prices'* on delivery." As for James Lenox, Stevens commented, "He gave me his money and his friendship, and I sought the world over to supply him with books and manuscripts." For Lenox, "collecting to shelve," Stevens collected "to disperse." In 1855, when Lenox came to London, he visited Stevens every day for nearly a month, checking the bookseller's stock of Bibles and books relating to America. Eventually, through "luck, perseverance and hairbreadth escapes," the Green Mountain Boy helped in assembling Lenox's "extraordinary collections of De Bry, Hulsius, Thévenot, . . . Hakluyt, Purchas," not to mention "the five Caxtons and the block books to which I helped him, besides the two early manuscript New Testaments by Wycliffe."

Supplying the British Museum—placing 10,000 desired American books in its library within a year and a half—Stevens also supplied other significant clients. To George Brinley, for example, he sold a collection of Mathers; weekly packets of books were shipped to the Smithsonian from England; the Library of Congress was the recipient of Stevens finds. Among his friends, Henry Stevens counted the printer Charles Whittingham and the publisher William Pickering. Among his customers he counted some of the greatest librarians and collectors of the nineteenth century. As he wrote to one of them, James Lenox, "One should never despair. All rare books turn up sooner or later in London."

Judging from the acquisitions handled by Henry Stevens, that statement seemed indeed to be true.[9] "Most American books of any value"— and a great many non-American rarities—"passed through his hands." His headquarters in Morley's Hotel, Charing Cross, and later at "The Nuggetory, 4, Trafalgar Square" became temporary treasure houses of great works on their passage from dealer to collector. During his first sojourn abroad Stevens arranged to "take the best of his Americana" from Obadiah Rich, the American bibliographer-bookseller who had preceded him in London. Since Rich had recently purchased the library of Henri Ternaux—"the most nearly complete collection of manuscripts and books" pertaining to America—the pickings were "rich" indeed, including four different editions of the Columbus Letter, thirty volumes of Jesuit Relations, and firsts of Peter Martyr, Cortés, Las Casas and Hakluyt.

Some of Stevens' major purchases were made in America, foremost among them the library of George Washington of which he wrote: "In 1848 I bought Washington's Library of about 3,000 volumes, for $3,000, to secure about 300 volumes with the autograph of the 'Father of his country' on the title pages, some rarities for Mr. Lenox, and many tracts and miscellaneous American books for the British Museum. Mr. Lenox declined. . . . I sold the collection to a parcel of Bostonians . . . and . . . was compelled to subscribe the rest myself." The Green Mountain Boy was undeterred by this setback. Two years later he acquired the Franklin Papers, some 3,000 manuscript items and over 200 Franklin imprints which went to Congress.

The acquisitions of later years need merely to be listed to arouse in the modern bibliopole the stunned amazement of the explorer upon the fabled peak of Darien: a "large and valuable collection" of the rarest books in the American Indian languages which went to Dr. Joseph Cogswell for the Astor Library; the "Wicked Bible" of 1631 which was purchased for James Lenox; a Bay Psalm Book acquired at a Pickering sale; some forty Shakespeare quartos; the libraries of Samuel G. Drake, E. A. Crowninshield and Baron Humboldt—all these passed through the knowing hands of the Green Mountain Boy who operated from the metropolis of London. In 1854, the "hearty, . . . plump . . . bachelor" traded his bachelorhood for yet another "acquisition," marrying the widow of a Polish baron, Mary Newton Kuczynski, who was also a descendant of Sir Isaac Newton. Two years later Nathaniel Hawthorne paid him a visit, recording in his English notebook the treasures shown him:

Mr. Stevens showed us some rare old books which he has in his private collection: a black-letter edition of Chaucer, . . . Dryden's translation of Virgil, with Dr. Johnson's autograph in it: and a large collection of Bibles . . . a Spanish

Document with the signature of the son of Columbus: a whole little volume in Franklin's handwriting, . . . the original manuscripts of many of the songs of Burns.

Working as he did in the currencies of two nations, Henry Stevens paid several extended visits to his native country.[10] Between 1847 and 1848, between 1857 and 1858, in 1863, and again between 1868 and 1870, he returned to the United States. At the time of his first return he placed Obadiah Rich in charge of his London affairs and "brought with him in six cases nearly $5,000 worth of books relating to America" designed for James Lenox and John Carter Brown and met with both of them. In the course of that journey he also acquired the library of George Washington, made sales to Peter Force, and bought copiously for the British Museum, his purchases including, for example, "all the duplicate newspapers from the New-York Historical Society." Later returns to America were almost as spectacular, including the purchase of a *Tamerlane* from Samuel G. Drake and the bookseller's proposal of a catalogue of the Lenox Library.

The Vermonter was becoming an authoritative figure in the book world of two countries. His specialties were wide ranging: early editions of the Bible, early voyages and travels, Americana, Caxton, fine bindings. As his reputation developed, his concept of the book crystallized. "A nation's books," he would write, "are her vouchers. Her libraries are her muniments." "Libraries are an index of a nation's, as well as an individual's wealth, taste, and character. . . . he who buys a choice library . . . spends not, but invests his money. Good books pay a liberal interest to their owner, and are an inheritance to his children." And again: "Books are both our luxuries and our daily bread. They have become to our lives and happiness prime necessities. They are our trusted favourites, our guardians, our confidential advisers, and the safe consumers of our leisure. They cheer us in poverty, and comfort us in the misery of affluence. They absorb the effervescence of impetuous youth, and while away the tedium of age."[11]

Such attitudes were reflected in the work of Henry Stevens as bookseller and as scholar. He aimed at all times to combine those functions. His catalogues were designed to become works of reference. As he wrote in the Prospectus to his *Historical Nuggets*, "All the Books described are in stock, and our object is firstly to catalogue them for sale, and secondly by carefully giving the titles in full with accurate collations and occasional descriptive, historical, geographical, and biographical notes, to form at the same time a useful bibliographical work of reference."[12] In a sense, Stevens became a philosopher of bibliography, cogitating its nature and purpose, and boasting of his "love of accuracy and fulness in scientific" description. His catalogues were, as he put it, "elevated into Bibliography." Complaining as late as 1872 that "Bibliography as yet is a mere jackall, or packhorse . . . doomed to work for other arts and sciences," he hoped to exalt it into a science in its own right. His years were punctuated by tangible efforts in that direction. In the *Catalogue of My English Library* (1853) he wrote: "If you are troubled with a pride of accuracy, and would have it completely taken out of you, print a catalogue."

Stevens followed his own precepts. Between 1854 and 1884 he published *A Catalogue Raisonné of English Bibles* and *A Catalogue of American Books in the Library of the British Museum*, the *Bibliotheca Americana*, reissued as *Historical Nuggets*, catalogues of the Crowninshield and Humboldt Libraries, *Historical and Geographical Notes on the Earliest Discoveries in America*, the *Bibliotheca Historica*, a catalogue of his father's library, *Photobibliography*, describing his invention for a universal bibliography and his plea for a Central Bibliographical Bureau, *The Bibles in the Caxton Exhibition*, and finally his castigation of inferior book manufacture, *Who Spoils Our New English Books*.

By the time *Who Spoils Our New English Books* appeared, Henry Stevens had left to him but few pages in his "Volume of . . . Earthly Labor." On 28 February 1886 he died in London. The firm he had founded had already undergone certain changes. Between 1860 and 1866 Henry Stevens' brother Benjamin Franklin Stevens was a partner. The period of the American Civil War, at the outbreak of which Henry Stevens served as arms agent for General Frémont, saw a decline in the business. Moreover, "Stevens' dilatory financial practices caught up with him and bankruptcy followed." Subsequently the business was rebuilt; Stevens' son, Henry Newton Stevens, became an assistant, and in 1885 the son's partnership led to the new style of Henry Stevens & Son, operating at first in a public shop at 115 St. Martin's Lane "over Against the Church of St Martin in the Fields" and subsequently at 39 Great Russell Street opposite the British Museum. So the firm continued after the founder's death until 1895 when Henry Newton Stevens became head of the new firm of Henry Stevens, Son, & Stiles, the result of a partnership between Stevens and his friend and assistant

Robert E. Stiles. In 1907 that firm issued a catalogue of rare Americana that included the Waldseemüller world-maps of 1507 and 1516 which had been discovered in the Wolfegg Castle Library. The same year another Henry Stevens, son of Henry Newton Stevens, was admitted to partnership. In 1926 Henry Newton Stevens' son-in-law Roland Tree joined the firm, and in 1962 Roland Tree's son-in-law Thomas P. MacDonnell became a partner.[13]

And so, the young man from Barnet, Vermont, who traded grandiosely in the printed records of two civilizations, exerted an enduring influence upon the antiquarian book trade of two countries.

THE CHARLES E. TUTTLE COMPANY

Like the firm founded by Henry Stevens, another firm that rose from Vermont soil has survived into the present, and that firm, interestingly enough, has traded in the currencies of two continents. Unlike the case of Stevens, whose letterbooks and ledgers have been preserved in various institutions, "there seem to be no extant [Tuttle] records." While the details of that firm cannot be reassembled into a colorful mosaic, the basic facts of its history can and should be recorded.[14]

The firm founder, George Albert Tuttle, was Henry Stevens' almost exact contemporary. Born in 1816, he started work as a printer in Vermont at the age of sixteen, and hence the firm traces its origin to the year 1832. A few years later young Tuttle started out on his own, printing books and selling wallpaper and all the paraphernalia associated with a nineteenth-century country bookstore. George Albert, who died in 1885, was followed in time by his four sons, and they by theirs. One of those grandsons changed the direction of the firm and brought it into the ken of the antiquarian.

Charles E. Tuttle, Sr., born in 1878, worked in a mail order house in Chicago before returning to Rutland, Vermont. There he was invited to add an antiquarian department to the Tuttle business. As a result, Charles Tuttle became an expert in Vermontiana, and some of his *Selections . . . from Vermont private libraries*—books, pamphlets, broadsides, manuscripts—turned up in Libbie's Boston book auctions. Expanding the range of his interests from regionalism, Tuttle ventured into diverse antiquarian fields from Cromwellian tracts to American blacks. By 1939 the Tuttle antiquarian department was sufficiently broad-based to become independent. Removed to Charles's tall colonial house on Main Street where fantail pigeons roosted in the eaves, it became a mecca for searchers after the old and rare.

Shortly before World War II, Charles, Sr.'s son, Charles E. Tuttle, Jr., joined his father as a partner. In 1943 Charles, Sr., died and Charles, Jr., was in the overseas army. The Rutland operation was continued with assistant Jane Wright in charge. Then, stationed in Tokyo after the war, Charles E. Tuttle, Jr., introduced to the ancestral firm his own individual predilections. Exporting Japanese books, old and new, to America, he also opened a shop in Tokyo, entering the field of publishing and establishing a rare book department in the heart of the city's book district. A stream of Japanese books flowed steadily to America. In Rutland, *Tuttle's Literary Miscellany*, compiled by the late Charles V. S. Borst, brought an exotic flavor to Vermont. One Vermonter had had a lifetime romance with England; another with Japan. And so, as Henry Stevens had linked America and Albion by his book operations, the Tuttle firm for many years linked Orient and Occident with "Books to Span the East and West." As the Stevens firm continues, so does Tuttle's Antiquarian Books, "builders of special collections—appraisers of literary property," still under the aegis of Charles E. Tuttle, still on Rutland, Vermont's, South Main Street.

ELIJAH LEROY SHETTLES

No part of this vast country seems entirely immune from the strange practice of antiquarian bookselling. Vermont in the Northeast and Texas in the Southwest have both spawned practitioners of that curious trade. In 1852, when Henry Stevens, Green Mountain Boy, was acquiring a collection of the earliest books in the languages of the American Indian, and George Albert Tuttle was printing and selling books in Rutland, Vermont, Elijah Leroy Shettles made his bow to the world.[15]

Shettles would become an antiquarian dealer only during the last twenty years of his long life, but the picaresque romance he lived during his first sixty-nine years prepared him for that trade. Through much of that strange foreground he loved books and collected them. In a sense, he served a lifetime apprenticeship for a comparatively brief period of mastery.

He was born in Pontotoc County, Mississippi, not, like Henry Stevens, to books, but to poverty. Against the background of Mississippi's Flatwoods Country he attended a log cabin schoolhouse, studied

McGuffey's Readers, borrowed books. In 1875, age twenty-three, with "a little paper-covered trunk, a fiddle, a brass horn, and a change or two of clothing," he left home to seek his fortune in the West.

During the next half-century, Elijah Leroy Shettles was many things—teacher and gambler, saloon keeper and Methodist preacher. He was also a lover of books. To the future bookseller much of his varied experience proved grist for his mill. Early on he spent some time in the Grange movement in Arkansas. Fifty years later he was to handle "the most extensive single collection of materials in the nation on that organization."

In 1881 the future antiquarian arrived in Texas, an enormous man with an immense frame, a bushy mustache, a prodigious memory, and a predilection for book talk. When, ten years later, he was converted from the riotous life of a gambler and entered the ministry of the Methodist church, the opportunity of acquiring books was one of the rewards of his "new life."

From his youth Shettles had been a constant reader. "I do not know when I first began to read," he was to write. Now, as Methodist circuit rider, he began to collect. Despite his affection for Dickens and Bulwer, Smollett and Fielding, Shakespeare and Sterne, he made no attempt to collect English literature and history, but foraged for Americana in specialized fields. As he put it, "I have done considerable grazing." He grazed for books not merely at Gammel's book establishment in Texas where he purchased Parker's account of the Fort Parker Massacre for $8, but wherever his ministry took him—Nashville and New Orleans, Alabama and Arkansas. He grazed for Texana and Wesleyana, for books about the South and the Civil War, bad men and circuit riders. In Mobile, he found a cache of Confederate letters and order books; in Birmingham, a "lot of books piled up on the floor like corn."

From the beginning of this specialized collecting, Shettles was attracted to pamphlets. "I had a strong leaning toward pamphlets," he was to write, "and I have bought many. . . . on a trip to New York I bought over 800, all on the Civil War. . . . I have bought them for from ten cents to $275.00. . . . Pamphlets cover more subjects than books . . . Indians, Slavery, Lottery, Gambling, Dueling, Political and Religious Controversy, War, Overland Trips, Rangers, Vigilantes Committees, . . . the bad man of the West, . . . Ku Klux Klan, the Sons of Liberty, . . . the Knights of the Golden Circle." This aging antiquarian forager sensed the permanent value of ephemera and constantly sought it out, amassing catalogues and runs of newspapers, brochures, broadsides and letters. And so he was able to bring to Texas the documents of its own history.

In 1921 Elijah Shettles, a white-haired sixty-nine-year-old giant of a man, ceased being an amateur collector and became a professional bookseller. Despite the ups and downs of his already long life, he had equipped himself for the role. He had assembled the books and pamphlets of an expanding region. He had specialized where specialization was needed. Now he was able to help develop all the libraries of Texas—the University of Texas, the State Library, Southern Methodist University, the Rosenberg and San Antonio Libraries, and Rice University. His *modus operandi* was described by an admiring collector:

Mr. Shettles did business, mostly by mail, in his cottage home out in a plebian [sic] part of town. He might have had three thousand, maybe more, books, not counting duplicates, mainly Americana, with emphasis on Texas, the West, and the South. He was expert at acquiring remainders of privately printed historical material and then controlling the market on it. He was a great pamphlet man. He had been trained—as a professional gambler on cards—to remember concretely, precisely. He knew the bibliographical facts about almost every title stored in his capacious memory, and knew an extraordinary amount of the contents of thousands of books and pamphlets. He could gut one very quickly.

The ex-gambler and Methodist circuit rider had become a bookseller who "helped educate the educated people of Texas to appreciate their own history and records." He had become "a force in the development of bibliophilia in the Southwest."

In addition to the love of books and appreciation of the ephemeral, Shettles was endowed with an extraordinary bibliopolic memory. When a dealer from Kansas mentioned a rare pamphlet to him but regretted he had forgotten the date, Shettles "supplied it, told him where the pamphlet was printed, gave him some facts about the author, recalled how, when and where he himself acquired his own first copy of it, at what price, to whom he sold it and at what price . . . [and] noted casually certain printed items that had preceded it, and then named a still rarer pamphlet published in reply to it."

For nearly twenty years, until his death in 1940, Shettles honed that prodigious memory and helped build the libraries of the American Southwest. At his death a fellow Texan, J. Frank Dobie, said of him that "He had mental and spiritual powers that made him at home in many eras." "He cast a shadow." His shadow did not extend as far as Henry Stevens' or Tuttle's, but it covered the state of Texas. It was as large as the state, as large as the man himself.

CHARLES F. HEARTMAN

In 1916 the firm founded by Henry Stevens—Henry Stevens, Son, & Stiles—wrote to the bookseller-auctioneer Charles Frederick Heartman: "We think you are doing good work, and that your catalogues are prepared with a great deal of attention to bibliographical details, more so than any other we have seen, emanating from your side of the Atlantic."[16]

The praise, if a trifle condescending, was genuine and was merited. Charles F. Heartman was indeed producing catalogues of bibliographical distinction during the early twentieth century in America. Yet, though his work might be respected, he himself did not always evoke enthusiastic response from his colleagues. Heartman was something of an enigma, the key to which lies in several factors. He was, first of all, a German-American, and although he developed a perfervid addiction to Americana and rejected Teutonic attitudes, he inherited them. He was a man of many peeves and prejudices, which he did not hesitate to enunciate orally and in print. Throughout his professional life he struggled between the muse and the marketplace, between ambition for bibliographical excellence and the need of money. He was, finally, a rover who operated from more than half a dozen different localities in the North and South, few of which ever became noted as antiquarian book centers. He was, in short, a lone star.[17]

Heartman was born in Braunschweig, Germany, in 1883, and, having lost his mother when he was only two, was brought up by his father and grandmother. Educated at grade school and gymnasium, he became a journalist, and at one time served as foreign correspondent in the Balkans. As early as 1900 he edited *Der Literat*, a short-lived literary periodical, and later was editor-publisher of *Der Berliner Beobachter*. By 1907, when he left Germany, he had produced a small corpus of writing, mostly under pseudonyms such as Heinrich Hartmann and Dr. Heinrich Krohmann. He had also developed the characteristics that would persist throughout his life—his individualism and impatience with opposition, his temperament, his candor, and his love of books. "I collected books and prints," he recalled, "when a mere boy." He also liked to recall that his "scholarly mind" had been "trained in Europe."

In 1907 the young newspaper man who already foresaw a German collapse left his native land for London where he met and married Martha Esche and "started his activities as a bookseller in a small way." By 1911 they had emigrated to the United States. Heartman, who had only $40 with him, promptly secured employment as a janitor in an apartment house on Second Avenue and as promptly began frequenting the Fourth Avenue bookstores. One bookseller, Deutschberger, "promised to introduce him to the mysteries of the book business if he worked for him for nothing during his spare time." In the course of that brief apprenticeship Heartman managed to buy German books for pennies, "mainly first editions of early authors," and by 1912 he was able to open a bookshop on 22nd Street. Already a rover, later in the year he moved to 36 Lexington Avenue.

Almost from the start Charles Heartman combined his bookselling activities with his career as an auctioneer. He had had an encouraging experience at the Hoe sale where he met the dealer Eisemann of Baer & Co., Frankfurt. The novice bookseller had found on a cart in Houston Street a pile of German pamphlets on socialism and anarchism that included the printed report of the first Social Democrat Convention in Germany. He had paid $5 for the lot and, after meeting Eisemann at the Hoe auction, sold it to the foreign dealer for $200. This might have been enough to endear the auction sale to Charles Heartman. But he had other reasons for entering the auction business. "Since I was ambitious and hard working," he explained, "it was natural that I constantly overbought myself, and therefore . . . had to meet my obligations to auction houses through consignments." His experiences as consigner led him very soon to the resolution to "make auctions for myself and, (fighter for the underdog I always was) at the same time reform the auction business." In 1913, therefore, Heartman "took space on the second floor above his bookstore and engaged R. E. Sherwood . . . as auctioneer." His first auction sale was held on 9 and 10 June 1913—the precursor of hundreds that would follow. By 1938 Heartman had issued 283 auction catalogues. As for the auctions themselves, they were "more than commercial sales . . . they were gatherings of dealers, librarians and collectors." Whether or not they carried into practice Heartman's preachment, "I aim to protect the seller, because the buyer can protect himself," they attracted a notable collection of buyers. At one of his auction parties, Wilberforce Eames, William L. Clements, Lathrop C. Harper and Otis G. Hammond were among those present who "gathered in an upstairs room and discussed collectors and collecting for most of the afternoon." A famous Heartman sale, held on Washington's Birthday in 1927 in the auctioneer's Metuchen, New Jersey, headquarters, was a surprise party for the New York bookseller Gabriel Wells, who was presented with a booklet, *Gabriel Wells, the Philosopher. An Essay by Temple Scott.* The host hired a Pullman car to convey the crowd of buyers back to New York. A few years later, in 1931, Heartman held the sale of the "Eminent A. Edward Newton Collection, formed by the late George H. Sargent," at which A. Edward Newton himself and Barton Currie officiated as auctioneers. Heartman's practice was to serve a meal—frequently prepared by his wife—at every sale, and upon the occasion of the Sargent auction, "the food and liquor bill for the dinner consumed came very close to a thousand dollars." Heartman was developing his ultimate reputation for "skillfully" combining "country dinners, pecans and books."

He was also developing a reputation for the contents of his sales which, like his bookselling stock, consisted primarily of rare Americana. As one whose "scholarly mind" had been trained abroad, Heartman felt it incumbent upon himself to formulate and explain his intense devotion to Americana: "Americana," he wrote,

is not a hobby, it is a creed. . . . to me it seems that only the Americana collector has reached the heights of supreme contentment. . . .

I go over some letters written from Morristown by George Washington; . . . a document . . . by Lincoln. . . .

. . . I look at my set of sixteen Presidents, lithographed in color by Currier. . . . I am immediately enwrapped in a century crowded with historical incidents, unbelievable romantic and decisive. . . .

Within a year I sold a number of items printed in Cambridge, Massachusetts, two of them earlier than 1660. I had eleven hitherto undescribed Indian Captivities, . . . I sold unique Primers; the manuscript of a forty-niner who went over the plains; Revolutionary Orderly books . . . What would I have rather handled? A Gutenberg Bible? A Shakespeare folio? A Keats letter? A Royal binding? Not me.

Why this pronounced feeling towards Americana. After all, I had a European training. . . . Because it is not a hobby, it is a creed. Americana . . . represents not merely an accumulation of utilitarian and quaint objects of the past . . . . but with it goes the assimilation of a state of mind . . .

Americana is something that if it grips you once, will change your habits, temperament and view of life. Pity the one that never came under its spell.[18]

However turgid his style, however Germanic his phrasing, the message shines through. Heartman has been called "one of the best 'scouts' in the book-hunting game." He traveled "frequently to inspect dealers' stocks in other cities"; he made "contacts with many libraries to secure their duplicates." As a result, he auctioned and sold "thousands of unrecorded imprints" and an array of rare Americana that attracted prospective purchasers to his premises and collectors to his catalogues.

Between 1913 and 1953 Charles Heartman issued 312 auction catalogues and 160 special priced catalogues and lists containing his Americana discoveries. One noteworthy catalogue, circulated in 1919, was entitled *Six hundred Pamphlets, Broadsides, and a Few Books . . . relating to America . . . prior to eighteen hundred. Bibliographically, Historically and Sometimes Sentimentally Described.* Another, *Americana, Printed and in Manuscript,* issued in 1930, has been called "a model of careful cataloguing." It included the Stuart-Bute Papers relating to the Revolutionary War priced at $47,500, and the manuscript of the first eight stanzas of Poe's poem, "For Annie," priced at $17,500. Heartman's Americana Catalogue Number 120 offered a collection on slavery and blacks and included the gold medal presented to the first black voter in the United States. The prefaces to many of his catalogues, such as the 1929 preface on "First Editions," are bibliographically informative.

Heartman's catalogues were issued from a variety of places, many of them bearing little or no relationship to the antiquarian book trade. Whatever relationship to that trade may now accrue to them stemmed principally from Heartman's association. His first major move, to Rutland, Vermont, took place in 1920. By the following year he had moved again, to Perth Amboy, New Jersey, where he remained one year. His next venue was Metuchen, and there his "old New Jersey mansion, filled with colonial furnishings," attracted crowds of "bookish people" who came to participate in Heartman's famous auctions and enjoy Martha Heartman's famous cooking. After about thirteen years in Metuchen, Heartman moved again, this time to New Orleans where he "established the Pelican Galleries, conducting a retail business and holding auction sales of books, at 723 Toulouse Street" in the French Quarter. There Charles R. Knight became his associate. After a year in Louisiana, the nomadic antiquarian moved again to the place that would henceforth be closely associated with his name. In Hattiesburg, Mississippi, he purchased a 400-acre farm from the United States government which he dubbed "The Book Farm." "His intention was to establish there a cooperative colony for intellectuals," but Heartman soon found bookselling and auctioneering more lucrative and more appealing, and he compromised by holding week-end barbecues to which he invited neighbors and bibliophiles. After only three years in the South, Heartman concluded that the region was "hungry for books" and needed "an intelligent force who . . . can be helpful to librarians as well as to collectors." After filling that role in Hattiesburg for seven or eight years, Heartman moved to Biloxi in 1943, and thence to New Braunfels, Texas, in 1947. By 1951 he was back in New Orleans, where he would remain until his death.

Through all the migrations—occasioned no doubt by economic stress as well as personal predilection—Charles Heartman pursued his multiple career not only as bookseller and auctioneer but as scholar and writer. As early as 1915 he launched Heartman's Historical Series which continued until his death and comprised seventy-eight numbers among them The "Blue Book"; a Bibliographical Attempt to Describe the Guide Books to the Houses of Ill Fame in New Orleans and A Bibliography of First Printings of the Writings of Edgar Allan Poe. Also in 1915 Heartman published his Checklist of Printers in the United States from Stephen Daye to the Close of the War of Independence, pleading:

If somebody will co-operate with me, we will bring this work down to 1815. I would also like to have a collaborator for a Checklist of Mexican Printers from the beginning till . . . 1800; and also one for a Checklist of Printers who worked in South and Central America from the beginning till about 1800; thus giving a complete Checklist of American Printers (North and South) from the beginning to about 1800. I consider this a most necessary reference book and would gladly welcome assistance in this work.[19]

Charles Heartman labored during much of his life to supply such reference books in his specialty of Americana. Among his bibliographical and literary productions were his Phillis Wheatley . . . A Critical At-

tempt and a Bibliography of her Writings (1915); *Charles F. Heartman Presents John Peter Zenger and his Fight for the Freedom of the American Press* (1934); *American Primers, Indian Primers, Royal Primers, and . . . Non-New-England Primers Issued prior to 1830* (1935). In his study of *The New-England Primer Issued prior to 1830* (1934) he revealed his ambitions, shortcomings and handicaps: "To say that I am satisfied with this work would not be telling the truth. For more than twenty years it was my ambition to write a real history of the New England Primer and to give the bibliography as an appendix. However, such a work must again be postponed for . . . it would take two years of constant work. . . . If one only had no debts and a Guggenheim Fellowship . . . one could do interesting work."[20]

In 1916 *Heartman's Bibliographical Leaflets*, No. 1 presented "the first complete bibliographical descriptions" of the rare work on the American Revolution, *Geschichte der Kriege in und ausser Europa vom Anfange des Auffstandes der brittischen Kolonien in Nordamerika* of which he himself had offered the first complete set at auction. In addition to his manifold labors, between 1925 and 1927 he took on editorship of *The Americana Collector*, "A Monthly Magazine for Americana—Lore and Bibliography," in which he enunciated candid and not always palatable views on "Rare Books As Merchandise," and ran a series of articles on "Famous American Booksellers Past and Present," including Joseph F. Sabin, Walter M. Hill, Lathrop Colgate Harper, George D. Smith, Charles Eliot Goodspeed, and "Gabriel Wells, The Philosopher." In 1932 Charles Heartman became editor-publisher of the *American Book Collector*.

As prickly as he was productive, Heartman enjoyed engaging in literary skirmishes. One attack he directed in 1934 against the forger Thomas James Wise, remarking, "I do these things in my own temperamental way."[21] Another—in the form of a critical pamphlet—was leveled toward the end of his life against Wright Howes' contemplated bibliography of U.S.Iana.[22] In between, Heartman sought and found occasion to fulminate against a variety of "fakes, forgeries, dishonest bibliographical statements." Neither collectors nor booksellers escaped his arrows. Among the former he described the nation's president as "Franklin D. 'Piker' Roosevelt (no piker in using the country's funds)." Among the latter he dubbed a king of antiquarians as "George D. 'Try to take it away from me' Smith." He expostulated against "The asinine

desire . . . to deal only in certain names and certain classes of literature,"
and he continued his expostulations until the end of his life.

His seventieth birthday was celebrated in April 1953. The following
month he attended a meeting of the National Society of Autograph
Collectors at Columbus, Ohio, and a few days later, on 8 May, he
succumbed after a heart attack. The catalogue of his final auction had
already been compiled, and the sale was held on 24 May. Only one
personage was missing on that occasion—the lone star himself who had
brought to Perth Amboy and Metuchen, to Hattiesburg, Biloxi and
New Orleans his enduring romance with rare Americana.

FRED A. ROSENSTOCK

Charles Heartman had little in common with Fred Rosenstock except
the love of books and Americana.[23] It is true that Heartman hailed
from Germany and Rosenstock from Austria, but in character, family
background, and center of operation these two lone stars were literally
poles apart.

Fred Rosenstock came to Denver by a circuitous and fortuitous route.
As a child in Biala Potok, Austria, he spent his boyhood in the Carpathian Mountains and by age seven had not only learned Yiddish,
Ruthenian, Polish and German, but could read English. The family
sailed west aboard the *Patrizia* in 1904, and the nine-year-old Jewish
immigrant from Austria-Hungary began a new life in Rochester, New
York. There he was early introduced to American mores and American
literature, especially the literature of the Wild West. "As a boy in
Rochester," he would recall, "I was avidly consuming all sorts of reading
matter on the so-called Wild West, including the dime novels of that
day. It was natural to fall under the spell of the Western illustrators as
well. I came to know and to be charmed by the work of Russell and
other artists." He came to know also the charm of Mayne Reid whose
adventures he read in Yiddish translation while working in the library
of a Jewish clothing local. His growing passion for Western Americana
would one day be crystallized and shared with others against an appropriate western background. Meanwhile, in Rochester, in 1913, Fred
Rosenstock made his first book sale. Finding a copy of a work on Niagara
Falls for twenty cents, he sold it to the Niagara Falls Public Library for
$5. He was on his way.

Already a racy storyteller and avid reader, wearing the glasses he would wear all his life, Fred Rosenstock was developing into the "volatile, excitable, enthusiastic, generous man to whom conversation about the things he loved was the savor of life." During World War I he worked in the surgeon general's office in Washington, D.C., where, he would remember, "I continued to add to my library. I suppose—even then—you could call me a collector because I bought enough books to deserve the designation. I always had books, and it was one of the delights of my life."

Following the war, Rosenstock worked as bookkeeper-stenographer for the Thomas Cusack Outdoor Advertising Company. After a bout of pneumonia his health began to fail and the doctors advised him to resettle in the West, in Arizona or California. In August 1920, therefore, he left Washington, and so raised the curtain upon the Professional Adventures of Fred Rosenstock. En route to the Far West, he lost his sorely needed only pair of glasses, and was forced to make a "stopover" in Denver to order a new pair. That "stopover" would last a lifetime.

Though Denver, the "focal center of the Rocky Mountain West," was scarcely a distinguished book center in the 1920s, the mile-high city did boast some secondhand bookstores. On his third day in the city, Rosenstock swooped down upon them. By 1921, having elected to remain in Denver, he was working for the Curran Company, a billboard concern, and he was haunting the bookshops. Fine sets and collectors' items, French books, first editions, fifty-cent bargains—all were acquired. In time Rosenstock bought entire libraries, some on the installment plan, obtaining Charles T. Wilder's collection from his widow, the library of Henry S. Winans, and a "windfall" found in the basement of Grimwoods' bookstore in Colorado Springs.

It was time for Fred Rosenstock to enter the ranks of the antiquarian booksellers. On the first of March 1922 he opened his Denver Book Shop at 1758 Stout Street for the sale of rare and out-of-print books, sets, fine bindings and first editions. The venture was apparently ill-conceived, ill-financed, or ill-placed, for it failed. Denver was not yet ready for a bookstore of that nature. Staging the city's first book auction, Rosenstock sold some of his stock in June 1923 and the same year the Denver Book Shop closed its doors.

The next Rosenstock bookstore would not make its bow in Denver for another five years. During that period, Rosenstock—now married to Frances Goodman—raised money by auctioning his recently acquired collection of modern first editions at the Anderson Galleries in New York. Despite the flush times of 1927, the sale did not come up to expectations. A presentation copy of Louisa Alcott's first book, *Flower Fables*, for example, went under the hammer for only $5. At the same time, the prospective bookseller made a book-buying journey east, acquiring a new stock in Kansas City and St. Louis, Chicago, Cincinnati, Washington, Baltimore, Philadelphia, New York and Boston.

On 20 November 1928 Rosenstock's Bargain Book Store opened its doors at 406 Fifteenth Street. It was "crammed with old books, some very rare," and it soon became "a mecca for Western historians and buffs." In his office on the balcony, in a "lofty cubicle," the proprietor would ferret out "priceless bits of Americana" and talk fascinatingly about the ephemera that "made history come alive." Despite its precarious timing, the Bargain Book Store fared well and endured. It surmounted the depression years during which Rosenstock abandoned his specialty of first editions for Western Americana and Charles Russell paintings and sculptures. Drawing most of his income from the sale of textbooks—"Sound, Sanitary, Secondhand Schoolbooks"—he could satisfy his personal taste for books of the Wild West. In time the Bargain Book Store "became a warm and friendly haven for students, teachers, collectors, and authors, as well as bookish characters seeking refuge and conversation." It expanded its services, announcing "New and used books bought and sold; New and back number magazines; High School books and supplies; Rare Books—Fine Bindings—Autographs; Libraries Appraised; Special Supply Service to Public Libraries." It survived the years—the Second World War, the fire of 1949, the economic changes of the 1950s.

Rosenstock issued his first catalogue in 1931, offering such Americana as items on Colorado and the Indians, overland expeditions and the Far West. He converted his automobile into a pioneer "bookmobile," bringing "the bookstore to the library." He toured the East to buy and sell to Scribners, the Bennett Book Studios and Harzof of G. A. Baker & Company. He built up the Denver Public Library's holdings in early diaries and documents. He numbered among his customers Frank Dobie, David Lavender, Irving Stone, James Michener and Frank Waters of New Mexico whose gaunt, weathered face gave him a strong resemblance to Abraham Lincoln.

The books he sold he found in a variety of likely and unlikely spots. Years before he had bought a fine first issue of *Leaves of Grass* at

Lowdermilk's in Washington and sold it the next day to Alfred Gold-smith. Transactions were not always that swift or that easy. But Rosenstock amassed a fine stock, purchasing through his agent William Jackson of London, foraging through family attics and warehouses, even buying from Goodwill Industries.

In 1934, in his Catalogue of Western Americana, Rosenstock wrote: "Many of these rarities represent thrilling adventure in their acquisition; and the process of packing off some pamphlet to a person in Rhode Island will at once bring the thought, 'I'd like to tell him how many times my heart was in my mouth coming down that slippery, wet, narrow mountain road that night, with the brakes "on the blink," to Breckenridge and back; all for that pamphlet.' "

The Adventures of Fred Rosenstock were beginning to resemble the Adventures of his boyhood hero Mayne Reid. Especially after 1940, when he launched the Old West Publishing Company and combined the activities of antiquarian bookseller with those of publisher, his adventures accumulated. Rosenstock liked to publish what he owned. Buying the journal of John Doble, for example, a day-by-day narrative of life in gold rush California, he subsequently published it between boards. His first such publication was one of his most adventurous. Warren Ferris' *Life in the Rocky Mountains*, a record of the author's fur-trading during the 1830s, had appeared in issues of a Buffalo weekly, the *Western Literary Messenger*, between 1842 and 1843. Gradually, Rosenstock acquired all those issues. Then, in a bibliophilic want list, he chanced upon a notice inserted by the owner of Ferris' original letters to his family and his map of the fur country. With the resultant haul, Rosenstock was able to issue Ferris' *Life in the Rocky Mountains* as the first publication of his Old West Publishing Company.

In a delightful paper delivered before the Denver Westerners, Fred Rosenstock recounted his adventures under the title of *Small Miracles in My Life as a Book Hunter*. His "small miracles" included the purchase of biographer Edwin L. Sabin's "working material" on Kit Carson, a purchase that was climaxed by the later acquisition of a rare Carson daguerreotype and Brady's portraits of Carson signed by the trapper-soldier. From the great-grandchildren of Jefferson Davis, settled in Colorado Springs, the antiquarian bookseller purchased Jefferson Davis' library, later adding at least one hundred items to it and selling the whole almost at cost to the state of Mississippi. Throughout his adventurous career Rosenstock watched, waited and seized, so creating one "small miracle" after another. Having acquired the sketchbook and manuscript diary of Lieutenant James W. Abert, explorer of New Mexico, he was able, years later, to purchase a copy of the published version of the Abert *Narrative* which included the author's corrections and additions in his own hand.

The Rosenstock finds were themselves Rosenstock adventures: the discovery of the original letters and will of Jim Beckwourth lying scattered on the basement floor of a Denver house; the finds of diaries of the nineteenth-century western explorers and guides Alexander Barclay who arrived in Fort Bent in 1834 and Philander Simmons of the Cherry Creek gold country; the gradual amassing of ephemeral programs about the early Colorado theatre.

By 1955 Fred Rosenstock could read in the *Rocky Mountain News*: "Who is Denver's best-known bookman? If you asked that question in Glen Dawson's shop in Los Angeles, at Peter Decker's in New York City, John Howell's in San Francisco, or in any other of the famous bookshops of America, you'd get the same answer: Fred Rosenstock." By 1962 Denver's "best-known bookman" had sold his general stock of 100,000 volumes to Brigham Young University in Provo, Utah, where it was hauled in seven trips. Thanks to that sale, the bookseller was able to purchase a building where he set up anew, first as Fred A. Rosenstock, Books, and then as Fred Rosenstock, Books and Art, specialists in Western Americana. By the end of the 1960s he could place on exhibition "One Hundred Years of Western Art," and his reputation as "art collector and dealer" was "nationwide." In 1971 he was given an honorary doctorate by Brigham Young University. Four years later the octogenarian antiquarian closed his firm of Fred Rosenstock, Books and Art, but shortly thereafter, unable to endure retirement, opened an art gallery. Today Fred Rosenstock has just published "a new edition of his first book *Life in the Rocky Mountains*, Warren Ferris' memoirs of the fur trade in the 1830's." The lone star of Denver who traded the Carpathian Mountains for the Rockies is indeed "the rarest of the rare." His adventures, his enthusiasm, his finds and his collections have spurred "the growth of interest in Western history."

In varying ways, all antiquarian lone stars have stimulated interest in their chosen fields, bringing to the farflung reaches of the continent the fresh force of their knowledge, their enthusiasm, their excitement. One collector has written, "I incline to judge the civilization of a city by its bookstores." If bookstores are indeed the measure of civilization, these lone stars from Vermont and Texas, Mississippi and Colorado have civilized as they traded in books.

NOTES

1. Henry Stevens, *Catalogue of My English Library* (London: Whittingham, 1853), p. [v].

2. Wyman W. Parker, *Henry Stevens of Vermont: American Rare Book Dealer in London, 1845–1886* (Amsterdam: Israel, 1963), pp. 21 and passim. (Any one writing about Henry Stevens is deeply indebted to his biographer Wyman W. Parker. I also acknowledge the help of John Buechler, Head, Special Collections, University of Vermont, and Thomas P. MacDonnell of Henry Stevens, Son & Stiles); Henry Stevens, *Recollections of James Lenox and the formation of his Library* (New York: New York Public Library, 1951), pp. xviii and passim.

3. For Stevens' early life, education, and connection with Force, see Adolph Growoll, *Book Trade Bibliography in the United States in the Nineteenth Century* (New York: Franklin, 1939), pp. xlviii–lviii; Wyman W. Parker, "Henry Stevens: The Making of a Bookseller," *Papers of the Bibliographical Society of America* 48:2 (1954), pp. 150–155, 159–163; Parker, *Henry Stevens of Vermont*, pp. 21, 23, 27, 36; G. W. Smalley, "A Tribute to Henry Stevens," *Publishers Weekly* (17 April 1886), p. 521; Stevens, *Recollections of James Lenox*, pp. xix f, 12; "Henry Stevens," DAB.

4. Parker, "Henry Stevens: The Making of a Bookseller," *Papers of the Bibliographical Society of America* (1954), p. 156.

5. Stevens, *Recollections of James Lenox*, p. xii.

6. [Henry Stevens], *Photobibliography* [London: Norman, 1872], p. [1].

7. For Stevens' first sojourn in London, see "The House of Henry Stevens, 1839–1907," *Publishers Weekly* (29 June 1907), p. 1913; Parker, "Henry Stevens: The Making of a Bookseller," *Papers of the Bibliographical Society of America* (1954), pp. 149 f, 168 f; Parker, *Henry Stevens of Vermont*, pp. 9, 13–16, 69, 127, 174; Stevens, *Recollections of James Lenox*, pp. xx ff, 13; Philip John Weimerskirch, "Antonio Panizzi and the British Museum Library," *The 1981 AB Bookman's Yearbook*, pp. 44, 65.

8. For Stevens and his clients, see Information from Anne Caiger, Historical Manuscripts Librarian, University of California at Los Angeles, where some of the Stevens Papers are deposited; Parker, "Henry Stevens: The Making of a Bookseller," *Papers of the Bibliographical Society of America* (1954), pp. 163, 166; Parker, *Henry Stevens of Vermont*, pp. 15 f, 136–139, 147, 149; Stevens, *Recollections of James Lenox*, passim.

9. For those acquisitions, see Parker, *Henry Stevens of Vermont*, pp. 50 f,

55, 183, 186, 199, 210, 217, 232; Stevens, *Recollections of James Lenox*, passim; Weimerskirch, *Antonio Panizzi*, pp. 63, 67.

10. Wyman W. Parker, "Henry Stevens Sweeps the States," *Papers of the Bibliographical Society of America* 52:4 (1958), pp. 249–261; Parker, *Henry Stevens of Vermont*, pp. 105, 197, 255, 269, 276; Stevens, *Recollections of James Lenox*, pp. 62, 64, 145 f.

11. For Stevens' comments on books, see Stevens, *Catalogue of My English Library*, pp. vi f; [Stevens], *Photobibliography*, p. [1]; Henry Stevens, *Who Spoils Our New English Books* (London: Stevens, 1884), unpaged.

12. *Stevens's Historical Nuggets Bibliotheca Americana or, A Descriptive Account of Our Collection of Rare Books Relating to America* (London: Stevens, 1885), Prospectus, p. [1] and pp. vi f. See also, for Stevens on bibliography, "Obituary. Henry Stevens," *Publishers Weekly* (6 March 1886) pp. 338 f; Stevens, *Catalogue of My English Library*, p. [v]; [Stevens], *Photobibliograpbhy*, p. 3.

13. For firm changes, see Information from Anne Caiger, Historical Manuscripts Librarian, University of California at Los Angeles; "The House of Henry Stevens," *Publishers Weekly* (29 June 1907), pp. 1912 f and 1916; Parker, *Henry Stevens of Vermont*, pp. 239, 243, 301 f; "Benjamin Franklin Stevens," *DAB*.

14. For Tuttle, see Charles V.S. Borst, "The Charles E. Tuttle Company," *Antiquarian Bookman* (25 November 1957), pp. 1715 f; John Buechler, Head, Special Collections, University of Vermont, to Madeleine B.Stern (17 May 1982); George L. McKay, *American Book Auction Catalogues 1713–1934* (New York: New York Public Library, 1937), #7939, 8010, 8151; Charles E. Tuttle to Madeleine B. Stern (26 May 1982). According to John Buechler, "In 1917 or 1918, the father of the present Charles broke with his brothers and went into the business of bookselling exclusively, but why the father auctioned his Americana collection in 1917 [sic], I do not know, unless it was to get funds to start his new bookselling operation."

15. For Shettles, see J. Frank Dobie, "The First Bookseller to Enrich My Life," The Southern California Chapter Antiquarian Booksellers Association of America, *Bulletin Number Two* (Summer 1957), p. 2 (Courtesy Barbara Rootenberg); J. Frank Dobie, "E. L. Shettles, Man, Bookman and Friend," *The Southwestern Historical Quarterly* XLIV:3 (January 1941), pp. 350–356; Elijah L. Shettles, *Recollections of a Long Life. Edited With an Introduction by Archie P. McDonald. Foreword by J. Frank Dobie* (Nashville, Tenn.: Blue and Gray Press, 1973).

16. Harry B. Weiss, *The Bibliographical, Editorial and Other Activities of Charles F. Heartman* (Privately Printed, Christmas, 1938), p. 8.

17. For Heartman's characteristics, life and activities as auctioneer and bookseller, see *American Book-Prices Current*, ed. by Colton Storm (New York: Bowker, 1944), p. xix; *The Americana Collector* I (1925–1926), unpaged in-

troduction on "Americana"; James R. Canny, "Charles F. Heartman 1883–1953," *Antiquarian Bookman* (13 March 1954), pp. 732–735; Charles F. Heartman, *Twenty-Five Years in the Auction Business and What Now?* (Privately Printed, June 1938), passim; George L. McKay, *American Book Auction Catalogues*, pp. 27 f; Weiss, *The Bibliographical . . . Activities of Charles F. Heartman*, passim.

18. *The Americana Collector* I (1925–1926), unpaged introduction on "Americana."

19. Charles F. Heartman, *Checklist of Printers in the United States from Stephen Daye to the Close of the War of Independence* (New York [1915]), p. [9].

20. Charles F. Heartman, *The New-England Primer Issued prior to 1830* (New York: Bowker, 1934), pp. x-xi.

21. William B. Todd, *Suppressed Commentaries on the Wiseian Forgeries* (Austin: University of Texas, 1969), pp. 9–13.

22. James R. Canny, "Charles F. Heartman 1883–1953," *Antiquarian Bookman* (13 March 1954), p. 735.

23. For Rosenstock, see Donald E. Bower, *Fred Rosenstock A Legend in Books & Art* (Flagstaff, Ariz.: Northland Press, 1976), passim; Information from Terence Cassidy, A. Dean Larsen of Harold B. Lee Library, Brigham Young University, and Linda M. Lebsack of Rosenstock Arts, to all of whom the writer is most grateful; George L. McKay, *American Book Auction Catalogues*, #9071; Fred A. Rosenstock, *Small Miracles in My Life as a Book Hunter* [Denver 1965], passim.

Bibliographical Essay

Unlike the printer-publisher whose name is remembered from his imprints, the more ephemeral antiquarian bookseller leaves few records other than his catalogues which are themselves ephemeral. As a result, the primary bibliography of booksellers and bookselling is meager.

The business papers of some antiquarian booksellers have, of course, been preserved. Thomas H. Morrell of New York City, specialist in the American Revolution and the history of New York, left over 500 items relating to his career now in the New-York Historical Society; some of the papers of Henry Stevens of Vermont have been deposited in the University of California at Los Angeles; the Zeitlin and Ver Brugge Archive in twenty-seven boxes is also there. By and large, however, booksellers' records have seldom been preserved.

Booksellers' catalogues form prime sources for their careers. Many of these are available in the Catalogue Room of the Grolier Club, New York City. Also useful in this connection are George L. McKay, *American Book Auction Catalogues 1713–1934 A Union List* (New York: New York Public Library, 1937) and Robert B. Winans, *A Descriptive Catalogue of Book Catalogues Separately Printed in America 1693–1800* (Worcester, Mass.: American Antiquarian Society, 1981).

Local directories provide important information regarding dealers' locations and specializations. C. N. Caspar compiled a *Directory of the Antiquarian Booksellers and Dealers in Second-Hand Books of the United States* (Milwaukee, Wisc.: Caspar, 1885).

An invaluable source for bookselling history is the series of scrapbooks compiled by Adolf Growoll, known as the Adolf Growoll Collection of *American Book Trade History*. This is deposited in the Melcher Library of R. R. Bowker Company, New York City.

Issues of *AB Bookman's Weekly*, *American Book Collector*, *The Professional Rare Bookseller*, and *Publishers Weekly* yield information regarding antiquarian booksellers in articles and obituaries.

Few attempts have been made to record the general history of the antiquarian bookselling trade in America. Henry Walcott Boynton's *Annals of American Bookselling 1638–1850* (New York: Wiley, 1932) is, as the author describes it, "an informal chronicle" focusing on the eastern seaboard. Hellmut Lehmann-Haupt, *The Book in America* (New York: Bowker, 1951) is a useful comprehensive survey. Other relevant titles are "Famous American Booksellers Past and Present," *The Americana Collector*, ed. by Charles F. Heartman I (1925–1926) and Dorothea Lawrance Mann, "Our Ancestors and Their Book Business," *The Bookman* (1930–1931).

While only indirectly concerned with antiquarian bookselling, the following works yield considerable information on the subject: J. C. Derby, *Fifty Years among Authors, Books and Publishers* (New York: Carleton, 1884); David Kaser, *Books in America's Past* (Charlottesville: University Press of Virginia, 1966); Madeleine B. Stern, *Imprints on History: Book Publishers and American Frontiers* (Bloomington: Indiana University Press, 1956; reprinted, New York: AMS Press, 1975); Madeleine B. Stern, ed., *Publishers for Mass Entertainment in Nineteenth Century America* (Boston: G. K. Hall, 1980); G. Thomas Tanselle, *Guide to the Study of United States Imprints* (Cambridge, Mass.: Belknap Press of Harvard University Press, 1971), 2 vols.; John Tebbel, *A History of Book Publishing in the United States* (New York: Bowker, 1972, 1975), Vols. I and II; Isaiah Thomas, *The History of Printing in America*, ed. by Marcus A. McCorison (New York: Weathervane, 1970); Lawrence C. Wroth, *The Colonial Printer* (Portland, Maine: Southworth-Anthoensen Press, 1938).

Thanks to the efforts of local scholars, the history of regional bookselling has not been entirely neglected. Sources for the antiquarian market in Boston, where the trade may be said to have begun, include: Edwin M. Bacon, "Old Boston Booksellers," *The Bookman* 4 (February 1897); Worthington Chauncey Ford, *The Boston Book Market 1679–1700* (Boston: Club of Odd Volumes, 1917); George Emery Littlefield, *Early Boston Booksellers 1642–1711* (Boston: Club of Odd Volumes, 1900). For individual Boston houses the following are useful: [Drake] *Samuel G. Drake. His Life-Work and His Library* (N.p., n.d.) and John H. Sheppard, *A Memoir of Samuel G. Drake, A. M.* (Albany: Munsell, 1863); [Goodspeed] Charles E. Goodspeed, *Yankee Bookseller* (Boston: Houghton Mifflin, 1937) and George T. Goodspeed, "The Bookseller's Apprentice," *The Professional Rare Bookseller* 5 (1983); [Lauriat] Raymond L. Kilgour, *Estes and Lauriat A History 1872–1898* (Ann Arbor: University of Michigan Press, 1957) and George H. Sargent, *Lauriat's 1872–1922* (Boston: Privately printed, 1922).

The antiquarian trade in Philadelphia is investigated in George Allen, "Old Booksellers of Philadelphia," *Four Talks for Bibliophiles* (Philadelphia: Free Library of Philadelphia, 1958); Carl Bridenbaugh, "The Press and the Book in Eighteenth Century Philadelphia," *The Pennsylvania Magazine of History and*

Biography (Januray 1941); W. Brotherhead, *Forty Years among the Old Booksellers of Philadelphia, with Bibliographical Remarks* (Philadelphia: A. P. Brotherhead, 1891); H. Glenn Brown and Maude O. Brown, *A Directory of the Book-Arts and Book Trade in Philadelphia to 1820* (New York: New York Public Library, 1950); Howard Mumford Jones, "The Importation of French Books in Philadelphia, 1750–1800," *Modern Philology* 32 (1934); William Reitzel, "The Purchasing of English Books in Philadelphia, 1790–1800," *Modern Philology* 35 (1937). For specific Philadelphia dealers the following should be consulted: [Carey & Lea] David Kaser, Messrs. *Carey & Lea of Philadelphia: A Study in the History of the Booktrade* (Philadelphia: University of Pennsylvania Press, 1957); [Cobbett] Mary Elizabeth Clark, *Peter Porcupine in America: The Career of William Cobbett, 1792–1800* (Philadelphia 1939); [Leary's] John T. Winterich, "Leary's Centenary 1836–1936," *Publishers Weekly* (6 June 1936); [Rosenbach] Edwin Wolf 2nd with John Fleming, *Rosenbach A Biography* (Cleveland and New York: World Publishing Co., 1960).

Among studies of the antiquarian book trade in New York City are William Loring Andrews, *The Old Booksellers of New York and Other Papers* (New York 1895); John W. Francis, "Reminiscences of Printers, Authors, and Booksellers in New-York," *The International Magazine of Literature, Art, and Science* 5 (1 February 1852); Edwin D. Hoffman, "The Bookshops of New York City, 1743–1948," *New York History* 30 (January 1949); Thomas E. V. Smith, "The Book Trade of New York in 1789," *Publishers Weekly* 35 (27 April 1889). For individual New York City dealers the following are useful: [Philes] Harry Miller Lydenberg, "George Philes: Bookman," *Papers of the Bibliographical Society of America* 48 (1954); [Sabin] William S. Reese, "Joseph Sabin," *American Book Collector* N. S. 5 (January/February 1984); [Smith] [Charles F. Heartman], *George D. Smith G.D.S. 1870–1920 A Memorial Tribute* (Beauvoir Community, Miss.: The Book Farm, 1945).

An invaluable source for Cincinnati bookselling is Walter Sutton, *The Western Book Trade: Cincinnati as a Nineteenth-Century Publishing and Book-Trade Center* (Columbus: Ohio Historical Society, 1961). Other sources include "The Book Trade of Cincinnati," *The Literary World* 5 (10 November 1849); Edward A. Henry, "Cincinnati as a Literary and Publishing Center 1793–1880," *Publishers Weekly* (10 July 1937); William C. Smith, *Queen City Yesterdays: Sketches of Cincinnati in the Eighties* (Crawfordsville, Ind.: Banta, 1959). Individual firms in the area are surveyed in [Clarke] "Robert Clarke 1829–1899," *Ohio Archaeological and Historical Publications*, Vol. VIII; [James] "In Memoriam—U. P. James," *The Journal of the Cincinnati Society of Natural History* 12 (April 1889); [Smith] R. E. Banta, *William C. Smith, Gentleman Bookseller: A Tribute* (Hattiesburg, Miss.: Heartman, n.d.).

For bookselling in the Chicago area the following surveys are informative: "The Book Trade in Chicago," *American Publishers' Circular and Literary Gazette*

(4 October 1856); Guido Bruno, *Adventures in American Bookshops, Antique Stores and Auction Rooms* (Detroit, Mich.: Douglas Book Shop, 1922); "Chicago's Book Trade," *Chicago Times* (Supplement) (14 June 1884); "Chicago's Book Trade," *Publishers Weekly* (5 July 1884); D. B. Cooke, "My Memories of the Book Trade," *Publishers Weekly* (18 March 1876); [Albert D. Richardson], "Western Bibliography. The Book Trade of the North-West," *New-York Tribune* (16 October 1869). Among books on individual Chicago houses are [Abramson] D. B. Covington, *The Argus Book Shop: A Memoir* (West Cornwall, Conn.: Tarrydiddle Press, 1977); [Hill] Walter M. Hill, *Reminiscences and Results of A Quarter Century* (N.p., 1923); [Kroch] Adolph Kroch, *A Great Bookstore in Action* (Chicago: University of Chicago Press, 1940); [McClurg] John Drury, *A. C. McClurg & Co. Centennial 1844–1944* (Chicago: A. C. McClurg & Co., [1944]); [Morris] *The Morris Book Shop Impressions of Some Old Friends in celebration of the XXVth Anniversary* (Chicago 1912); [Powner] Samuel Putnam, *Powner's "The House of a Million Books": A Retrospect 1908–1925* (Chicago 1925).

Of interest for the bookselling history of the St. Louis and Kansas City areas are Eleanora A. Baer, "Books, Newspapers, and Libraries in Pioneer St. Louis, 1808–1842," *Missouri Historical Review* 56 (July 1962); David Kaser, *A Directory of the St. Louis Book and Printing Trades to 1850* (New York: New York Public Library, 1961); John Francis McDermott, "Everybody Sold Books in Early St. Louis," *Publishers Weekly* (24 July 1937). For individual dealers see [Glenn] Ardis Glenn, "Frank Glenn and the Glenn Bookshop: Pioneer Rare Book Dealer in the Midwest," *AB Bookman's Weekly* (7 September 1981); [Miner] J. Christian Bay, "William Harvey Miner," *The American Book Collector* 5 (March 1934).

Prime sources for San Francisco bookselling are Hugh Sanford Cheney Baker, "A History of the Book Trade in California 1849–1859," *California Historical Society Quarterly* 30 (June, September, December 1951); Robert Ernest Cowan, "*Booksellers of Early San Francisco*" (Los Angeles: Ward Ritchie Press, 1953); Warren R. Howell, "Exploring California Book-Trade History," *AB Bookman's Weekly* (8 January 1979). Books by or about individual dealers include [Bancroft] John Walton Caughey, *Hubert Howe Bancroft: Historian of the West* (Berkeley and Los Angeles: University of California Press, 1936); [Holmes] Harold C. Holmes, *Some Random Reminiscences of an Antiquarian Bookseller* (Oakland, Calif.: Holmes, 1967); [Magee] David Magee, *Infinite Riches: The Adventures of a Rare Book Dealer* (New York: Eriksson, 1973).

The antiquarian booktrade in Los Angeles is explored in *A Bookman's View of Los Angeles* (Los Angeles: Zamorano Club, 1961); Ernest Dawson, *Los Angeles Booksellers of 1897* (Claremont, Calif.: Saunders Press, 1947); Lawrence Clark Powell, *From the Heartland: Profiles of People and Places of the Southwest and Beyond* (Flagstaff, Ariz.: Northland Press, [1976]); Ward Ritchie, *Bookmen &*

their brothels: Recollections of Los Angeles in the 1930s (Los Angeles: Zamorano Club, 1970); Jacob Zeitlin, *Small Renaissance: Southern California Style* (Los Angeles 1972). The careers of the two major Los Angeles antiquarian dealers are recorded in [Dawson] Fern Dawson Shochat, *The Fiftieth Anniversary of Dawson's Book Shop: 1905–1955* (N.p. [1955]); [Zeitlin] *Books and the Imagination: Fifty Years of Rare Books Jake Zeitlin Interviewed by Joel Gardner*. Oral History Program (University of California at Los Angeles 1980) and J. M. Edelstein, ed., *A Garland for Jake Zeitlin* (Los Angeles: Dahlstrom & Marks, 1967).

Among useful studies of Southern regional bookselling are John F. Coyle, "Memories of Washington Bookstores," *Publishers Weekly* (21 May 1892); James Gilreath, "Mason Weems, Mathew Carey and the Southern Booktrade, 1794–1810," *Publishing History* 10 (1981); John M. Goudeau, "Booksellers and Printers in New Orleans, 1764–1885," *The Journal of Library History* 5 (January 1970); Lewis Leary, *The Book-Peddling Parson: An account of the life and works of Mason Locke Weems* (Chapel Hill: Algonquin Books, 1984); Roger Philip McCutcheon, "Books and Booksellers in New Orleans," *Louisiana Historical Quarterly* 20 (July 1937); Rollo G. Silver, *The Baltimore Book Trade 1800–1825* (New York: New York Public Library, 1953); Emily Ellsworth Ford Skeel, ed., *Mason Locke Weems His Works and Ways* (New York 1929), 2 vols.; Joseph Towne Wheeler, "Booksellers and Circulating Libraries in Colonial Maryland," *Maryland Historical Magazine* 34 (June 1939).

For the so-called "Lone Stars" who hailed from or operated in regions remote from American antiquarian book centers, the following are most useful: [Heartman] Harry B. Weiss, *The Bibliographical, Editorial and Other Activities of Charles F. Heartman* (Privately Printed 1938); [Rosenstock] Donald E. Bower, *Fred Rosenstock A Legend in Books & Art* (Flagstaff, Ariz.: Northland Press, 1976); [Shettles] Elijah L. Shettles, *Recollections of a Long Life* (Nashville: Blue and Gray Press, 1973); [Stevens] Wyman W. Parker, *Henry Stevens of Vermont: American Rare Book Dealer in London, 1845–1886* (Amsterdam: Israel, 1963) and Henry Stevens, *Recollections of James Lenox and the formation of his Library* (New York: New York Public Library, 1951); [Tuttle] Charles V.S. Borst, "The Charles E. Tuttle Company," *Antiquarian Bookman* (25 November 1957).

Increasing consciousness of the need to preserve our bookselling history is evidenced today by the development of oral history programs which aim to record on tapes interviews with or reminiscences of leading antiquarian booksellers. Columbia University and the University of California at Los Angeles are two of the many universities developing such programs. The trade itself is making a significant attempt to preserve its past. Under the direction of James Lowe of New York City, the Rare Book Tapes were conceived and produced and now consist of two volumes available from the Antiquarian Booksellers Center, New York City.

Index

Mackenzie, William, 27, 28
MacManus, George, 42
MacManus, George S., Co., 42
Madrid, Spain, 139
Magee, David, xv, 146-147, 220;
    Infinite Riches, 146-147
Maggs, Ernest, 163
Maggs Brothers, 187
Malkin, Sol M., 78
Malter, George, 141
Manchester, Ohio, 94
Manierre, George, 98
Manigault, Peter, 170
Mann, Charles, 30, 33
Mann, Horace, 9
Mansfield, Ohio, 79, 80
Marguerite de Navarre, *Heptameron*,
    101
Marks and Company, 163
Marshall, Richard, 166
Martin, François-Xavier, 185
Martyr d'Anghiera, Peter, 196
Marvin, A. S., 133-134
Marvin and Hitchcock, 134, 146
Maryland Journal, 172
Mason, O. T., *Indian Basketry*, 155
Massey, Ernest de, 132
Matador, Texas, 161
Mather, Cotton, 3, 5
Mather, Increase, 3, 4, 8
Mathers, publications of the, 195
Mathews, Herbert L., 120-121
Maugham, Mrs. Somerset, 103
Mayo, Frederick A., 179
McAllister, John, 33
McArdle, Patrick, 121
McCance, Andrew, 15-16
M'Carty, William, 36
McCarty (M'Carty) and Davis, 35,
    36
McClurg, Alexander Caldwell, 89-
    93, 94, 95, 97, 220; "Saints and
    Sinners Corner," xiv, 92-93, 158

McClurg, A. C., and Company, 93,
    97, 102, 104, 106 n.19, 143, 158
McCormick, Cyrus Hall, 98
McCormick family, 159
McGuffey, William Holmes, 201
McIntyre, J. W., 114
McKay, David, 43
M'Kean, William, 185
McKenney, Thomas L., and James
    Hall, *History of the Indian Tribes*,
    31, 177
McShane, Arthur, 177
McShane, Betsey, 177
Medici family, 127
Meech, Stephen W., xv, 111
Meech & Dinnies, 111
Meech & Loring, 111
Mein, John, 6
Melcher, Frederic, 13
Mendheim, H., 136
Mendoza, Aaron, xvi, 59
Mendoza, David, 59
Mendoza, Isaac, 17, 59
Mendoza, Isaac, Book Company, 59
Mendoza, Mark, 59
Menzies, William, 54
Mercer, John, 170
Mermet, 183
Messenger, Southern Literary, 179
Metcalf, Edwards Huntington, 164
Metuchen, N.J., 205, 206, 209
Mexico City, Mexico, 125
Meynell, Francis, 163
Michener, James, 211
Middlebury College, 192
Midland Notes, 80
Midland Rare Book Company, 80,
    84 n.14
Millard, Alice Parsons, 158-159,
    161
Millard, George M., 92, 93, 94, 158
Millay, Edna St. Vincent, 101, 102
Miller, Henry, *Catalogus von . . .
    Deutschen Büchern*, 25

About the
Author

MADELEINE B. STERN is Partner in Leona Rostenberg and Madeleine Stern—Rare Books in New York. She has written, edited, and coauthored a number of books, including A *Phrenological Dictionary of Nineteenth-Century Americans* (Greenwood Press, 1982); *Imprints on History: Book Publishers and American Frontiers*; *Publishers for Mass Entertainment in 19th-Century America*; *Books and Book People in Nineteenth Century America*; and *Old and Rare: Thirty Years in the Book Business* (with Leona Rostenberg).